BLOW
AWAY

DEAN SELMIER and MARK KRAM

THE VIKING PRESS   NEW YORK

LIBRARY OF CONGRESS CATALOGING IN PUBLICATION DATA
Selmier, Dean.
Blow away.
1. Selmier, Dean. 2. Crime and criminals—United States—Biography. I.
   Kram, Mark, joint author. II. Title.
HV6248.S428A33   364.1'523'0924   78-12299
ISBN 0-670-17447-5

Printed in the United States of America
Set in video Stymie Light

ACKNOWLEDGMENTS

Chappell Music Company: From *Do-Re-Mi* by Richard Rodgers & Oscar
Hammerstein II. Copyright © 1959 by Richard Rogers & Oscar Hammerstein
II. Williamson Music, Inc., owners of publication & allied rights throughout the
Western Hemisphere & Japan. International Copyright Secured. All rights
reserved. Used by permission.

Paul Simon: From *The Dangling Conversation*. © 1966 Paul Simon. Used by
permission.

THANKS TO HOWARD PORTNOY

AUTHORS' NOTE

The events and happenings depicted herein really oc-
curred. The conversations described are as accurate as
memory can provide.

The characters are at times amalgams of more than one
person, and the names of some individuals have been
changed to ensure their anonymity. The chronology and
location of certain events have been rearranged to protect
our safety.

Dean Selmier
Mark Kram

PROLOGUE

Toward the end neither of us could agree on how we got there, on who we were, or on the color of the desert. There was only this confused sense of place. Crawford once saw it as the steaming, pressing bedroom he shared with six brothers back in Alabama, or the skull-baking open hearth in Pittsburgh that he ran to later. The worst I could do was the humiliation of a September sun, with drops of water trickling down my leg to a classroom floor when I was too young even to know what a desert was. But toward evening, when the sun had moved well behind us, we would both calm down and agree that this desert, our desert, looked like a lovely naked woman caught in a certain touching light. The softly contoured shadows of evening would chase the meanness of the sand, bringing back some sanity, as we took off the wet white towels about our heads and listened for the launch.

The launch to and from the ship was our future. The launch saved us when the sun had no use for us anymore, and it served us up like a couple of eggs each sunrise for three months at the mouth of the Suez. There, Crawford and I would make our way up to a hole, ten feet by ten, which was called "the Oven." We were there to pull guard duty, though it was never clear who would be crazy enough to come near this emptiness. We were also there because Crawford and I had been AWOL for two weeks, all of that time having been spent in a Beirut whorehouse, where we had been found—with six women and a bottle of cheap gin in each hand.

"Three months," said the officer. "Behind bars, or in the Oven?" Crawford and I looked at each other and decided: we would be better off outdoors. Two weeks later I asked the officer, "How 'bout the night shift, sir?" He looked at me, with a big grin on his face, and said, "Now, that wouldn't be punishment, would it. Everybody wants the nights out there to beat the heat here on ship."

"Officers are smart," I said, reporting to Crawford.

"Motherfuckers ain't smart, boy; they *mean,*" said Crawford. Later, in the Oven, Crawford said he was being treated this way because he was black. I said it was because I was from Indiana; we were serious: the effects of isolation and boredom had begun.

After a while out there, it was obvious there were only two positions of relative comfort: facing the sun, and facing away from it. Crawford had made this remarkable discovery, causing me to examine again the capacity of his brainpan. "Why you think I don't face the desert with you, and turn back to the canal at certain times?" I said. "The sun, the goddamn sun, Crawford." If I was so wise, Crawford wanted to know, "Whatch you doin' out here, boy, bein' cooked for?"

There were also only two views: either facing the desert and looking at nothing, or turning around and seeing only the stacks of ships floating by on the canal. Once or twice, on the desert side, we saw, or thought we saw, a speck of a figure on a camel; after two months, Crawford began to see more.

So there we sat, day after day: Crawford, twenty-two, with a gold tooth shining in the front, trying to show the patience learned from years of being forgotten; and me, only eighteen, with no exit for the energy crackling through a young body and mind; I would learn here: to wait like a cat. The two of us sprawled in our desert cavity, with a water canister and rifles, sometimes talking with enthusiasm, sometimes aimlessly; sometimes we were as still as little night animals, though there was nothing small about Crawford. He was an immense creature, with a back as big and wet as the deck of a freighter, with a neck like the face of a mountain, and long, heavy legs that often seemed to make territorial claims on my side of the Oven. For all his ominous size, he was as kind and gentle as an old friar.

"What you gonna do, Crawford, when your time is up?" I asked him one day.

"Re-up, I guess," said Crawford. "But I ain't goin' out there where the big bear is."

"What bear?" I asked, figuring the heat may have got him.

"Bear ass and bear table, boy," he said. "He worse than any two-legged grizzly."

The boredom and frustration bit at our minds until we frantically searched for any object that would fascinate us. The stacks of the ships, the color of the desert, had long ago become worthless; when I stopped counting stacks, the number was one thousand. We took to watching the thermometer mock us—100 degrees, 105, 112—and I bet Crawford it would reach 120 one day; the loser would have to pay for a whore in Beirut; the highest it ever hit was 116. We studied the scorpions, but we were divided in our sentiments: Crawford wanted no part of them; I liked the company. One day, who knows for what reason, I picked up my rifle and blasted one crawling down the side of the hole.

"Whatch you go do that for?" Crawford asked. "He weren't botherin' nobody. Should've let 'im be."

It was a scorpion that started trouble between us. Crawford was dozing, his helmet down over his face with a wet cloth tucked under it. I scooped up the scorpion with the butt of my rifle, and put it gently on his hand. He jumped up cursing, looked at me stonily, and began to laugh. A few minutes later I took my helmet off and poured water on my head. Crawford took his helmet off, filled it with sand, and emptied it on my head. Covered with wet sand, I flew at him. He did not flinch. He thought I was joking. I caught him on the corner of his mouth, and a stream of blood ran down the side of his chin. He seemed shocked, looking at the blood on his hand, then at me. Not speaking, he walked over, picked me up, lifted me over his head until I was horizontal, and hurled me nearly eight feet out of the hole. I lay there, trying to sense if anything was broken. Nothing was, so I crawled slowly back into the Oven. We didn't talk. And then, looking sideways, I noticed a big drop sliding down Crawford's left cheek. It wasn't sweat.

"Hey, pal," I said. "You should've broken my neck. I deserved it."

"You and me friends?" he wanted to know. "Nearly killed my best friend."

"You can say that again," I said. "I ain't never had a better friend."

We had a week left in the Oven when Crawford spotted another one of his specks on the desert horizon. The sky was cloudless and relentless. My helmet weighed like a tank sitting there; my hair inside felt like wet steel wool. Christ, were we ever going to be free of this hole! I didn't pay any attention to Crawford. I had a headache; my eyes were sore; the bottoms of my feet were burning.

"Here he come," said Crawford. "He comin' right toward us."

"Have a drink of water," I said. "Rub some on your eyes while you're at it."

"Motherfucker's real, Dean," he said.

"Yeah, what's he in . . . a Rolls-Royce?" I asked.

"He on a camel."

"Aw, come on, Crawford," I said. "Cut the shit, will ya? It's bad enough out here without you seein' things."

"That's it," he mumbled slowly, to himself. "Come closer, baby."

"Crawford!" I yelled, turning toward him and then looking out. "I think—" I squinted. Barely perceptible, a dot jiggled in the shimmering heat. I turned away, then looked again. It was still there, but getting bigger.

Crawford raised his rifle.

"What the fuck are you doin'?" I asked.

"Havin' some sport, that's all."

"Put that thing down," I said. He wasn't hearing me.

Now it was no longer a dot but a heavily clothed figure on a camel. Crawford adjusted his rifle sight. The figure was two hundred yards away.

"Keep comin', motherfucker!" Crawford whispered. I grabbed his arm, and he pushed me away. My nerves were unraveling. My mouth had suddenly become dry with fear, and then a sharp thrill shivered up my spine until horror took over. Finally I thought he was playing with me, pawing at me like an old tomcat with a ball of yarn.

"There you are, baby, right where Crawford want you," he said to himself, looking down the sight. The man was a hundred yards out now. He was waving to us. Crawford was frozen. Big drops of sweat ran down his nose and cheeks. He parted his lips, his gold tooth catching the sun. I watched his finger slacken on the trigger.

"That's a man out there, you crazy sonuvabitch!" I hollered. "You can't kill a man!"

His rifle cracked. Sand kicked up from the desert. Riderless, the camel stopped.

"Yes, I can," said Crawford, tilting his rifle toward the sky, his eyes vacant. His fatigue jacket was soaked, his hand watery with sweat. He was drained. We sat there in silence. The sun was overhead.

Finally I said, "I guess we should go out and see who he is." Crawford did not answer. His eyes were still empty. Minutes passed like hours.

"Maybe the wind'll come . . . come and blow him away," said Crawford, turning back to the canal, he and I both knowing we would never be the same again.

PART ONE

1960

"What are you looking at?" the commandant asked, looking up from my dossier.

"The plants, sir," I said, standing erect.

"Why did you ask to see me?" the commandant wanted to know.

"I would like another half hour of exercise and sunlight, sir," I said. He looked sharp: like a high note on a trumpet if you could catch it and look at it. He was a short thread of a man. Every *i* about his dress and manner had a dot over it. They called him Commandant Squeak because of his high-pitched voice, which could drive a dog to howling, and because of his all-military tight-assed ways; they said he squeaked when he walked. But he wasn't any commandant. He was a warden. I didn't think he liked it much. He'd rather have been in Washington, running messages down the corridors of the Pentagon.

He burrowed into the sheaf of papers in front of him. "Let's see . . . you've been here three months," he said. "How long is your sentence?" He knew what I was carrying. It was all there in the papers.

"Fourteen years, sir," I said.

3

"Yes, I remember now," he said. I think he just wanted to hear me say it: fourteen years. But he wasn't a cruel man. The prison had just turned him some.

"For about the worst crime you can commit," he added. "Assaulting an officer." He looked down, and read on. "With the butt of a rifle. It says here you tried to kill him."

"With all respect, sir," I said, "if I'd wanted to kill him, I would have."

"You're a fresh kid," he said.

"No, sir."

"If you didn't want to kill him, why didn't you use your hands."

"I could have killed him with my hands, too, sir."

He cleared his throat, and started to go on.

"I'd like to add, sir," I said, interrupting him, "that I pulled the butt. It wasn't a clean blow."

"Clean enough for a broken jaw in three places, four teeth, and a severe concussion," he said.

"I was provoked," I said. "But I knew what I was doing, sir."

"I don't want to know," he said routinely. Nobody ever did, I thought. Officers protect their own. He pulled another paper out of the folder. All I wanted was some more sunlight. I wasn't asking for a three-day pass out of the joint.

"There's nothing here to indicate that kind of violence," he continued. "Nearly five years of service. Not much advancement. You're not very ambitious, are you? But very capable. At the top of your class in training camp." He stopped and looked up. "Everybody else was out of the swimming phase of the survival course after an hour, but you swam on for four hours. Is that right?" He didn't seem to believe it. "Tours of duty, ordinary: Asia; Mediterranean; Caribbean. You got around. That's not unusual. Not much trouble. AWOL once in Beirut." He paused to go back for a detail. "After basic training, you were assigned to radar training. What happened?"

"I wasn't bright enough, sir," I said. I had never been to

4

radar-training school in my life. He moved through some more papers quickly.

"Your IQ doesn't say that," he said, not looking up.

"I just washed out, sir," I said, still standing erect.

"Too bad," he said. "It looks to me as if you settled into becoming just another one of those bums. This place is full of them. Sooner or later, you all get into trouble." I didn't say anything. He turned the screw. "What do you think of that?"

"Yes, sir," I said.

"Yes, sir, you're a bum?"

"No, sir, I got into trouble."

"Now, about your request," he said, lowering his eyes to the folder. For all his bookish attitude, he wasn't the kind of man who could look another man in the eye and tell him he could not have more sunlight.

"Request denied," he said.

"Thank you, sir," I said, turning to look at all the plants, an elaborate montage of them in front of a draped curtain overlooking the prison yard.

"Haven't you ever seen plants before?" he snapped.

"Yes, sir," I said. "It's just that they're so brown and lifeless. They're dying, sir."

"Do you know anything about plants?"

"I know how things grow, sir. I was raised on a farm." He looked over at the plants. He knew they were dying. I wondered if maybe he wanted them to die.

"Dismissed," he said abruptly, motioning for the MP standing near the door.

Back in my cell—you could still call it a hole—I again went over my situation, something I hadn't done since I had been transferred from the real hole a month ago. I had been there for two months, surviving in the dark on only bread and water and a half hour of walking each day in a private yard; that was automatic policy for new inmates; the military was not nice to its rapists, killers, and near killers. These new digs weren't much better. Quietly gray. Close. Short rations

5

brought to me by an old trustee. And still alone, walking in the private yard.

"What'd you do, Pop?" I asked the old trustee one day.

"Knifed an officer," he said. "Subic Bay. 1948. The rainy season. I hated the rain."

"Did he die?"

"Deader than I am now," he said, handing me the slop for the day. "Do it again, I would. Those punks have no respect."

"Ya ever come close to gettin' out?"

"*Sheeeet,*" he said, "they don't even know I'm here."

I would do it again, too. I hoped that prick officer couldn't even eat a steak now. He had it coming. For weeks he had stayed on my back, making me his private project, dishing out every filthy, demeaning duty he could think of, needling me with his sarcasm in front of the other men: "Men, Selmier here is the perfect example of a man who will not adapt. Five years, now—right, Selmier?—and he still won't conform. I told you all to shine your boots. Look at Selmier's boots. I told him to buff the floor. Look at the floor." I did. You could see your face in both the boots and the floor. "Selmier's a pig, men. He doesn't belong." He looked at the other men. "You're not going to re-up, are you, Selmier?"

"Yessir."

"You see, men. Pigs never leave home."

I didn't deserve the abuse. Who knows why he did it? Every now and then, you'd find a young officer with a mean streak running through him like an angry scar. You see the same kind of people in offices sometimes, the kind who stay on you for their own strange reasons and never let you breathe. I was the best man there. He knew it. I didn't want any favors. I only wanted him to leave me alone; he wouldn't. So one day, after weeks of his tongue, after days of not sleeping because of all that anxiety shooting through me, I was standing by my bunk for inspection, with my rifle at parade rest, and here was this prick lacing into me again. All I heard was "pig." The rifle shot up into my hands, and I just flicked it against his jaw, sending him crumbling to my

6

buffed floor with blood coming out of his mouth and the teeth lying next to him.

Until that officer came along and his jaw got in the way, I couldn't knock the service. But I didn't know where the warden got that radar-school item; as I said, I'd never been near the place. After training camp, an officer had called me into his office and told me I was to report to this quiet little island in the Caribbean. They weren't cutting any orders; I was just to go to this island. When I got there, I checked in at a small compound into which twenty-five men drifted within the next several days. Finally, the officer in charge called a meeting. He stood there, in front of the small deck of bleacher stands, and said, "You are here to learn how to kill. And survive. Any questions?" Nobody had any, because it was clear from the way he said it we were not exactly on the floor of the Senate. The meeting was over. So was the picnic, if that is what I was expecting from the easy atmosphere of the island.

The program and the group had no name, but if there is something similar to it today, it would be the Navy Seals, who are trained for clandestine and highly sensitive operations. The training was long and brutal. After six months we knew how to kill with a newspaper rolled up a certain way in our hand; we could use a knife as well as a Madrid gypsy; we could operate as frogmen, parachute into the ocean and swim, hike and climb forever. (I didn't do well with guns at a distance, though.) When we split up, I was assigned to regular duty in the Pacific, like any other enlisted man. And for months I waited, wondering when I would be called on to activate this special training of mine.

Then, one day, an officer came up to me and told me I was to be flown to Okinawa. There, I joined another officer and two enlisted men. Eventually we were dropped off the coast of Laos for the rescue of a high Laotian official and his wife and two children. It was uneventful.

I was transferred to the Suez Canal area, where I spent six months, whored around with Crawford, and got into trouble by being AWOL. No officer showed up and told me I was going to be flown anywhere. I was getting restless.

I was ready to go AWOL again when I was given orders to report to Subic Bay, in the Philippines. From there, over the next two years, I was involved in three operations in Vietnam, all carried out in civilian clothes. We blew up a freighter. I rigged a bomb and put it under a communist leader's bed. And I took a bullet in the meat part of my arm as six of us sprang a Frenchman from North Vietnam. Along with a hunk of my meat, we left two of our group behind. Dead.

After spending several months back at Subic, I was sent to a base in California, where I ran into that prick officer and prayed for another transfer to come into my life.

But, I thought, sitting in my cell and looking at the slop on my plate, what I missed most was the food and fresh air. I dwelled on the old trustee's words: "*Sheeeet,* they don't even know I'm here."

It had been two weeks since I had seen Warden Squeak. I was on my third psychiatrist since I had been there. I began to hate them, as they came and sat smugly across from me with their tape recorders, throwing out a hundred silly questions and giving me inkblot tests.

What did I think of my father?

He was in the hotel-linen business, sir. He's dead.

What did I think of my mother?

She's a good cook, sir.

That's not what I mean, Selmier.

What did you mean, sir?

I mean . . . did you love them?

No, I hated them, sir.

Why?

Because they gave me life, sir.

(He shut up for a moment, then began drumming his fingers on the desk as if he were on to something. I'd better stop this fucking around, I told myself. This could hurt me. But I couldn't resist.)

Do you like death, Selmier?

8

What do you mean, sir?

Let me put it this way. What would you do if a hundred men were lined up outside and shot?

I'd worry that I was going to be 101.

Hmmmmmmmm.

What's that, sir?

Nothing, Selmier. Nothing.

I thought so, sir.

What's that?

I said, I see, sir.

Do you like baseball, Selmier?

I don't like the uniforms, sir.

How about football?

Same thing, sir.

Do you like any sports?

Yessir. Swimming.

Why?

I like the uniform, sir.

That will be all, Selmier. Until next week.

Thank you, sir.

That was the tone of most all of the psychiatric sessions. I was trying to stay sane, while they were probing to see just how crazy I was. They were, after all, officers. It was beyond them to see how any sane man could try to kill a fellow officer.

I was anticipating questions from the next psychiatrist who would come my way when a guard worked his nightstick on the steel door of my cell. He said the warden wanted to see me. When I got to his office, the warden was bent over and looking at his plants. He saw me and stood up straight.

"You say you know about growing things, Selmier?" he said.

"Yessir," I said, standing stiffly.

"I'll tell you what," he said. "You got two weeks to make these plants shape up. You can have all the sunlight you want. And you can take your meals with the rest of the men. You can work here from noon to two o'clock, when I'm taking lunch. If at the end of two weeks there is no improvement, you will be back on the same program you are on now. If you are successful, the job is yours permanently. And you will be taken out of isolation."

"Yessir," I said, trying to remember the shape of the plants so I could go to the library that night and find out what the hell kinds of plants they were.

"Do you know how much those plants cost, Selmier?" I didn't.

"My wife spent five hundred dollars of taxpayers' money on those plants. Remember that, Selmier. That's all."

"Thank you, sir."

"Don't thank me. Thank my wife."

The library books told me that Squeak's plants were philodendron and bougainvillea, with many mounds of plumbago. I read on. The philodendra, according to my reading, might make it; they didn't need much moisture and not all that much light. But the bougainvillea and plumbagos were in real trouble. The bougainvillea needed to be cut back heavily, and also watered. The bushy plumbagos needed sun, and plenty of water, too. Could they be saved? How far gone were they? I'd soon find out.

Each morning I would be out in the yard, scooping birdshit from the ground and off the walls and ledges with a paper. By the end of the morning I would head up to the warden's office whistling, while all the other prisoners stared at me and wondered who the hell this guy was walkin' around holding a hill of birdshit in front of him like he was a waiter in a good restaurant. I would try anything to get those plants back to health. And, too, it made the warden think I knew what I was doing and kept me out in the sunlight and fresh air. Up in the office I would throw open his curtains and let the sun pour in, water the plants, and never stop begging them, Grow, babies, grow! If you don't have any more growing to do, then get green, get green, sweethearts. Dean likes sunlight, too.

I must have been working on the plants a week when one day the warden returned from lunch and stood there listening to me talking. He coughed, and then moved toward his desk.

"Sir," I said, "do you think we can keep these curtains open so they can get more sun?"

"No. It's the view of the yard. It disgusts me."

"Well, sir," I said, "is it possible to keep a few floodlights on the plants up here all night?"

"All that electricity, Selmier." He frowned. "Waste of taxpayers' money." He looked over at the plants. "They're not so brown anymore, are they? Well, all right, you only have a week left anyway."

A week was all I needed.

The Friday before the warden left for the weekend was the big day. I knew he would probably pass judgment sometime that afternoon, then be off to wherever wardens go on weekends; me, except for this Friday, I didn't know one day from the other. I pulled back and looked at the plants; I drew close, and the fact was that they were better, though still struggling. They had started to stretch and grow, and tiny buds could be seen, but would it be enough to convince him? I had to believe in them; I had to make him believe. Put on a show, Dean; sell it. I heard the quick little cough as he came back from lunch. I started to gather my things and began an elaborate explanation of my objectives, of what I had done, of what had been accomplished against such great odds. Every time I thought he was going to say something I would press on with yet another detail. If I couldn't convince him, maybe I could wear him out.

"They're alive, sir," I pleaded, finally. "They're alive. Look at them." I hoped he wouldn't look too closely. He was staring at the plants and trying to put what I was saying together with what he was seeing.

"Sir. The plants, sir," I said.

"Oh, yes. Well done, Selmier," he said.

You betcha, I thought.

Three weeks later, at eight in the evening, the guard came by my cell and took me to a bare, small room with

just a table and two chairs. I was there fifteen minutes before a large, neat-looking man walked in with a briefcase
in his hand. He had on a smart felt hat and a thin tie with
a peanut of a knot between his button-down collars. He
was wearing a gray flannel three-button suit with narrow
lapels. On the street I would have picked him for an insurance man. Life. The kind of guy who sits across the coffee
table from you, measuring you with the actuarial tables in
his brain and saying, "God forbid you die, but . . ." (He
always whispers the first part, and comes down hard and
loud on the "but.") I figured this man now sitting across
from me as outside help, a psychiatric consultant, not one
of the rookies who went into the service so they could
practice on people like me. He opened his briefcase and
pulled out a folder. My life had been full of folders. I didn't
have to guess what was in it.

"You have nice color in your face," he said, his hat tilted
back above his pallid face. "Your skin tone's good, too. All
that sunshine, eh? Like it here now, do you?"

"Yessir," I said. "Everything I expected."

"Oh, you're a beauty, Selmier," he said. "They're calling
you a necrophile."

"What's that, sir?" I said. "And may I ask who?"

"The people that have been examining you. That's the
opposite of 'biophile.' "

"What's that, sir?"

"A biophile loves life, Selmier. All things living. He likes
to look at life. You don't like life, Selmier."

"Since when?" I asked.

"You like death. You're a necrophile. Got it?"

"If you say so, sir."

"I don't say so. They say so—all those kids on Uncle Sam's
tit. You've had three of them, right?"

"And you're the fourth, sir."

"Forget the 'sir,' " he said. "I'm not a psychiatrist and I'm
not in the military." He spat the words out like they were bile
in his mouth. "That's not all they say," he continued. "You're
antisocial. Hostile. And a dangerous young man. That just

about covers the field. You're going to be here a long time, Selmier."

"I'll make the best of it," I said, loosening up now. "I know where I am. I'll survive. I knew what I was doing with that rifle butt. I'll take what they got to give me."

"What we are here for, Selmier, is to try and find a solution to your problem. A young man with a fine service record gets into a jam . . . he shouldn't suffer the rest of his life."

"Thank you, sir," I said. "You're the best shrink I've had."

"I told you: I'm not one of them," he said. He let it slide. "You can call me James."

"Well, I'm all for a solution," I said. I hadn't heard positive words in months.

"You bet you are," he said wryly. "The military does things its own way. Fella like you has no chance against it. They spend all their time sniffing around Defense Department budgets; makes it easy for them to forget about a fella like you."

"The solution," I said. "What is it?"

"You want to know, eh, Selmier?" he said, chuckling. "The place doesn't live up to the ads, eh?" Some more *hee-hee*. I let him have his joke. He continued, "You ever kill, Selmier?"

"I don't think so," I said, lying.

"I think so," he said. He put on his glasses and started to read from a paper.

"That was on orders," I cut in. "That was my job, what I was supposed to do."

"Was it, now?" he said. "I wasn't aware that we were in a war." He had me there.

"Orders are orders."

"You could have refused. There is no war."

"I suppose so."

"But you didn't, did you, Selmier? No . . . it appealed to you." I was being cornered.

"I wouldn't say that. But it didn't bother me none, either." I tried some offense. "Say, what's your interest, anyway?"

"Never mind about me, Selmier," he said. "Let's just say

I'm like one of those high-paid IBM guys who go to campuses and pick out the best engineers. You can forget the high pay." He moved his eyes around the room. "Only all my engineers are in places like this."

"What are you askin'?" I said. "You want me to kill for you, don't you?" He didn't react. He was a pro.

"Put it this way: whatever the assignments are; courier . . . whatever comes up."

"No dice," I said. "I'm not crazy."

"We don't want psychos, Selmier. We don't want punk kids looking for adventure. No dramatics. It's a job. It's work. It's necessary. That's the kind of men we want."

"No dice," I said again.

"Fourteen years, Selmier," he said. "How are you going to get out of here? Who's going to help you from the outside? Your mother's old and barely managing. Most of your dead father's money from his linen-supply business is gone. Who's going to get the lawyer to aggravate Uncle Sam long enough so that one day he'll let you go? You know the answer, don't you? No one."

" 'Necessary'?" I said. "Who's it necessary for?"

He picked at his fingernails. "Man cannot kill man except to the sound of trumpets," he said. "That's what they say, right?" He leaned forward over the table, knocking his briefcase to the floor, and said, "There *are* trumpets, Selmier. You're not dumb. You can hear them."

I didn't hear any trumpets. All I could see was two posters in front of my eyes: one was like a Marine recruitment poster, and the other had the big, empty eyes of the old trustee on it, with 14 YEARS in large print scrawled below the eyes. There really was no decision to be made. But get it on *your* terms, Dean, *your* terms.

"I don't wanna know about any trumpets," I said. "But here's what I want, and I'm not backing off any of them. One: I don't want to know who you represent. Two: I want a completely clean record. Three: I want the right to turn down any job; I want to be able to choose. Four: I want to work out a cover career before my first assignment."

"And I suppose you want us to finance the career?" he said, with a broad slash of sour wit.

"No. I know how to take care of myself."

"What do you have in mind?"

"Acting. I thought I might give acting a shot."

"What do you know about acting?"

"I've been acting all my life. I might even be acting here with you."

"You'd be a very foolish young man."

"Another thing," I said. "I don't need help. Just some pocket money to get me to New York. But I want to be well paid for what I do, for whoever it is I'm doing it for. And only two assignments; then I don't owe you anything."

"You're asking a lot with fourteen years on your back."

"I don't mind taking care of plants," I said.

"Yeah, well, how do you think you got that job, anyway." Hadn't thought of that.

"When can you arrange to get me outta here?" I asked.

"Let's go," he said.

I just stared at him.

"Let's go," he said again. "Unless they're going to give you a going-away party tonight." I was still staring. His words sounded far off.

"You don't have much of a sense of humor, do you, Selmier?"

"All right," I said. "I'll . . . I'll go back to my cell and . . ."

"You got nothing back there. You're just gonna walk out the door with me."

I walked out with him as if I had been a visitor. We got into his car.

There were guards all over, but nobody even looked at us. We drove to a Holiday Inn.

"I like these places," James said, as we walked to our rooms. "Good value for your money. Excellent salad bars."

We were in adjoining rooms. I could hear him through the thin wall: gargling in the bathroom, laughing at the television. I never did hear him turn the TV off. I made a bet with myself that he was one of those guys who fall asleep with the test pattern still on.

I couldn't sleep. I just lay there in the dark. I was out of bed before James. The sun was coming up. I knocked on his door. I had to knock several times before he opened it. He was wearing rumpled, bright pajamas, and his hair—what was left of it—was all over the place. He looked older now, stripped of his bureaucrat's uniform.

"I'm off," I said.

"I'll say you are," he growled. "You know what time it is?"

"You lose track of time in the joint," I said.

"Yeah, yeah, I know," he said, groggily moving to his dresser. He rummaged through his suitcase, and pulled out an envelope.

"Here's five hundred dollars," he said. "This should take care of your eats for a while and your bus fare."

I started out the door. "I'll be seeing you," I said.

"You can count on it, Selmier," he said.

I was at the door when he called out, "Hey, wait a minute!" He shuffled toward me with a piece of paper in his hand. "You gotta sign this voucher."

"Don't tell me you want my name on paper?"

"Just . . . put down . . . oh . . . put down 'Actor.' Sign it 'Actor.' "

That didn't make any sense to me. But since Subic Bay and long before, things had become more senseless each day. I signed his paper.

"Don't you think you oughta turn off the test pattern," I said, pointing to the buzzing television set.

"Oh, yeah, yeah, fell asleep."

"You need company that bad, you oughta get a Saint Bernard to travel with you."

"Go on. Get outta here," he said. "You're not funny, Selmier. I like you better when you're dumb."

As soon as I left him, at the door, the fear left me. It was not a dream. It was real. I was free. The Greyhound to New York droned me into a smooth, deep sleep.

(The following is a transcript from an interview with Michael Dunn and Dean Selmier on a radio station in New York City)

INTERVIEWER: Our guests tonight are Michael Dunn and Dean Selmier, both of whom are currently appearing on Broadway in Carson McCullers' *The Ballad of the Sad Café*, adapted for the stage by Edward Albee. . . . You've just finished a performance of the show, haven't you?

DUNN: Yes, we should be having a nightcap right now at Jimmy Ray's.

SELMIER: He doesn't drink. They don't have a glass small enough.

INTERVIEWER: In the play, you are one of the Rainey twins. And Michael, you are a . . . a . . .

SELMIER: How are you going to get out? Where do you go from there? Oh . . . call him a dwarf. He won't mind.

DUNN: Yes, that's what I play in *Ballad*—a dwarf. But I don't like people calling me a dwarf. This shmuck here, Selmier, is the only one I allow to do that.

SELMIER: Yeah, he gets very nasty with people who call him a dwarf. If he's in a bar, he sticks out his little arm and stabs them in the face. It's like being stuck on the lip with a toothpick. I've seen half a dozen people get toothpicks on the lip. And I'm the one who ends up going outside.

INTERVIEWER: How tall are you, Michael?

DUNN: Three foot ten inches.

SELMIER: More like three foot, I'd say.

DUNN: Pay no attention to him. He's an unlettered hillbilly. You'd be surprised, though, how often I have to defend myself. But I don't always use my arm. Sometimes I use my foot. I know just where to kick somebody to break his leg. The hillbilly here . . . he taught me how to do it.

INTERVIEWER: Michael, besides your great success in *Ballad*, what struck us was that touching picture in *Life* magazine of you two. You have a cane over your wrist, and Dean here is carrying you piggyback down the street, while you're eating a hot dog. One could feel the affection between the two of you.

SELMIER: I hate him. I hate geniuses. Go ahead. Tell him. He's got an IQ of a hundred seventy-eight. He'll lie about his height, but he won't lie about that.

DUNN: Certainly not. I have more than my share upstairs. If I had to be big and stupid, I'd rather be me. Look at Selmier, for an example.

INTERVIEWER: Where did the two of you meet?

SELMIER: I was doing *Escurial* at the Café Cino, Off-Broadway, and along came Jerome Robbins. Fine man. He was there six straight nights. I don't know what drew him. Me . . . or my work as the Fool in the play. Anyway, he introduced me to Carlo Menotti, who invited me to do the play, with Arthur Kennedy as the King, at the Festival of Two Worlds, in Spoleto, Italy. So, one night at a party there, I'm walking across the room and nearly trip over something. I look down. It's a dwarf. I said to him, "What the hell's a dwarf doing under my feet?" He said, what made a hillbilly like me think I could act. We've been close ever since.

INTERVIEWER: It seems to me, Michael, that you have far transcended your size in the theater. I mean, most people with your size have a limited future. You are respected as an actor.

SELMIER: His ego takes up the whole theater. Nobody has to feel sorry for him.

DUNN: Sure, I have a big ego. If I don't think I'm a superior person, then I'd have to think I was inferior. I get pissed off when people think I am inferior because of my size. They think I'm not human. Once, a woman had me on her lap at a party, and was stroking me like a child. I turned around and bit her. "Goddammit, I'm a man," I told her.

INTERVIEWER: Do you think your future might be limited?

DUNN: No. There are not many dwarfs who are actors. Some can speak lines, but that's all. So there isn't much competition. I knew that when I started out.

SELMIER: I wish I was a dwarf.

INTERVIEWER: How did you begin, Dean?

DUNN: He's still beginning.

SELMIER: That's right. I've been at it a couple of years now. When I first came to New York out of the service, I worked as a steeplejack, flagpole painter, washed too many windows on high buildings. I lived off and on with a girl named Melanie, a ballet dancer. She's now with the Paris Opéra Ballet. She helped me get into Herbert Berghof's acting school. My teacher was John Stix.

DUNN: You got stuck, Dean. He didn't teach you a thing.

SELMIER: I didn't know what I was doing. I remember I was called up to do a sensory-recall scene. What to do? I thought of an earache I had when I was a kid. I just let go. I bawled like a baby. They hadn't thought much of me before that.

DUNN: You'd be surprised. You can get awfully stubborn and strong when somebody says you can't do something, or doesn't think much of you. I'll show *you*, you say to yourself. And maybe you've never done it before. I once jumped off a thirty-six-foot-high board when I was ten. I couldn't even swim.

SELMIER: I was at the school, and I guess I was doing all right. Then, one day, I was doing a scene with my friend Louie Waldon from Arthur Miller's *View from the Bridge*. I was supposed to kiss Louie. The rest of the class was looking. What would I do? It was a scene that would have made a lot of them uncomfortable. It didn't bother me. I gave him a delicious kiss. The teacher was impressed. He said I was ready to go to work.

DUNN: The whole nature of acting is not to be inhibited. Express yourself. Put your tongue down your woman partner's throat. Grab her boobs. Anything. Let it out.

SELMIER: So Louie and I went up to the Shakespeare company at Stratford. Only minor roles.

DUNN: Yeah, you couldn't find the parts with a tweezer.

SELMIER: It's not very interesting.

INTERVIEWER: No, go on. We have plenty of time.

SELMIER: Well, we went up there, and being bored and

crazy, too, we sort of became a disruptive influence, they said, on the company. We were asked to leave. We had some fun with one of the leads, though. We kept teasing him about how he was always trying to get in this young actress's pants.

DUNN: Dean, you're on the radio.

SELMIER: Oh, I'm sorry.

INTERVIEWER: No, that's all right. This is free-form radio.

SELMIER: I came back. Didn't do much. Kept on washing windows. I met a fourteen-year-old runaway. Vera. Tried to straighten her out. She turned to hooking. Later, after I met the Dwarf, here, I introduced her to Michael. He wanted some of it. "Get that dwarf away from me," she said. She wanted me to introduce her to Richard Burton, who was always looking for young girls. I introduced her one night at Joe Allen's.

DUNN: He's cruel, isn't he?

INTERVIEWER: I hope you don't—

DUNN: I'm going to give him a kick in a second.

SELMIER: Then, I hooked on at the Café Cino. Did Genet's *Death Watch* there. I played the killer. Also *Escurial,* as the Fool. I rigged up a hunchback, and would come somersaulting out onto the stage. It was a helluva shocking entrance. Once, I almost landed on Jerome Robbins's lap.

INTERVIEWER: How did you get the part in *Ballad?*

SELMIER: I used to drink occasionally with Albee in the Village. He's a nice guy, but . . . what's the word?

DUNN: Like a chameleon. He can be lovely, he can be cruel.

SELMIER: He arranged for me to see the director, Alan Schneider. And, of course, knowing Michael here didn't hurt me.

DUNN: Don't blame me for your obscurity.

INTERVIEWER: Do Broadway people have much to do with each other offstage, or do they just go their separate ways? I mean, all those egos always bumping into each other.

DUNN: Of course. Who else understands them?

INTERVIEWER: Where does all this socializing take place?

DUNN: Well, Dean and I are at Downey's often. Usually drinking with Jason Robards or Albert Finney, who's in *Luther*. I like it there because not too many people stare at me, because there are fifty other people more famous than I am. Sometimes I'll see somebody looking at me, but I think it's because they know me from the play. Right or wrong, I pretend that's the reason why they are eyeing me.

SELMIER: Now and then, we go to a place called Harold's. Burton and Chris Plummer and Jason Robards are in there often. Burton will have a few, and usually nudge me and say in that big booming voice of his, "Can we get one of those young things over?" No wonder his wife picks him up at the theater whenever she can.

DUNN: He's got a thing about a woman's mammary glands. I find them vastly overrated.

SELMIER: And Shakespeare. He talked to me one night for an hour about him. I said I didn't like all those kings runnin' around in baggy clothes and talking funny, giving all those flowery speeches after cuttin' off heads. That set him off. He's good company, though. One night a bunch of us went back to someone's apartment on the West Side, and we were so drunk we were pissing off his balcony. His wife came out and we turned, all of us with our things out. She screamed, "Get these drunks out of here." Our host pulled himself up royally and said, "If they go, I go." He went.

DUNN: You see, there's a lot of strain in the theater. Actors have to let go. So do actresses. They like actors. It's incestuous, in a way.

INTERVIEWER: In what way?

DUNN: I mean there are many affairs between actors and actresses. After all, they work closely together. You're taught to touch and feel. To be uninhibited. It's like this radio station: free-form.

INTERVIEWER: Do you see any actresses steadily, Michael?

SELMIER: It's not *that* free-form, for Chrissake.

INTERVIEWER: Well, Michael here has a handsome face.

DUNN: Don't listen to Selmier. Sure, I escort actresses here and there. But like other girls it's hard for them. Sometimes there are vicious remarks from guys. Not to me: to the girls. I can handle it. But the girls aren't used to it.

INTERVIEWER: What about you, Dean? Are most of your women interests in show business?

SELMIER: I spread them out. I had a couple of dates with Barbra Streisand. Informal. You know. "I'll meet you for a hamburger" type of thing. Not even dates, I guess. She was in *I Can Get It for You Wholesale* at the time. I really liked her. Great ass. The trouble was this: I was dating her roommate. One evening, she went to shower. I was sitting on the bed with Barbra, talking and kidding with her. I was just going to make a move, and out comes my girl from the shower. Bad luck. Too bad she wasn't a little dirtier. I never did get off the ground with Barbra.

DUNN: Those things are always happening to Selmier. He's a screw-up.

SELMIER: It's catching in this business.

INTERVIEWER: So what are your plans for the future? Michael?

DUNN: I'll run out the string with *Ballad*. And then I'd like to make a big picture. Something that's going to be noticed. Then I want to go to Rome and get a lot of clothes made. American tailors seem to forget that the function of a suit is to cover your body. They ignore my size. They make a suit for a six-footer. That kind of look. It doesn't work on me.

SELMIER: I hope Michael and I are going to make our own movie. We've written the script. And now all we need to find is a little money.

INTERVIEWER: Thank you, and good luck.

SELMIER: I hope you don't lose your job.

(End of transcript)

"For Chrissake, Michael," I said. "If you play that thing one more time, I'm going to flush you and that tape down the toilet."

"I murdered you, Hillbilly," he said. "You're no match for me with give and take. Listen to it." He started to turn the tape recorder on again. I chased him around his backstage dressing room as he screeched and finally hid in a small closet. There was a knock on the door. I opened it, revealing a tie with a peanut knot. That was the first thing I saw.

"Ahhh, Selmier," James said. "Good to see you again. Put on a little weight, haven't you?" He walked into the dressing room. I hadn't seen him since I left him at the Holiday Inn and caught the bus to New York. I was hoping he'd died. Michael walked out of the closet.

"What's that?" James asked, surprised.

"That's . . . a star," I said, keeping an eye on Michael's kicking leg. "Michael," I said. "Could you give us a few minutes?" James watched the dwarf limp out. He slammed the door.

"That's a star?" James said. "Queer business you're in, Selmier." He nosed around the room, picking up a makeup kit, looking into the mirror. "*Yessssir.* A real beauty. Can never count you out, Selmier. Here you are, Broadway play, your own dressing room."

"It's not mine," I said. "It's the dwarf's. I only have a small part." He seemed disappointed.

"Still, it's Broadway, Selmier," he said. "You're a real actor. Who would have ever believed it?" He offered his hand. I took it tentatively.

"I didn't think I'd see you again," I said. "It's been a while."

"I bet you didn't. I just bet you didn't."

"Can't blame a man for tryin'."

"We're never in a hurry. You wanted time, you got time."

"Look, I keep my bargains. I owe you fourteen years. I know what the price is."

"Ohhh, of course you do. I don't pick deadbeats."

"How'd you find me?"

"You were never lost."

"So? It's only an hour till curtain."

"Yes, yes. Business. You actors are busy people. You're on, Selmier." He watched for a reaction in my eyes.

"Where? When? Who? Maybe I won't like it."

"You can't turn this one down, Selmier. We waited too

long for you. And you can forget the three W's. You'll find out when you have to. You'll take this one, Selmier. No questions. Still in shape?" He looked me over.

"I always am," I said.

"How about up here," he said slowly, pointing to his head.

"It's still on my shoulders."

"Yeah, yeah. Once you've done it, you never forget. Not the good ones, right? But you're drinking a bit much, aren't you?"

"Come on. Get on with it. How's it work?"

"What?"

"The process."

"It's simple, Selmier. Like a devil's-food cake. You don't ask, Why does yeast make dough rise? It doesn't matter. It just does."

"All right, what are my moves?"

"What are your plans?"

"I'm going to make a movie. If I can get my mother to borrow fifteen thousand dollars for me. Maybe they'll let her have it on my father's good name. I don't know."

"Make it in Europe."

"That's more money."

"Don't worry about the money."

"Okay, it's Europe."

"You go to Paris. You call this number." He wrote it down on the back of the envelope he gave me. I signed his voucher: "Actor."

"That's it?"

"Simple as that," he said, walking to the door.

"I won't see you anymore?"

"I don't think so," he said. I was closing the door behind him. He stuck his arm in the way and said hoarsely, "Oh, one other thing: the trumpets. Remember the trumpets, Selmier. You won't go wrong."

"Yeah, I know all about those trumpets," I said, closing the door. "Fuck you and your trumpets."

24

PART TWO

PARIS, 1965

Lying back on the bed in the Hôtel Scribe, near the Avenue de l'Opéra, I waited for the phone call. Up to now, I had never met him, didn't know his name, nothing except that a contact would reach me by phone. All James had said, while handing me the cash in an envelope and a plane ticket, was that I was to rely on the contact, who could supply me with anything short of a guarantee to heaven. Being a wiseass never seemed to fit James. He always reminded me of a piece of buttered white bread, face up to the sun. I would never see him again. That was fine with me.

The minutes ticked by while I played with a patch of sunlight on the wall, working my hands until they formed the likeness of a huge bird, and then of other animals. Bored, I got up and called room service for some ice-cold Stolichnaya vodka and a pepper shaker. I walked to the window and looked up at the sky, seeing in the mountains of bright white clouds all sorts of shapes and forms, mainly big, wild-eyed chariot horses thundering heads apart. It had become a habit of mine since those days in the desert with Crawford, this looking at things—say, wallpaper, or giant waves—and seeing something else.

I felt completely calm, but my mind was racing. I thought of the movie I was going to make and of my first assignment for James. How would it be? I wondered. I thought of myself on the set, of how he would look—whoever "he" was—just before I killed him. I wanted to be in both places right now: on the set, and next to *him*. The vodka came just in time.

The bottle came in a bucket of ice, and next to it was the pepper. The waiter fussed about, trying to get the maximum con out of a simple bottle of vodka. I tipped him, but he hesitated. I poured a big drink into the rocks glass, then shook several bits of pepper onto the surface. The pepper drifted toward the bottom, taking the waiter's eyes with it as I looked up. Smiling, he shook his head and left, probably thinking that here was another American who would ask for catsup at a three-star restaurant. Adding the pepper wasn't vulgar to me. It was an old habit I had picked up from my agent on Broadway, Barna Ostertag, who told me that there was a lot of fusel oil on the surface of vodka and that it was poisonous; that before the refinements of distilling, they used to make a lot of bathtub stuff in Russia. In Russia, she said, it was still common to use pepper in your vodka. James Bond used the same trick. Besides, the taste had started to agree with me.

A couple of tugs on the glass, and my anxieties started to melt. The phone rang a half hour later.

"Is this the actor?" the voice wanted to know, between large gulps of breath.

"Yeah, the name is—"

"I don't wanna know your name," the voice said, as if I should know better.

"There's a hot-dog stand by the Arc de Triomphe," he said. "Meet me there tomorrow at noon."

"I don't know where that is. Make it Notre-Dame." He didn't say anything for a long moment.

"When you're in Paris, you do what I say." The voice paused again, and then grumbled, "Okay, Notre-Dame it is. Get yourself a Paris street map. Next time, know where it is."

"You'll know me by my black boots," I said. "They're scuffed up. Like me."

"Look for a bright scarf and a pair of Hush Puppies," he said, and then roared, "What the hell, you crazy? I know what you look like. This ain't no fashion show."

I had to smile. I liked him. Whoever he was, he had a sense of humor. He didn't seem to have enough breath, though, to last another day.

The voice was sitting on the steps of Notre-Dame when I arrived. He was wearing a checked suit, big bow tie, and beret. How could you miss him? He was jotting something down on a piece of paper when he looked up and saw me. He walked toward me, almost with a penguin's waddle. I wanted to laugh, mainly because he looked so funny but also because I felt foolish, having expected someone maybe about six-three, with steel-gray eyes, someone so big that he could sit down and you wouldn't notice the bulge of a .44 Magnum in his shoulder holster. He added a name to the voice. "Puffy," he said. He wanted to know why I was smiling. I told him the truth, figuring anybody that could dress like that was certainly a man who did not take himself seriously. My innocence he chalked up to the James Bond movies.

"Too much gloss," he said. "But Fleming got close about a lot of things. People'll never know how close. I got nothin' in common with Bond." He looked me up and down. "You don't, either. Put you in a suit, and a tie around your neck, and you'd still look like an old card in a brand-new deck. Some people ain't made for clothes. Me . . . my body won't let me like them. You . . . your personality ain't made for clothes. Look at those handmade boots you got on. Beautiful! But on you they look like they just come out of Woolworth's."

"Okay, okay," I said, laughing.

"You know what finally stopped me on clothes," he went on. "Socks! Socks. They drove me crazy. I'd lose one of a pair. Or I'd get a little hole that turned into a big hole on the

29

toe. Even took to cutting my toenails real short. Still, the holes came. One day, one of them was cuttin' my toe so bad that I walked out, went home, and ripped apart every sock with a hole in it. I've gone downhill ever since." He caught me staring up at the cathedral.

"What the hell you lookin' at?" he asked. "It's just a church."

"I've been wanting to see this all my life," I said. "I've seen the film so many times."

"It looks better in the film. Come on, let's go. First, let's go to that stand over there and I'll warm up for lunch with a couple of hot dogs. Then we'll go over to my place and have lunch and talk business."

Three hot dogs vanished from his chubby little hands in five and a half bites. I counted them, while wondering about his digestion. We reached the Metro in mid-bite, and he wiped his hands on his beret. I pointed to a streak of mustard on it, and remarked that with another five or six hot dogs the beret would soon be yellow.

"Sometimes I use my jacket or pants," he said, winging past the comment and onto the train. "I love mustard."

I tried to draw a bead on him. Some of it was obvious: he ate like a hippo; he dressed as if he'd just stepped out of a pawnshop window; he should have been carrying a tank of oxygen on his back; he knew how to laugh at himself; he was from the South.

So far, so good. I've always liked Southerners. They're tricky in their own way, but if they're with you, they'll stick to you like gum when hands are called. I've never found much loyalty in the East, or any character at all on the other coast, which is only a gigantic bivouac for Easterners and Midwesterners who haven't made it yet. And the real Southerners know how to survive. This guy, I thought, would survive forever if his heart held out. I tagged him for an odds-and-ends man; a junk man for the CIA, maybe, living hand to mouth on little jobs that were chucked at him now and then like bits of raw meat; a guy who might meet you in a room somewhere and give you a name and address, and would never be seen again. Hundreds of them work the shadows of Europe and Asia. Later, I'd know how far off I'd been. I should have guessed it that first day, in his office in Montmartre.

We were hardly through his office door—which read INTERNATIONAL THEATRICAL BOOKINGS—and there he was, grunting and fighting for breath, racing for his desk. He pulled out a big oxygen cylinder, and quickly fell back into his rickety chair and clamped the mask over his mouth. He sat there, still, with the sweat pouring down his jowls and his stomach beating out and in like the heart of a magnificent elephant. Finally he began to stir. He removed the mask and then reached down and pulled a loaf of French bread out of his desk drawer.

"It's those goddamn four flights of stairs," he said. "If I take 'em too fast, they nearly kill me. If I take 'em too slow, they only wound me. It's bronchial asthma. By now, maybe emphysema. Who knows?"

"You book acts, do you?" I asked.

"Yeah," he said, smiling. "The last one I booked was four years ago. I sent an Italian juggler to the Oktoberfest. Those crazy Bavarians cracked a bass drum over his head." He pulled a penknife out of his pocket. "Hey, go over to the icebox there and get us our lunch. There's some salami in there. And some mustard."

He was not exaggerating. That's all there was: a roll of salami, six jars of Colman's mustard, and about ten roaches that had been chilled to death and were on their backs. The refrigerator and its decor blended well with the rest of the place. Now, I'm not what you'd call a gourmet, nor do I care much where I flop or under what conditions I have to work —I can make do—but why anyone would walk up four flights of steep stairs, let alone one flight, for this place was beyond me; the bums in Grand Central shacked up better than this, I thought. The room was cold, and the walls were cracking. There was no rug on the sagging floor, nor any furniture to make it sag more—only the desk and a small couch in the corner. A big poster of Clark Gable was tacked to the wall. I placed our lunch in front of him, and he began to chop at the bread and salami with his penknife.

"Quite a place you got here," I said.

"Pay it no mind," he said. "I only stay here during the hot weather. When it's cold, I stay in a little hotel near here. Paris is always cold now, it seems." He chopped at the goods, stopping only to brush aside bits of cards with numbers on them.

"What're those?" I asked.

"Tierce cards," he said. "I'm only nuts about three things: tierce, my work, and the movies." He looked up at the poster of Gable. "They don't make 'em like the King anymore. Tierce," he explained, "is a French passion that has replaced the traditional Sunday picnic. Now millions of Frenchmen sit over apéritifs in cafés, studying these maddening puzzles, which require that you select the first three horses in a certain race. But the French don't stop at anything so simple. There are six thousand eight hundred forty combinations if there is a twenty-horse field. The variations go on and on, like three horses for three francs, four for twelve francs, five for thirty francs." Puffy said he didn't know anything about horses. He only put numbers down. "Being addicted to tierce," he said, "often leaves you talking to yourself on crowded street corners.

"Now, to my work," he went on, tucking a piece of salami back into his half loaf of bread. "I'm what is known as a 'moth' in this business. Maybe the last of the pure moths left. There are other moths, but they are only quarter moths. The rest of the time they're butterflies. That means that the positions they hold, the way they look, would never make anyone think that they are quarter moths. Their range is limited. Me—I'm a real moth. Can fly forever, and you'll never know where I am next. Call, and I'm available."

"I prefer working alone," I said.

"Suit yourself," he said. "But nobody's alone in this business except the dead. All that is asked of you is perfection. They don't care how, or with whom. Make a mistake, and you'll be the smallest caribou on the ice floe, with a thousand polar bears movin' toward you. They'll let you rot in some prison. They'll let you die. You won't count. I know. I used to be a settler."

"What's a settler?" I asked.

"A settler settles . . . people," he said. "Another thing: sometimes you'll know what the work is about, sometimes not. You'll know only what you have to know. Whatever suits them. It's all cut and dried. Get the Bond crap out of your head. It's all just a piece of work. Unless you're nuts. Or a patriot."

"You must know I'm neither," I said. "I get the job done."

"What's your fancy?" he asked, finishing off his sandwich and taking a long drink from a bottle of red wine on his desk. "Explosives? Guns? Everybody's big on guns these days."

"Whatever I think of. Whatever works."

"Experimental, huh? How old are you? I'd say twenty-seven, twenty-eight. You won't see thirty." He waited for a reaction. He tried again. "I'm sick of dealing with amateurs. Kids like you who can't even make their way through a subway turnstile. Where do they find you? It's enough to make me gag." He waited again, while pulling on the wine bottle, squinting over at me with his left eye. I said nothing.

"You're not pissed off?" he finally said.

"Why should I be?" I said. "I know a con when I see one. You know who I am. You probably know more about me than I can remember. Besides, it's all just a piece of work."

"I knew I'd like you." He smiled.

"For a slob, you're all right, too," I said.

"Okay. Now, for business," he said, pulling a folder from his desk and lighting up a corncob pipe. Thinking of his lungs, I winced inside each time he inhaled the long drafts of smoke.

"The money," he said. "You know how much, right? James told you about that. No more cash from now on. Everything is bank-to-bank transaction. No envelopes passed along by blind men in dark alleys. Expenses? They go into the bank, too. Start off with a few thousand, usually, and if the cost is going over, let me know. Which bank, where, and what name. Also the account number."

"I'm not sure yet. I'll get it to you later."

He tossed the folder across the desk. There were a dozen pictures, five by seven, all of them taken from a distance: a fat man on the deck of a boat, wearing a white yachting cap and blue blazer and holding a drink in his hand; the same fat man around a pool with some bikini-clad girls; again the fat man, holding up a large fish as he is getting off a boat; and always in the background the blurred shape of a much bigger man.

"Don't mind the big slug," said Puffy. "His name is Lutz. A bodyguard. Man Friday. He's always with him. If he gets in the way, which most likely he will, send him packin', too. The fat man—he's the one you have to settle. Name's Stoessel, Hermann Stoessel. Playful-lookin' fella, isn't he? Now, where'd you say you're goin' to shoot your movie?"

"I didn't. I thought I'd take a look around first. Most likely Italy."

"Make it Spain. Save us some expenses."

"Hey, you gotta stay out of my movie work. That's none of your business."

"Look at it this way: Spain has fabulous locations; you'll be able to handle the unions better there; it's a beautiful country; and it's cheap. There's also one other item: Stoessel lives right off the coast of Spain, on an island near Ibiza. It makes sense."

"Okay, I'll take a look."

"Stay at the Hilton in Madrid. That's the hangout for the film industry. Everyone from grips to actors. It's sort of a job center."

"Anything else?" I asked.

"That's it for now."

"I'm off," I said. "Here, why don't you finish my sandwich."

"No, it'll ruin my afternoon snack." I started for the door. He called out, "Be very cautious at first."

"Stoessel?"

"No, the setups. You guys making a first film always use

too many setups. You don't have to cover every scene from every angle; they cost money."

He was working on my sandwich before I was out the door. Puffy stayed in my thoughts as I walked. In a way he was like a favorite uncle, who had been deeply stained by life, who was all alone, who was the first one drunk at all the weddings because he couldn't stand being there sober, on the brink of such sure-to-be sadness. I understood his aloneness. In another way I saw him as a tough old razorback who could handle who he was and what he did, a hard case who could be dangerous behind his pose of lovable eccentric. Maybe he was all of this. I knew only that I felt responsible for him in some way. I'd let him act in one of my movies one day. I wanted him to live long and to die in bed. Sentimental? No . . . only an unexplainable feeling I grafted onto the few people I loved, like Michael Dunn, Crawford, and some others. All of them strays in life, maybe—strays like myself —looking for themselves in their own way and knowing only —as the song goes—that "nothin' ain't worth nothin' but it's free."

I wanted to see what had made Dr. David Goldman turn his back on Park Avenue gold.

By taxi, David's clinic was about an hour outside Paris. When I got there, the kids were playing on the lawn, running and jumping and wrestling; they looked like normal kids. I got out of the taxi and walked closer, toward a young woman who was down on all fours in the middle of the lawn as squealing and grunting kids leap-frogged over her. Most of the time, with their degree of strength and coordination, they didn't make it, and she would collapse and grab them to ease their fall. Up close now, I studied the kids; they still looked normal. I walked around to the front of her, hating to give up the rear view of her in jeans. And when I got there, she was on her back with a kid up on her hands, her chest heaving in an Irish wool sweater and her long, straight hair tangled in her face. She and the kid stopped giggling, and her head and eyes tilted back at me. She did a quick flip-flop onto her belly and elbows and looked up at me and said with a wry smile, "Just a night out with the boys." Lucky boys.

"I'm looking for Dr. David Goldman," I said. "I'm an old friend." She got up, but didn't bother to straighten herself; she didn't have to. A couple of kids draped themselves around her legs.

"An old friend with money, I hope," she said, gesturing with her hand toward the house. "This way. He's in his office working on the books."

"He's not too good with money," I said. "He likes to run away from it." I cut it off right there. I didn't know how friendly she and David were.

"You know how much it takes just to heat this old dump?" she said, as we neared the house. "As much as it would cost for a couple weeks at the Ritz. The expenses here eat you alive. I don't know how he makes it."

"Those kids looked all right to me," I said. "Where are all the defectives?"

Her hair whipped around; then there were eyes flashing like sparks. Just as quickly, she said, her voice even and controlled, "We don't call them that here. They are children. Three kinds: those who can be educated to a modest level, those who can be trained, and those who are totally dependent. You saw all of the first group. They just look like other children."

She left me by the stairwell, pointing to David's office. There was arctic ice in her eyes. I didn't care. I still saw her on the ground, with her ass sticking up, that solid back, her hair dangling.

David's office door was open, but he wasn't there. I sat down behind his desk and waited. The office was plain, with old simple furniture. There was a small bookshelf in back of the desk, filled with fat clinical-looking books. A map of the world was tacked to the wall and had pins stuck in many cities—Tel Aviv, Stockholm, and others. Off the landmass of the U.S., where Long Island would be, there was a deep blackening made by a felt-tip pen. On the desk in front of me were a thin accounting ledger, a book, and a half-written letter, which began

Dear Monsieur and Madame Dibault:
   I can deeply understand your pain and the feeling of, first, inadequacy, and now, emptiness. As I told you when you brought Jacques here several months ago, these feelings were only natural, but that you and Jacques would both learn in time. Your son seems to be learning faster. He is not—as you suggest —a living vegetable. There is no such identification at the clinic. Like many children here, Jacques is in a lonely fight for dignity . . .

In the margin was scrawled "Have Sandra translate."
   David's voice filtered in from the hallway. I quickly moved to the wall in back of the door, and doubled my fist. He entered, and I stuck the fist into his back, growling, "Don't move, you crazy shrink!" His hands went up and his body stiffened, until I said, "Now who would want to knock off a Jew who doesn't like money?"
   He turned, the fright receding from his face. He looked at me oddly for a second; then we grabbed each other by the shoulders in welcome. He had changed. His cocksure eyes, once so certain of the future, of the line of movement in his life, seemed vague, tentative. His face was pale and dry, with jagged etchings beginning to form around his eyes where his dark and heavy eyebrows cut away. His thick hair was mussed, his tie loose and crooked around his neck. His brown tweed jacket looked as if it had been cleaned and pressed too much.
   "How many times do I have to tell you?" I could hear him saying. "You farmers from the Midwest think all Jews have money. So why do they keep getting hit over the head in

Brooklyn. They should be in Miami with their money." He paused. "What are you looking at?"

"You look older," I said.

"Yeah, we Jews also grow old fast." He laughed. "Well, you don't look any different. You still look like a scout for General Custer."

"What's with the map?" I asked, sitting down.

"That's where my heroin shipments go," he said, trying to make a sinister face. He wasn't very good at it.

"And that book? I never used to see you read anything except those schoolbooks of yours. And the society page of the *Times.* To see what rich Jewish girls you had screwed were getting married."

"The man with a million questions. You're worse than a Jewish mother. Make that a Jewish father who's a surgeon."

"Yeah, and he's getting old, very old. Look, I might as well come out with it. Your father came backstage at *Ballad.* He doesn't look well. When he held his hands up, they were trembling. He asked me if I was going to be writing you. I told him I was going to Paris. 'Dean,' he said, 'tell him to come home; tell him his father needs him. He'll listen to you,' he said. Where'd he ever get that idea? . . . I've delivered the message."

"Dean, what can I tell you? He just doesn't understand. Never did. He chose his way in medicine, knife-happy and fee-crazy. Let's say I've chosen my way. My work here is important and sensitive." He picked up the letter in front of him. "Take this, for an example."

"I read it. Kinda personal, isn't it?"

"Everything's close to you around here. Look at Monsieur and Madame Dibault. Embarrassed. Guilty. Can't even stand to look at Jacques. They've been here once in six months, and they wanted to know when he'd be able to read and write. Read and write. Hell, it will be a triumph if we are ever able to get him to wrap strings around a package."

This was the serious David now, the natural bent of his character since he had risen up against the values of the

AMA, his father, and, as he once put it, against his mother's chicken soup. Glibness was not his style, only a device among the baggage he used when he tried so hard to keep up with that fast and trendy Long Island crowd: weekends of horseback riding and sailing in the fall, almost all sailing and sunbathing during the summer, and parties outdoors with long buffet tables under Chinese lanterns, parties that ended at Sunday dusk with everyone looking vacantly at one another and trying to remember who was the young man or woman who had shared his or her bed the night before. On the cold Sunday mornings in winter, if they were really bored, if they had already done the Caribbean, they would meet at Allen's, up on the East Side of Manhattan, for a bloody mary, and then drive slowly through the Bowery in their sports cars and look at the freaks littering the sidewalks, or the winos who would jump out and try to clean their car windows for a coin; then the caravan would end up in some quaint, sawdusted place for brunch.

"Look at it as an anthropological mission," David once cracked when I balked at one of those impromptu trips. That was his crowd speaking, not David, I would learn later. Keep it light, and don't be a bore with talk of politics and the world's end. There were no bells tolling for them. Did these emotional sixties ever finally reach that crowd? I wondered, looking at David now. I knew they had spun David around, but the trigger had been not so much a slow shift in consciousness as a personal shock of recognition on a lazy, faraway autumn day of boating that I had almost forgotten but that he never would.

I first met David at one of those parties in Great Neck. I didn't know what I was doing there, except maybe that the girl who took me thought I was a curiosity piece: my being a steeplejack and a hungry actor might provide some off-flavor for the dull periods between bed and bar. She slept with someone else that night; so did I. "You don't sleep with the guy you bring, silly," she said. As if I cared.

It was the second afternoon of the marathon when David sat down next to me near the pool. He said he had heard that I was a steeplejack. He looked to be about my age, but with a pampered face, evenly suntanned, and without a hair out of place; a guy whose life figured to have few surprises, no sudden turns of fortune or mind. He said he was studying psychiatry. I told him psychiatrists sucked. He smiled thinly, and went on. Why was I such a hostile person? Was I ever afraid being a steeplejack, and could I define the fear? Did I feel irrelevant in such a technological age? I didn't know what "irrelevant" meant, I told him. "There you are," he said. "You are hostile. Everybody knows what 'irrelevant' means." I didn't.

We talked about fear and violence, and I told him about Crawford's sporting kill in the desert. The incident shocked him, but he finally said he could understand, because "Boredom does strange things to the mind." He didn't have it quite right. I said that I could kill him right there, and not give it a second thought. He dismissed that as bullshit, but later came back to it, saying, "Maybe you are completely without conscience." Fabulous. For this he goes to shrink school. Three hours passed before he got up and said, "That'll be fifty dollars." I told him I got paid the last time I was asked so many questions. "How much?" he asked. "With bread and water in a dark room," I said. I didn't elaborate.

After that day we would hook up twice a month or so for dinner in Manhattan, usually at Frankie & Johnnie's. Or I'd go out to Long Island, and we'd go sailing, usually the two of us and a couple of girls. He seemed to have a lot of free time, I thought then, for a kid up to his neck in studies. I mentioned it to one of his friends. "Oh, David," he said. "He's so brilliant he's a bore. I keep waiting for him to fall on his face, but he never does. Everything comes easy to David."

He fell, all right! It was during an afternoon on Long Island Sound. I can still see him there, with an impish grin on his face, and then, suddenly, his mouth open and a terrible fright in his eyes, like only a few minutes ago when I stuck my fist in his back. The clouds seemed to be frozen in a high sky, the water was choppy, and the mood was light and aimless. We had gone through half a case of champagne in a couple of hours. I was fiddling with the sail, with my back turned to David and the girls, and I could hear him saying, "Now, really, girls, let's be intellectually honest. How many times have you come when making love? Once? Twice? That's the most. You fake it, don't you? How clever women are."

On that note I turned, and there he was, his arms and legs at wild angles, his body falling backward into the cold water. One of the girls had pushed him, and the champagne had done the rest. The champagne had worked on me, too. I figured he'd be back on deck in a few minutes. But the current was carrying him farther away. Twenty feet. Thirty feet. I thought of throwing him a rope, but he wasn't in any shape to catch one. There wasn't any time to turn the boat around. He panicked; his motions were spastic. He was forty feet away now. React, Dean; dammit, react!

I grabbed a life preserver and hit the water on my belly, my head up, the water feeling like a thousand icy needles. I couldn't find him. I yelled his name several times before he bobbed up, to the left, thrashing even more furiously than before. He'd been down once. I knew he couldn't hold out much longer. He was about sixty feet back and to the left, but the current was carrying him toward shore. The current, the hundred push-ups I did every day, the long, barely endurable survival course that I had mastered in the service—all of this was working for me now. I didn't take my eyes off him as I swam. Hard! Long, smooth strokes. Harder! Long, strong strokes. He was in my arms. I dropped the preserver around him, cradled his head upward in my arm, and kicked for shore. The current was running like a Greyhound bus, and had it not been with us, or had it been less rapid, we might never have made it. Once on the beach, I put him over my right shoulder, head down, and slogged to the nearest house. The people called an ambulance, then the Coast Guard, to pick the girls up, while I did some basic lifesaving work on David. The water soon trickled out over his blue lips. I didn't feel so good myself. My legs grew heavy, my body shivered uncontrollably, and my lungs ached. Then, I passed out.

David changed. He had been a sponge soaking up the juice of life up to this time; he had been a frivolous creature who had a gifted mind. But now, as the sixties began to rumble, he changed. No more sailing, no more long weekends of sex and booze. He took long rides south in buses filled with blacks through the fires of Montgomery and the police dogs of Birmingham. Twice he would be locked up with Dr. King, once with a cracked head.

"I could understand, maybe, if my son was eighteen," his father moaned, "but he's twenty-four years old."

It took only a little more than a year for David to turn his back on movements—at least physically. He did not go back to his old Long Island weekends but instead saw himself as a sort of mixture of Albert Schweitzer, Tom Dooley in Laos, and Thomas Merton.

By now, his old man was pulling his hair out. "He acts as if money were poison," he growled. "What does he think is sending him through all his schooling. Buttons?"

Old Dr. Goldman didn't want any credit. He just wanted David to face the American facts of life as he knew them, wanted a son to carry on "the profession" through the next three decades, and for that son to have a son who would do the same. Neither of them backed off an inch. And David finally left it all behind—without guilt and as coldly as if he'd sliced a dangling button off a jacket.

"How personal is it with you and the broad?" I asked, interrupting his monologue about his work at the clinic.

"What girl?"

"The one that was out front with the kids. You said everything's personal around here. Does that include her?"

"You mean Sandra. Well, let's put it this way: she will get very personal if you call her a broad. This is 1965. That's a name out of *Guys and Dolls!*" There was a slight impatience in his tone.

"Okay, then," I said. "Suppose you bring Sandra with you to dinner when I get back from London."

"One doesn't bring Sandra anywhere," he said. "I'll ask her if she wants to join us."

"Do that," I said. David could still get pompous as hell. His dad would be proud of that.

LONDON, 1965

Cut away all the theories of psychology applied to people, all that crap about *what* they are, *why* they are, and where they're going, and I think you have only two kinds of people: those who stay behind, and those who keep on movin'. Few know where they're movin' to; they just move on. Whether it is the next step up the office ladder or the last dart from behind a tree in some godforsaken jungle war, hardly a man is ever really prepared to do what he has to do. You just do it. And then you know that you were ready. And you keep doing it, taking the one extra lunge, jacking up the stakes in your life, until one day you stop and say to yourself, Am I what I think I am? Am I really prepared? And that's when you can call off the dogs and piss on the fire: the hunt is over; you won't be movin' anywhere anymore.

All of this passed through my mind on the plane to London, where I would meet the Dwarf, who helped write the film that everybody thought I couldn't make because I didn't know a thing about making films; to London, where I would also take that first step toward my first killing for men who ordered them up as if they were reading off a menu. I was movin' on, I thought, away from fourteen years in prison that they could drop on me anytime if I didn't perform; away from the fantasy of making a film, to reality. No doubts tracked through my mind. There were no secrets to either —filming or killing. The two only become muddled through too much talk and interpretation: in film, because of high-brow critics who love to smother a story with technical fuzz, like with long prose songs on Antonioni's lens choices; in killing, for industrial or national expediency, talk of how it somehow must reach far beyond everyday life, of how it illustrates dark secrets, has a magic of its own no matter how one might feel about the deed itself. What bullshit! There is no magic in method or motive or style; the magic comes later: when it is done, when you are still alive and sitting there behind your "cover" and thinking of all that could have gone wrong, all that could have made you very dead.

"Hey, Hillbilly!" a voice yelled as I passed through the lobby of the Piccadilly Hotel. I knew whose voice it was, but when I looked around, I couldn't see him. The Dwarf could be tough to find even when you were looking for him. I finally spotted him. His tiny feet were sticking out of a deep chair. He toddled over, looked up, and said, "Look, I have to meet a reporter now at the Mermaid. That's a pub below a small theater down off Fleet Street, a theatrical and press hangout. He wants to interview me. He wanted to come here, but I said I'd rather go there. I want to have dinner around the corner at the Wig and Pen. I'll be with a guy. John Thorstan. Acts a little bit on the stage. Runs a small watch-repair shop on the Kings Road. Check in and come on down."

"Well, the financing is all set," I said.

"How much?"

"Enough," I said. "If you lay off the booze and don't fuck up the shooting." He faked a karate chop to my knee.

"What are your plans?"

"I figure we're here a couple of days. . . ."

"Why don't you come to Rome with me for a couple more? I have to have some suits made."

I remembered what he had told me about the last time he

was there, the first time he walked into the shop. The Italian tailors didn't know what to do. They only stared: at his feet, at his arms, at his legs. None of them said anything, until one of them picked him up and placed him on a stool, and then they all began fluttering and squeaking around him like hungry birds. He was clearly a challenge to them, and when he came back for a fitting, he got a leg caught in his tiny new jump suit and toppled off the stool. They picked him up as if he were a rare piece of sculpture.

"I'd love to see you and your tailors," I said, "but I can't. I have to be back in Paris. We'll hook up in Madrid. Say, in ten days. We'll be ready to get started on the film. Go on. I'll see you in an hour or so."

"I'm too big now, Hillbilly," he said, referring to his recent success in *Ship of Fools,* the picture in which he played a strolling narrator and bemused observer on a ship bound from Mexico to Germany before the war. "I don't think you can afford me."

"Dwarfs don't get any bigger," I said. "And besides, we're partners. It's our film. Remember? It was your idea."

"But you don't know a camera from a baseball bat," he continued.

"Quiet, or I'll put you in my suitcase," I said, starting to drop down and grab him.

Laughing, he ran to the door.

The Dwarf, his friend Thorstan, and the reporter were at a table in the corner of the Mermaid.

"It could be a rumor," the reporter was saying, "but have you heard anything about the fact that you may be nominated for an Academy Award for *Ship of Fools?*"

"I've heard the same rumors," said the Dwarf, "but I think it's too early to tell right now. Maybe in another month or two we'll know. I'm not thinking about it. Doing the picture was enough for me. You got enough?" The reporter nodded, thanked him, and left.

"Let's go over to the bar for a drink," said the Dwarf. "Thorstan, here, is what they call a villain. Not like you,

Hillbilly, who's always playing at it. Retired now, though, aren't you, John? He's also not bad with a line."

"You might say I'm retired there, too," said Thorstan. "I like the peace and quiet of my watches. Old watches. You can count on only two bloody things in London these days: old dogs and old watches. I make a living."

I lifted the Dwarf up on the bar, and as we drank, he pointed to a man with a girl down at the far end.

"Look at that, will ya," said the Dwarf. "The guy's got a goddamn viewfinder around his neck. I thought that sort of exhibition went out with casting couches and whipcord riding britches. Has to be an amateur. Directors don't wear those things in bars."

"What's it for?" I asked.

"It's used to put the scene in a frame," said the Dwarf. "Looking through it, you see how the scene will look on the screen. A lot of directors keep one around their necks on the set to check out all the possible setups and camera angles."

"There are three buttons on the end of it," said John, "and it comes apart in three places. An easy bit of gadgetry. Nothing at all like the beautiful madness of some of my timepieces in the shop."

"You see what I mean, John?" said the Dwarf. "Amateurs. All over the place. One down there trying to impress his girl. Here's another, Dean, who's going to waste his money and my time. And he doesn't even know what a viewfinder is."

"I have one in my shop," said John. "Come on up and I'll explain how it works."

The next morning the Dwarf and I went over the script changes I had made, and then I made my way up to Thorstan's. He didn't look up as I entered. He had a jeweler's glass in one eye, and was bent over with a thin, half-inch tool between his thumb and forefinger. The place was quiet, and then, suddenly, a series of chimes went off. The noise didn't bother him; it was familiar. Finally he looked up.

"Oh, there you are, Dean," said John. "Close and delicate work, this." He held up a big pocket watch in the palm of his hand. "This was made about 1910. It only has a thread of life left in it. I'm trying to bring it back all the way."

"John, about the viewfinder," I said. "Is it possible for a trigger mechanism to be placed inside, and then released by one of those buttons?"

"What do you want to release?"

"A cylinder of smoke. In the script, one of the characters is drugged, and the Dwarf and I didn't want to go with the old pill-in-the-drink routine."

He thought a moment, then opened the drawer below him and pulled out a viewfinder. He dismantled it in three pieces and inspected the insides of each piece.

"Yes, it can be done," he said. "It will take me a week or so."

"Will you do it?" I asked.

"Sure, but I have to ask you for a few bob. I have to put my other work aside here and there."

"Here," I said, putting one hundred pounds down on his table. "This is for the viewfinder and your work."

"No, Dean," he said, "this is far too much. Especially for a friend of Michael Dunn."

"You don't tell him"—I winked—"I won't tell him. Just make sure it works."

Maybe it *will* work, I thought.

And if it doesn't?

There are other ways. When you keep on movin' on.

PARIS

The dinner talk was boring. David was going on about the French people's rudeness to strangers, particularly Americans. They were never rude to me, I thought, and Sandra closed the topic. "David, speak the language and they're pussycats."

I didn't want to seem like a jerk by asking Sandra all those dumb first questions, like, What do you do? Where do you come from? What are your interests? I wanted to know, but I wanted it to flow naturally. I wanted to ease into her; this was not a woman you tried to impress.

"David, I'd like to use the clinic's bank account," I said as the brandy came. "It's convenient for me, and it's important. I'm going to be getting sums of money from time to time. The money will go right into your account. Use five thousand for now. I'm sure it will help the clinic some."

David studied the brandy, swirling it in his glass. "What money? Where from? Who—" His eyes showed nervousness.

"No, it's not from your father."

"Then why are you letting me take—"

"I'd like to help your work. That's all. If you don't like that one, then call it an exchange for the use of your account." David said he didn't much like the idea. Sandra said he was a fool. She meant it. She blew the brandy down with one swig, and asked me to order another. David said he would accept the arrangement. He'd like to know more, though. I told him there wasn't going to be any more—ever. He sulked. Bring on the chicken soup, Mama, I thought.

We parted outside the restaurant; David went to his car and Sandra to hers. I said I would walk back to my hotel. I didn't want to push my luck with her by riding in her car; the nearness of her might set me off. I knew I wouldn't get anywhere that way. Her smell stayed with me during the ten-block walk to the Scribe, but my mind was on David.

I tried to piece him together. Punk rich boy. Committed idealist. Prodigal son. Schweitzer. Damn, if that was what money and brains and training did to you, who needed it? I remembered an incident at Downey's one night when Michael Dunn and I were there with him. The Dwarf never liked him, never liked all his questions about his size and

48

feelings; David was not being insensitive, only a bit clinical, trying to understand and learn. But Michael put up with him until that night at Downey's.

"Dean, I've come to . . . the conclusion," David slurred, "that you're evil, that you're an . . . evil . . . hillbilly." He laughed so loud that heads turned our way; it was a mean laugh. "If you . . . don't believe me," he continued, "just . . . just you ask the . . . Dwarf here."

He was on the first octave of another laugh when the Dwarf's tiny paw stabbed his nose. Michael was ready to give him his left paw when I grabbed it in midair. Blood dripped from David's nose, but he just stared out at the strong left arm of the Dwarf, frozen in my hand, then at the two of us, with horror in his eyes. I put a napkin up to his nose, and helped him get a cab.

When I got back to the table, I said to Michael, "Dwarf, why go and do that? He's only a rich kid trying to forget he's rich."

He didn't say anything then, but a week later, the Dwarf said, "You don't know much about people. The rich never forget they're rich, Dean. I see them every night in the theater—the old rich, the new rich, the expense-account rich. But the real rich never turn their backs on money. They know what it is: power. You may believe he's running from his money, he may believe it, but he can't run away from the smell of power. That will always be with him. Dean, I'm not a dwarf if it doesn't turn up in him someday."

There seemed a strain between David and me. We no longer seemed to have anything in common. Once, maybe, my craziness had given him a sense of freedom. Now, through his work, he had outgrown our friendship. He didn't want me around, and yet he did not like the thought that he felt that way. The conflict made him irritable. Maybe that was it. I was a burden to him, a reminder that he could never be entirely free, because he owed me.

I wished I didn't need his bank account. I wished I would have let the Dwarf get through with his left paw. I wished

... What the hell—I still admired him for what he had given up, for what he was doing with those kids at the clinic, the private research he was engaged in whenever there was time for it.

"Why work your ass off when the parents don't even care?" I had asked him over dinner.

"Because I love my work," he said. "And that may be the dumbest motivation for doing anything these days."

No, Michael Dunn, I thought, you are not a dwarf.

 MADRID

Common sense, instinct, desire, and a lot of pluck is all you need to direct your first film. The same with a killing. It is odd how similar the steps are: first the idea, or the objective; then the preproduction planning, the selection of locations, the rounding up of equipment and technicians, the casting. And then the production schedule itself: the number of shooting days, making each one count because loss of time can break you, can take your short money and destroy the building of mood. Then a certain motion begins, until it becomes a force, and you can sense that the story or victim is yours, and that there is no way that either can get away.

The motion moved into another gear as soon as I touched down at the Hilton bar on my first evening in Madrid. Puffy had been right: the bar looked like a stock exchange for the film business of Spain. One sweep of the bar and I had already made a couple of faces: Nicholas Ray, the expatriate director; and a noted screen villain, a fine actor whose name I could never remember and who had never caught on the way he should have. I knew him slightly, from Broadway, but I wasn't going to say hello. Besides, his back was turned to me. He even looked like a mean bastard from that angle. He had been a great soldier in World War Two. When Patton was driving through France, pictures appeared in U.S. newspapers of German officers hanging from meat hooks. Who in hell was hanging them from meat hooks? Patton was asked. He didn't know, but he would find out. He did. It was Old Nameless there at the end of the bar. He was called in front of Patton. He figured on a court-martial. Patton gave him a medal.

I had been in the bar half an hour when a dark little sparrow lighted next to me. He started shoveling peanuts into his small mouth.

"Señor, are you in film?" he asked.

"Why?"

"I always ask, señor. Everybody here in film. Spain like Hollywood now. My uncle Elorito, he is producer."

"And you?"

"My name, señor, is Luis. I work for my uncle."

"Yeah, I'm in film."

"An actor?"

"Yeah, but I'm here to *make* a film."

"You never make film before in Spain?"

"That's right."

I waited for his graft. He shoveled some more peanuts into his mouth.

"We can be of help, señor?" he asked.

"Maybe. What kind of help you got?"

"Come, señor. You talk with my uncle."

I followed him out of the hotel. We got in a taxi and rode for seven blocks until we stopped in front of a storefront. It wasn't MGM, but it looked all right. A blast of garlic hit me as I opened the door. The old man behind the desk looked like a piece of fresh leather that had been too long in the sun. He was sucking on some fishbones, and it looked like the rest of the fish was on his sleeves.

"This is my uncle Elorito," Luis said.

"A pleasure, señor—"

"Dean," I said.

"He is to make film, Uncle."

"Ah," said Elorito, picking at a back tooth. "The Americans, the English, the Germans—everybody want to make film in Spain now. So cheap, so beautiful."

"This American wants to make a little film," I said.

"How little, señor?" he asked. "Little little? Little big? Big little?" He paused, and then got to the point. "What is your financing?"

"Under thirty thousand dollars," I said.

"Little little," he said, picking up another bone.

"Too little, right?"

"Nothing is too little in Spain, Señor Dean."

"What do you want for your end?"

"Nothing. Just all distribution in Spain."

"It's a deal."

"So what do you need from us?"

"First, a cameraman," I said.

"Do you want to look at some footage?" he asked.

"No, I know the man. Luis Cuadrado. I've seen a few of his films. He's perfect. Can we get him?"

"If he is not working, yes."

"Tell him I'll treat him fairly. He's got talent."

I pulled a checklist out of my pocket and scanned it.

"The script has to be translated."

"No problem."

"And actors?"

"No problem. What about raw stock? You can get very good deal from my cousin's lab."

"Yeah, that's fine. Now—"

"Sixteen or thirty-five, señor?" Elorito asked.

"What's that?"

"The raw stock. Sixteen or thirty-five millimeter?"

He had me there. I didn't want to look stupid. If I did, this old pirate would come down on me like an oak.

"What kind of question is that?" I said, somewhat annoyed. "You know it's going to be shown in big theaters."

"Thirty-five," he said, writing on a pad next to his fish.

"And two cameras," I said.

"Aeroflex?"

"Yeah, that's it. Aeroflex. Now, what about the unions? How many men do I need?"

"Twenty-one," he said.

"Now, there *is* a problem."

"The unions, señor. You know how they are. They are always a problem. The actors, they are cheap. But the unions. One big problem."

"Let me see the union by-laws that say I got to have twenty-one men," I snapped. I didn't see him coming up with any book. He didn't even make a move to the drawer. He paused only a beat.

"Well, then, it is seven, señor."

"Elorito, don't fuck me around," I said, reaching over and purposely knocking the dish of fish and its juice into his lap, "and I won't fuck around with you." I apologized.

"A way of life too long," he said, shaking his head.

"Now, what about the sound?"

"Two men. One on the boom mike, one with earphones, checking the sound levels."

"No, Uncle," Luis interrupted. "He can shoot the film *en silencio* and dub it later." Uncle Elorito glared at his nephew. "That's the way it's done here," said Luis, nervously looking at me.

I looked at Uncle. "Ah, yes, señor," he said, "I forget. Old men forget so easy."

"All right, I'll be back in two weeks," I said. "Everything will be ready?" I pulled out my money. "Here's five hundred dollars for odds and ends and as a bond of good faith between us." I started for the door with Luis.

"We will be ready, Señor Dean," said Elorito, counting the money.

"Yeah, and one other thing," I said, turning back. "I figure on twelve shooting days. Then, two more with just a cameraman to pick up some loose scenic footage on Ibiza."

"Where, señor?" Luis asked.

"*Ibeeza,*" I said.

"There is no such place."

53

I spelled it out. "I-B-I-Z-A."

"Ah, *Ibeetha*," he said.

I could hear it now. The motion was humming like a huge electric cable in and around me.

 PARIS

Even Paris can be dreary in the morning. The rain slapped against the windshield of Sandra's Fiat. Because of the rain, she had picked me up at the hotel. I didn't want to leave the hotel. I wouldn't want to leave the hotel on a good day, I thought, looking down at the stretch of her long legs between a miniskirt and black boots. I figured she'd try to make a run for a museum, especially when she began to drop Rembrandt on me.

"A good friend of mine had an opportunity to buy a small Rembrandt oil at a private auction. He brought in three art critics to guarantee its authenticity. They all agreed it was genuine, and he bought it for a small fortune. When he had it prepared and cleaned, they found another painting and signature underneath. He had bought himself a Lucas, not a Rembrandt. I haven't read an art critic since."

She pointed to a building. "The Louvre is up ahead." I didn't like that. I couldn't see three hours being spent in a museum. Goddamn rain! If it wasn't pouring out, I probably could have got away with a few monuments, an intimate lunch, and then a nice, long walk. I do well on nice, long walks. I was silent, trying to figure a way to get her out of the Louvre.

As we came upon it, she gunned the Fiat, and before I knew what to think, all those dead masters were behind us. She turned and said, "I wouldn't put you through that."

"How'd you know?"

"I can feel it in a man. A lot of men don't seem to go for museums, but that has nothing to do with being a man. A man is no less a man if he can stand in front of a Van Gogh for fifteen minutes and see something, and he's not less a man if he can't."

"I can't. They bore me. I'd much rather look at you."

"Great artists don't bore. If you can see. If you try to understand. . . ."

The windshield was fogging like crazy with all the talk. No rag under the seat, so I popped open the glove compartment and fished around. I felt a cold object against the back of my hand. A handgun. It was attached to the roof of the glove compartment. I found a cloth, closed the compartment, and wiped Sandra's window first. I said nothing.

"By saying that they bore you, you're implying that you know something about it."

"They're like Antonioni. He puts me to sleep."

"He's a great painter."

"But a bad director," I added.

"Are you a good director?"

"We'll see. But I'll settle for being as good as Sergio Leone."

"Blood and guts. All those big Italian close-ups."

"Hey, where are we going?"

"Well, we're going back to my apartment. And then we're going to have a huge salad with French bread and wine. And then we're going to do the only civilized thing there is to do on a day like this." She adjusted the radio, then looked at me.

"What's that?"

"We're going to bed."

I felt the adrenaline. "Kid me some more. I like it."

"Who's kidding. It's better than masturbating. But I can't complain about that. It's been good to me."

"How so?" I asked. I felt like a tongue-tied ventriloquist.

"It freed me. Once I found that I could give myself pleasure, I was free to pick and choose. I didn't have to settle for some sweating clod, panting like a horse. Some jerk who doesn't know that making love is an art, too. I had enough of them in the army."

"You're direct as hell, aren't you?"

"Why not? I'm not a mannequin in a store window; I'm not the pedestal type. I'm a woman, with the same drive between my legs that you have. Nothing shocking about that. It's elementary. But a lot of men can't handle it. They want the whole wine-and-roses thing. Wine and roses is nice, but that comes afterward. If I care. I might not want any wine and roses later. I might not seem hard to get, but I am. You don't get my mind—or me, for that matter—with what's there in your jockstrap." I listened to that marvelous voice and kept my eyes on her profile. The voice was soft and velvety, like the smile on her face.

"How do you know I have a jockstrap on," I asked. I was smiling now, too.

"The firm bulge there," she said, looking down. "It's not natural. What are you—penis-proud or an ex-dancer?"

"No . . . it's more convenient," I said, fumbling. "I don't believe in having many clothes. I find this comfortable and easy to wash." It was the truth. It wasn't much, but it was the best I could do. If she made love like she talked . . . The adrenaline came again.

"That thing can stand up on its own," she said. "Give it a break. Let it breathe."

"How can you tell?" I asked.

"Your thumb. It's immense." Like a jerk I started eyeing my thumb. "And your big toe is probably gigantic, too."

She changed the subject back to the salad she was going to make—a mountain of salad, she said, with chopped-up walnuts, tomatoes, radishes, lettuce, prosciutto, strips of leftover chicken, and roquefort dressing. The car ride was endless, and it wasn't until later that she told me she had gone well out of her way while she made up her mind for certain about me.

"I am what I am," she said, "and usually do what I say, but I wanted to be sure about you. Because I liked you, and

I didn't want to feel that I had made a mistake, that you were some fool who would come in two minutes and have his clothes on by the third minute."

"Wrong guy, Sandra."

In bed now. The next morning. Having hardly moved out of it since she made the salad the afternoon before. She was still wearing the Irish wool sweater I had told her to put on; I wanted to feel the way it was when I first saw her on the lawn of the clinic with the kids. She was bare from the waist down. She was still half sleeping when I got up to make breakfast. Unusual woman, Sandra. No last name yet. Knew only that she was born in Israel and very proud of being a Sabra. In an ass-backwards way, she reminds me of me. She was free the day she popped out of her mother's womb. She was a natural. The kind of woman who didn't want to be a man, who liked being a woman; it came easy to her and she wasn't afraid of it. Or of being feminine. Sandra knew how to be a woman; she had that elusive presence that can't be spelled out, only sensed and valued like a cool desert wind when it first comes at night. You wouldn't find her at singles bars. You wouldn't find her worrying about fashion; what she wore soon became fashion. You wouldn't find her barricaded behind useless possessions; she cared only about her paintings, all of them by unknown artists. I knew that no matter how close we would be, there would always be some dark tunnel of her mind through which I would never be allowed. Nor would anyone else.

She came into the kitchen as the toast popped up. She was still bare from the waist down, the sleep still in her eyes. She had a great ass.

"What's that?" she asked, leaning on my shoulder and staring into the frying pan.

"I call them 'mess-hall eggs,'" I said. "They look like eggs; they smell like eggs; they might even taste like eggs. But if you threw them against the wall, they'd bounce back and hit you in the head." She ate them anyway.

"Can you earn a living working for David at the clinic?"
The apartment was nice. Real nice.

"David can't even earn a living working for David," she
said, and laughed. "I work there whenever I can, usually
two or three mornings a week, but David can't afford to pay
me."

"And this place, the car . . ."

"I'm a social secretary," she said. "For Monsieur Garrotte."

"That's a nice name. What's he do?"

"What does Monsieur Garrotte do? Well, he's got his
hand into a little bit of everything."

"And what's a social secretary?"

"I keep his appointment schedule. Go to business dinners
with him."

"You meet a lot of men, eh?" I said, feigning jealousy, but
maybe it wasn't fake.

"Always," she said. "Some I like. Some I don't. Some I
like very much. You fall in the last category."

"And David—does he fall in the last category, too?"

"Of course not. David's a saint." I liked the message.

"Then it's wine and roses," I said. She got up and opened
the white-shuttered windows. She turned toward me, folded
her arms, and smiled.

The sun came in first as a ribbon that split the room in half,
then ended up on an oil painting of a woman that hung on
the wall. The woman was nude to the waist and looked like
Sandra. I cleaned off the table and did the breakfast dishes.
I always do the dishes when I stay over with someone; I
always did them for the Dwarf when I would stay with him,
and his maid didn't like it much. I'm also good with a vacuum cleaner and a hell of a show at a Laundromat. I'd say
I was neat in a quiet sort of way, very patient, careful, and
precise. I'm fond of planning, making lists, checking things
off as I go. You'd never know that by my appearance, which
says I play life on instinct and follow no plans. Plans can put
you in a tight jacket, sure; but that doesn't stop me from

going through the motions and making them and then throwing them out if I want to. It's always good to have a script. A script for filming. A script for killing.

Winter sunlight filled the room now, making it warm and soft. She had six large pillows under a lamp next to a high bookcase in the corner. I moved the pillows to the center of the room and stretched out naked, letting the sun wash over me. When she came out of the bedroom, she dropped down and rested between my legs, her head on my thigh, her face looking up. The sun made her eyes glow. She closed them.

We must have slept for a couple of hours, and when I got up, she had gone into the bedroom. I went to her. She was sprawled drowsily in bed, a book opened on her chest, and I bent down and kissed her. She told me to walk over to the top drawer of her bureau.

"You see those four long sashes there," she said. "Bring them here. Now tie my hands and feet to each post. Tight, but not too tight."

"Why don't you take off that sweater. You look uncomfortable."

"No. It feels good." I tied her feet first, leaving those long legs spread wide apart, then her arms.

"They're not cutting your skin?" I asked.

Kneeling between her legs, I stared into her eyes. They were glassy. She was breathing hard. I lifted her sweater up to her shoulders. Her nipples were fine, hard points of blazing pink. I worked with my fingers first, starting them gently on the soles of her feet and then up and down her thighs. Her arms pulled at the posts; her legs tried to lift from the bed. Then I sucked furiously on her toes.

"Oh, my God," she moaned.

Slowly I began, from the bottom up, licking and biting hard all the way until I reached her breasts.

"Eat, eat," she said.

I wouldn't. She would have hit me if she had not been tied. Catching my breath, I slipped down and brushed my penis over the wet hollows that tapered from her thighs, and finally put it in my hand and maneuvered it up and down the neatly cut and creamy passage between her legs.

"Please, Dean," she shouted. "Now, Dean!"

I wouldn't. I went up to her ear, and kissed and nibbled around it. Finally, unable to control myself, I plunged into her, using a pattern of ten strokes: three shallow, two quick-deep, three shallow, two slow-deep. Then, I pulled out, let myself cool down, and then began with ten more strokes. On the seventh round I untied her legs. I never reached that tenth stroke. I started to come and she exploded under me. I could feel her contracting, grasping and milking my penis. I knew what she was doing. So did she. Her legs kicked out like a wild mare's, and she nearly drew blood from my shoulder with her teeth. She let herself play out like a string of firecrackers.

"Paris is glowing right now," she said, "and so am I."

We lay in bed for another hour. Silent. Watching the shadows moving along the living-room wall through the door. She picked up the bedroom phone, and began to rattle into it in French.

"Yes, it's Sandra," she said. "Now, let's see." She turned to me and asked if I liked garlic. I was game. Dinner was in English.

"Okay, one order of shrimp in garlic sauce. Two orders of fried rice. Two orders of fried dumplings. And that spicy lamb of yours. And some ribs."

I wondered if she would lick her fingers. She did. I loved her. And I would never tell her.

 LONDON

The Dwarf had been to Rome and back by the time I returned to London. I walked down the hall to his room at the

Piccadilly, and as I got closer, a blonde about five-six came out of his room like a shot and flew by me. I knocked on the door. It opened, and I looked down at the Dwarf, who was in a blue robe with yellow piping. The smile on his face faded as soon as he saw me.

"Oh, it's you," he said, turning and walking back to his bed.

"Who did you expect?" I said. "That hooker who just left nearly knocked me over."

"Yeah, I thought she might have changed her mind," he said, hopping up on his bed. "You see how big and beautiful the bitch was?" She wasn't big. They all looked big to him. "Well, she came in here, and we talked for a while, and she finally says, 'Where's the fellow?' I tell her I'm the fellow. She started to run out right then, but I got her back. I talked to her calmly. I told her I was like any other man, except that I was built funny. I had her on the side of the bed now. She seemed to understand. Then I stood up on the bed and leaned her back gently. I took off my robe. I lifted up her dress and opened her legs. Her eyes were closed. I started moving between her and clutching her waist. Then she suddenly jumped up, knocking me off the bed and yelling, 'No, no, I'm sorry! I can't. I just can't! It's like something crawling on me!' "

"It's an old story, isn't it?" I said.

"As old as hell," he said, the frustration clear in his face. "Why is it when you're here in the room with me, they always stay?"

"I don't know," I said. His life had been so full of this shit. I tried to brighten him up. "Maybe . . . they figure that if you fall in, I'm there to pull you out. I mean, what girl wants to walk around the rest of her life with a dwarf inside her." He laughed uncontrollably. Then the phone rang.

"Yeah, this is Michael Dunn," he said. "Who? Yeah, put him on." He listened for a couple of minutes. Then he got up on his feet and started jumping up and down on the bed with the phone still at his ear. "When did you hear?" he yelled, catching his breath. "A good chance, you think?" He talked some more, and slowly the expression changed on his face. "No, no! I can't do that. I promised. We start in another week or so. I promised. . . . All right. If you think so. But you got him all wrong." He put the phone down and turned to me. "I've been nominated for an Academy Award, Hillbilly," he said. "That was my agent. He wants me back right away. He said I can't make the film with you. 'How would it look in Hollywood,' he said."

"He's always been against it," I said. "What're you going to do? What did he say? I know he said something."

"He said you're not worth the chance. You're bad news."

"Bad news?"

"He said you bopped an important Hollywood executive once."

"He had it coming. . . . So, what's your decision?"

"I don't know, Dean. I don't want to let you down, but—"

"I'll get you laid in Spain," I cracked, trying to quell my rising temper. "Those Spanish whores think dwarfs are good luck."

"I—"

"Forget it, Michael," I said. I didn't want him to say no, and I guess I knew he shouldn't say yes. "You've had the stick all your life. You deserve the best of it now. You don't owe me anything."

"Thanks, Dean," he said.

"But who can I use now?" I asked.

"How about John Thorstan?" he said. "He can act."

"The character's supposed to be a dwarf."

"So change it. All you lose is the grotesqueness. The scenes will still be funny with Thorstan. I've seen his work on the stage."

"Will he work? He's nuts about those watches of his."

"He'll pay you to work."

That evening I went to Thorstan's shop. He was flattered to be asked to work again. He pulled out the viewfinder, and broke it down in front of me. He looked at it admiringly.

"A bit ingenious, if I do say so," he said. He started to describe the mechanism.

"Which button triggers it?" I said, interrupting him.

"This one," he said, pointing to the middle one. "Here, let me show you how it works." He put the viewfinder back together, came up close to me, pressed the button, releasing the smoke in my face, and said, *"Pffft.* You're drugged."

You got it wrong, I said to myself. *Pffft.* You're dead.

I was back in Paris the same evening, thinking I would surprise Sandra, who didn't expect me for a couple of days. I opened her apartment with the key she had given me. I could hear the shower running in the bathroom. I undressed quickly, moved into the bathroom, and pulled the shower curtain open. In a flash her fist shot out and caught me on the mouth, stunning me and drawing blood from my lip. She had one leg in the shower, one leg out as she tried to reach desperately for her robe.

"Hey, darlin', it's me," I said, grabbing her and pulling her into the shower with me. "It's me. Dean." Fear was spread all over her face as I drew her close to me. Her heart was pounding. We stood quietly under the falling shower.

"You dumb bastard!" she shouted. "You dumb bastard!"

"I'm sorry," I said. "I thought you'd be scared for a second and then you'd recognize me."

"I didn't see anything. Just a man."

"You're sure quick," I said, turning off the shower. "Come on out, and let me dry you off." I worked the towel over her trembling body but stopped when I reached her shoulder.

"What the hell is this?" I asked, pointing to a scar.

"An old childhood scar," she said.

"Looks like a bullet crease to me. Maybe a month old." She pulled away from me and went for her robe. I might be a bastard, I thought, but I wasn't dumb.

"Do you take shorthand, too?" I asked, putting her robe around her.

"You're not funny," she said, her hair dripping and her eyes shooting out like laser beams.

"Come off it, Sandra," I said. "What are you up to?"

"I told you—I'm a secretary for Monsieur Garrotte."

63

"Yeah, a secretary with a bullet crease in her shoulder and a revolver in her glove compartment."

She drew on her robe, wrapped a towel around her head, and started out of the bathroom. "Ask him yourself. He's having a party tomorrow night. You want to go?"

"I wouldn't miss it for the world," I said.

"You coming to bed?" she called out from the other room as I dabbed at my lip in the bathroom mirror.

We lay there in the darkness, listening to our own thoughts and to the records playing across the bedroom.

"Does it matter?" she asked.

"How can it matter if I don't know what is supposed to matter to me?"

"I don't like a lot of questions."

"That makes two of us," I said. "You go your way, I'll go mine."

"I see," she said, a bit defensively.

"You didn't let me finish," I said. "As long as we meet in between. The way we are now. Close." She drew closer to me, and the music fell away.

Puffy was waiting for me in his office the next morning. On the way, I had stopped to buy another viewfinder, giving me two of them: Thorstan's invention and a regular one, which I would keep around my neck at all times now. I took the one from Thorstan out of my pocket and placed it in front of Puffy, along with the dummy cylinders.

"I need some business for a cylinder," I said. "About the size of this dummy here. About an inch and a half in length."

"How long you got?" he asked. "I mean, what's your timing?"

"Two minutes, I figure. In and out."

"I'd say that was very up close."

"I only need one cylinder made. But I want the guy who does it to make sure it works. The middle button is the trigger."

"You want the stuff in that cylinder to be quick and sure."

"Yeah, just like passing out after an all-night drunk."

"Dammit if you ain't a crazy cowboy," he said. "Where'd you ever come up with an idea like this?"

"I don't know, but I think it'll work."

"I told ya—you'll never see thirty."

"We'll see."

"You mean *I'll* see. You won't be around."

"Confidence—that's what I like."

"Selfish is more like it," he said. "Who's gonna talk to me about the movies? . . . Pick it up tomorrow night."

A SUBURB OF PARIS

As I came out of the hall, past a pair of gargoyles, around an old gas street lamp from London, a butler showing the way, size and space flooded over me. The living room was big enough for a couple of lion acts. Shooting an eye up to the ceiling, I threw in a high-wire act as well. As I faced the hall and the people, gathered around five enclaves of furniture spaced about the center of the room, an immense marble fireplace roared and threw up shadows on white walls that seemed more like the slopes of Everest. Off to the side, men in formal dress strung together like motionless wax figures, poised behind a vast table decorated with food. Out of an old period movie, a quartet worked nonchalantly at Mozart in a far corner near a shiny black piano the size of a giant stingray. My eyes fixed for a moment on the big shadow of the violin player, on the tilt of his head, the poetic swing of his arm—the way my own shadow looked in my mother's sunlit living room while a teacher frowned at my playing of the *Hungarian Dance #5*.

"Whatever Monsieur Garrotte does," I said, turning to Sandra, "he does it well."

65

"I don't see David," she said. "I hope he comes. He has to get away from that clinic for a while."

I hooked around a passing waiter for a couple of champagne cocktails. He looked at me as if I were trying to take his job. The stare couldn't have been for my getup: buckskin jacket, newly shined black boots, creased black pants; that was as good as I could get. Besides, this was a crowd for all seasons. I looked the crowd over: a handful of turbans here, some Saudi headdress over there, many more business suits than dinner clothes, a symphony of different accents.

"What kind of crowd you call this?" I asked Sandra.

"Eclectic," she said. That didn't help much.

We moved through the crowd slowly, finally ending up next to the fireplace, I looking up at a big painting above it. I couldn't figure out the rest of the cast, but it looked like Napoleon was right in the middle of a battle. Sandra didn't bother with the picture; she'd probably seen it a hundred times. I was still looking when I heard him.

"A remarkable man," the voice was saying. "Slightly demented, but no less remarkable. I would say he was without equal as a military strategist."

While trying to understand how someone could be only slightly demented, I turned and looked at the commentator. Sandra introduced him as Monsieur Garrotte. It was his eyes that caught me first: cold blue eyes that were as distant as stars. Looking at them, I thought of long-range missiles primed and waiting on a remote mountain somewhere. He was tall, blond, and formally dressed. His skin was bright and taut; he might know his way around a handball court. But no, I concluded, he belonged to the royalty of saddle and hounds, except there wasn't anything to chase in France. His speech was not rapid but rather clear and quiet, like the sound of a small stream. There was no halting between words or stumbling for the proper word. He knew what he wanted to say next and said it; his tongue was as sure as his mind. I guessed he was about forty-five or fifty. I didn't think I cared for him much.

"Consider this about Napoleon," he said, pointing up to

66

the squat figure surrounded by smoke and death. "In one conflict after another, with Europe running crimson with blood, no one could discern his simplicity, nor the greatness of his Army. Was he a devil? Were his troops better trained? His enemies sought, in panic, to attach magic to him, when all there was was a first-rate mind and a maneuver so astoundingly simple that it is laughable today: that is, Napoleon knew that all opposition, by nature and habit, would come at him from the right side. For months, he trained his lancers to fight with their left arms, from the left side. Can you imagine the confusion and surprise that the enemy felt in battle? By God, that is genius. Alas, it was Wellington who saw the obvious. He trained his men to attack from the left side against Napoleon's left-handed lancers. The rest is history. Except for this: to this day, the English drive on the left side of the road. And though much of the world thinks right-handed, do not let anyone tell you, my dear Selmier, that genius is not left-handed."

Abruptly, he changed the subject. "Sandra tells me you're in film," he said. The man did his homework. "So how do you find Paris?" he asked, passing me a glass of champagne from a waiter's tray.

"It's a city," I said. It was a wise remark. He didn't call me on it.

"How do you spend your time?" he asked.

"I don't think of time," I said. "I let it worry about itself. I just blow in the wind." Sandra pinched my back. Did I have to be an asshole all my life? the pinch seemed to say.

"Well . . . Sandra takes me around," I said quickly, "but—"

"He's in love with Notre-Dame," Sandra interrupted.

"Why so?" Garrotte asked. The guy was full of questions.

"It's the film," I said. "I've seen *The Hunchback of Notre-Dame* thirty-five times."

"Have you read the book?"

"I can't read."

"My dear Selmier, you mean you *don't* read."

"Any way you want it—can't, don't. It's all the same to

me." Sandra kicked me in the ankle. Garrotte paused. I figured that last remark would chase him. It didn't.

"What a devil of a man!" said Garrotte, acting mock-serious. "I think it begins like that—Book One, Chapter Four, 'Quasimodo.'" He paused for a couple beats, and began again: "He shows himself, and you see he's a hunchback. He walks, and you see he's bowlegged. He looks at you, and you see he's short of an eye. You talk to him, and you find he's deaf. Why, what does the Polyphemus do with his tongue?" Garrotte lowered his voice, came up very close to me, and whispered, "He talks when he likes. He's lost his hearing from ringing the bells. He's not dumb." His eyes never left me.

We talked for several minutes more. He seemed fascinated by my interest in Notre-Dame and the story of Quasimodo. Somewhere along the way, I felt a needle. I parried with nonsense; I was out of my league. Soon he left, saying, "We shall see each other again, my dear Selmier. You are a most entertaining fellow."

"Your Garrotte can sure talk it," I said to Sandra.

"I've never met a man like him," she said. "All that I know, and maybe all that I am, I owe to him."

"What's that supposed to mean?" I asked.

"Nothing," she said, looking across the room. "Look, there's David."

She waved. David joined us. It wasn't long before he asked Sandra if he could have a word with me in private.

"Dean," he said, watching Sandra leave, "I can't stand still for this."

"Hold on," I said. "What can't you stand?"

"The money in the clinic's account. There's twenty-five thousand dollars in there. Where did you get that kind of money? It's against the law, what you're doing."

"What am I doing?"

"You're hiding money, that's what. Putting it through my account. I don't do things like that. It's against everything I stand for."

"You don't need some of that money for your clinic?"

"I'd rather see the clinic go under than do this sort of thing."

"Come on, David," I said. "Face facts. You want to be your own man. Then be one. If not, drop the clinic and go home to Daddy. I always thought this clinic shit was show for the old man, anyway." Attack was my only out.

"You sonuvabitch!" he said. "You know that's not true."

"Well, show me," I said. "You're helping me, and I'm helping you. There's going to be lots more coming your way. I'll get you even more help from some other people."

"No, I don't—"

"I say you gotta do it!"

"You calling me on that day off Long Island Sound?"

"Are you kidding?"

"Then why should I—"

"For the kids," I said. "For them and your research. Your work's more important than right or wrong."

For the kids! That one was still clanging around in my stomach. I should have been shot for that line. But I meant it about his work, because that is all a man ever has, and if he lets that go, he might as well go with it.

"Don't give me that bullshit," he said unconvincingly. He was wavering.

"Then do what you want," I said. "I'm going to get a drink."

I was heading toward the nearest waiter when the butler came up to me and told me that Monsieur Garrotte would like to see me. I followed him out of the room, then down a long hall with some more gargoyles and dim paintings. He knocked softly on the door, and a buzzer opened it. The door opened into Garrotte's study. He met me halfway, and said, "I will return in a few minutes. Make yourself comfortable. The liquor is over there—cognac, vodka, scotch. Oh, yes—Indiana, isn't it? Jack Daniels might be more to your liking."

I hadn't told him that I was from Indiana. I poured myself a vodka, and sort of eased into the room. Puccini swelled throughout the study; I didn't know where it was coming from, but I had always had a soft spot for anything by Puccini. The carpet was thick and dark blue. Another high ceiling. Heavy Indian red drapes with big sashes veered down from a big window that looked out onto a garden. The wallpaper had an eighteenth-century look to it; the design was intricate and busy. His desk, a gold-trimmed antique for sure, was clean and bare except for an ivory pen-and-pencil set. That was the first thing you saw as you entered the long room—the desk, the draped window behind it, and the high bookcases flanking the desk. The desk, I thought, fit the look of his eyes, the way he spoke. In the middle of the room a pair of leather couches faced each other in front of a lighted fireplace.

I let my eyes move across the books: a complete collection —it might have been, there were so many—of Balzac and Dickens, separated and with each section held up by heavy African sculptures. There were many sections: philosophy, medicine, politics; a lot of books on the military, including *The Rise and Fall of the Third Reich,* and one on Rommel. I didn't recognize many of the titles. On one side of the shelf were the Warren Commission Report, which I counted to have twenty-six volumes, and a single thin book called *Markings.* I was still there by the bookcase when he came back to the study.

"The music is not too loud?" he asked.

"No, I like Puccini."

"So do I," he said, pouring himself a cognac and then opening a gold case. He pulled an implement from his pocket and snipped the end of a medium-sized cigar.

"Some might call his music silver macaroni," he said between a sip of his cognac and a pull on his cigar, "but I am not one of them. I like his sentimentality."

"How's the United Nations out there?" I asked.

"Enjoying themselves," he said.

"I was just looking at some of your books."

"What interests you?"

"None of them. I don't know much about books. And I can't stand history. It's the past."

"I beg to differ, my dear Selmier. History is us. It is now. Santayana said it best: 'Those who cannot remember the past are condemned to repeat it.' The record of life's societies never varies. Owners protect their property. Men, or countries, without property will try to take from those who have. Big eats small; power gorges on the powerless as lions feast on lamb. Those who will not rule with the boot will feel the boot. Those who will not kick are generally simply unable to kick. I know of no other history. Do you?"

"I see the Warren Report there," I said. "You think there was some kind of conspiracy behind Kennedy's murder?"

"Would it matter to you?"

"No, he was just a politician. I was only curious."

"Most politicians are not much more—you are right. But he was different. He had an effect. He was a force in the minds of the people, of the world. He could not work the machinery of Congress, but he had a psychological effect on the world. He made it care, made it feel good about itself. Perhaps the people were stupid, and had he lived, they would have had to face their stupidity. But I think not."

"This one here, *Markings*," I said. "By that UN guy?"

"Dag Hammarskjöld, yes."

"Killed in a plane accident?"

He took another sip of cognac, fingered his cigar. "Accidents do not happen to the Hammarskjölds of this world."

"Anything in particular you wanted to see me about?" I asked.

"No, except that I thought that somehow I might have irritated you at our introduction. I do not want that."

"What does Sandra do for you?" I asked. "I shouldn't ask, but I have."

"Whatever Sandra chooses to do," he said. "She is like a daughter to me."

"I'd better be getting back to her," I said. "Listen, you and I have no problem. You're all right with me."

I was nearly to the door when he said, raising his voice a notch, "Let me do you a favor, my dear Selmier. The next time you need a viewfinder, it is not necessary that you go to London for it."

He was smiling. He looked like a lion who had just eaten a lamb.

Sandra and David were still by the fireplace when I returned to the living room. I looked at David.

"Well, what's it going to be?" I asked.

"All right," he said tentatively. "For now."

I turned to Sandra. "I know," I said.

"You know what?" she said.

"I know," I said again. "And it doesn't matter."

The next evening, I met Puffy in his office. I was a half hour late. He began by glowering, then looked hurt.

"I can't stand people who are late," he said. "People always comin' into movies late and blockin' your view and talkin' all the time while they're tryin' to find a seat. But this ain't a movie! You got to be on the nose with time. One day you're not—ain't where you're supposed to be—and whack, whack!" He clapped his hands twice.

"Everything ready?" I said.

"Yeah. When you leavin'?"

"Tomorrow afternoon."

"All right," he said. "Two things." He picked up the viewfinder. "First, what you got in here is Cyklone-K. A bit old hat and obscure these days, but perfect for the job. Second, when you let it go, make sure you count to a hundred twenty. Two minutes. And no wind. Nobody'll get hurt with it in the wind. Remember: two minutes, or you'll get a blast of it yourself."

"It's been tested, right?"

"Better than a water gun."

"Okay, I'm on my way."

"How 'bout a movie?"

"When I come back."

I was at the top of the stairs when I heard him call out, *"Two minutes, Dean! Ya hear me, Dean? Twooo minutes!"*

When I think of film, I think of dreams. I am in the center of
the dream, watching. People speak and move; places shift;
objects of no importance come into view, and then, when I
look again at them, they have taken on all importance. I am
the dream and the dreamer. That is the way I watch a movie.
How to make one, though, that is different, I thought. I sat
in the lobby of the Madrid Hilton, trying to decipher what
Raymond Spottiswoode was saying in his book *Film and Its
Techniques.* It was too late, I knew, for him to save me, but
I didn't need much saving, really. Mainly I wanted to become familiar with some technical terms. Couldn't look like
too much of an ass. The sparrow Luis arrived with a smeared
manila folder containing details for the film. He noticed the
viewfinder hanging from my neck.

"You are ready now, Señor Dean, I see." He chuckled. I
smiled thinly. I felt like a ham, looking down at the viewfinder. I had acquired the habit of fingering the middle
button. So what? I wanted that thing to become a part of me.

"All is ready, Señor Dean," he said. "Cuadrado will be
on the camera. You are lucky to get him. Only because it is
twelve days. He has big film coming up. Uncle will buy the
raw stock from his cousin's lab. It will be processed there,
too. Much cheaper for you."

I looked at the sheet where it said TECHNICIANS. I noticed
an extra man had been added. "Who's this?"

"He is the man with Nagra to pick up wild track we use
later in dubbing," he said. I'd have to look that one up in
Spottiswoode's book.

"Can we begin a week from Monday?" I asked.

"All that remains is casting," he said. "That is for you to
do."

"I'm mainly interested in a woman," I said. "She along
with me and John Thorstan, who'll be here tomorrow, are the
major roles. You can pick most of the minor roles. You know
the talent around here better than I do."

I trusted the sparrow. He knew what he was doing. And I saw him go up against his uncle over the head count.

"Half the movie we will shoot in the Casa del Campo," he said. "I have secured permits. I have picked two apartments for interior shots. They will not cost much: twenty dollars a day in pesetas for the people who live there."

"What else?"

"Equipment and crew are all set. We are ready to go."

"Great," I said. "So, do you know any good female leads in Madrid?"

He thought a moment. "Yes, there is one staying here," he said. "Her name is Ingrid Pitts. Shall I talk to her?"

I told him to go ahead. He went to a house phone. She was down in the lobby in a half hour. She looked perfect for the part. Blond. Willowy. Sensual. Great tits.

"Give her the script, Luis," I said. "The part is yours if you want it, Ingrid."

"I want it," she said. She probably hadn't worked for a while. Madrid was filled with Ingrid Pitts.

"You're hired," I said.

The next day, she phoned my room. "I still want the part," she said. "But I would like the character rewritten to fit me more."

"You're fired," I said, and hung up. It wasn't the rewrite. She would be trouble. I could see delays, my money dwindling, while she struggled with motivation. There were others. I found one two days later. Besides, the story was mainly my role and Michael's—Thorstan's now. It was hard to shake off that little dwarf, even from six thousand miles.

The shooting went well. It was mostly because of something I always believed: even a novice director can look good with the right people behind him. The Spanish were pros. The cameraman, Cuadrado, handled all of the technical puzzles and setups, selected the angles and shots, and even did most of the art direction. I worked hard on the pace and feeling of each scene and tried to keep enthusiasm crackling through the long days. I didn't play at being a director. I didn't comb my brain for clever camera angles. I didn't stand on a corner waiting for the sun to come out.

"The rain," Luis said one day. "It looks like we cannot shoot today. Not enough light. Will not match yesterday's light."

"Go out and get twenty-five umbrellas," I said. "We've got to shoot the gun-battle scene."

Luis came back with the umbrellas. Of course, the rain had stopped; the sun was out.

"Now what you going to do, Señor Dean?" he asked, as if I was cornered.

I turned to John Thorstan. "You got another line, John," I said. "Just say, 'Hey, it stopped raining!'" He looked at me strangely, the way he did after the first day's shooting.

Luis had asked me, "Do you want to look at projections, Señor Dean?"

"Sure," I said. "I wouldn't miss it for anything." I leaned over toward Thorstan's ear and said, "What the hell are projections?" He said he would find out.

"Projections are dailies," he came back and said, as if he were giving me the combination to a safe.

"And dailies are—?"

"You see in the screening room tonight what you shot yesterday," he said, with wonder in his eyes.

"Well, you know, John, I've done all my work on the stage. I'm not used to film language."

He understood, he said. But later on, when the picture was finished, there was something he didn't understand.

"Dean, we've never used the viewfinder scene," he said. "The one I hooked up with the smoke cylinder."

"Yeah, I decided against it. I didn't like it. I think the picture works without it, don't you?"

"Yes, that may be right," he said. "But I hope you don't mind if I don't close my watch shop and depend on your next picture for my living."

"Is it that bad?"

"*Nooo,* mate. It has its moments. You'll be able to edit it into better shape." He looked at the viewfinder. "I still liked that viewfinder bit. Christ, you haven't had this bloody thing off your neck. Oh, well, use it in the next picture. I hate to see my work wasted."

It wouldn't be.

Arriving with Luis and another cameraman—not Cuadrado—I explained what I wanted from them on Ibiza. From Luis I wanted half a dozen young girls, willing to have some footage taken of them for a film. They would get a day's pay —fifteen dollars each—and a nice boat ride; they would be back by nightfall. I also wanted him to rent a boat. "And tell them to bring their bikinis," I said.

One look around Ibiza, less than a hundred miles from the coast of Spain and one of the biggest of the Balearic Islands, and I knew the sparrow wouldn't have any trouble. Despite his gaunt look, he had a way about him.

By noon they were all outside the Montesol Hotel, where we were going to spend the night. Dozens of them, the cream of the world's runaways, from Scandinavia to Los Angeles, were sitting at sidewalk tables, some of them in native dress, one with a vest from Morocco, others with Afghan jackets, all of them looking for peace and love and enough hash to bring the high they had come so far to find. Here on Ibiza they had found the Riviera of the youth underground. It was a world without clouds.

At six the next morning, Luis had the chosen six girls and the cameraman waiting by the dock next to a boat and a driver, and I had replaced my director's viewfinder with Thorstan's rigged viewfinder.

"Señor," Luis said. "The girls, they want money now." I gave him ninety dollars, counting it out in the half light. Free spirits still knew about money.

"And the captain," he added. "He wants to know where to go."

"Tell him thirty miles, south by southwest." Luis spoke to him in Spanish.

"Does he know where I want to go?" I asked.

"Yes, señor, but he say nobody ever go there. It is private property."

"So let's make it unprivate," I said.

The big white house! It stood on a hill above a quarter mile of white beach. "Luis, we're going past it," I said. "There's where we want to go." The boat turned and soon we were pulling up to a pier. The girls jumped out of the boat and raced for the beach in their bikinis. I staged some shots. They went swimming. I set up some more shots. It was a shame that I would never bother to develop the film.

The whole time, I could feel someone watching us. Now and then, I squinted up at the big white house, hoping to see someone. The girls hit the water again. I didn't know how long we could handle this routine. We must have been there three quarters of an hour before I saw the giant coming down the steps of the hill. Standing next to me, he was even bigger than I had imagined. About six-seven. Maybe fifty-five years old. His hair was silver. His big face had a jagged, bony structure, which age was now starting to melt. He didn't seem to have any hands, only the longest and thickest fingers I'd ever seen on a man. He looked me over as if I were an unusual shell that had just washed up on the beach.

"Private land," he said. His accent was hard. "Nobody allowed here. What are you doing?"

"Shooting a film," I said. He squinted at the clapboard and read the title out loud, slowly: "Maybe ... You ... Don't ... Like ... It."

"We'll be finished soon. Then we'll leave."

"No," he said. He turned and looked up toward the house. There was another man up there now, on a balcony. The man waved down to the giant. The giant nodded.

He moved past the girls, and went for the cameraman, picking his camera up with a couple of fingers and examining it closely. He came back to Luis and me, and frisked us both. He pointed to the viewfinder around my neck. I took the viewfinder in my hand and looked into it.

"To see the picture before we film," I said. He nodded that he understood. Sure you do, Lutz.

"Come," he said. "All of you."

We followed him up the wooden steps, about a hundred of them. The man from the balcony was waiting for us at the top. He was in a gold silk robe with black lapels and black cuffs; the gold looked real. The sun bounced off him as if he were a dome on top of a building. He was all bulk, which is a nice way of saying that he was fat: Sydney Greenstreet-fat, Victor Buono–fat. Drop him into the ocean and he'd make a great life preserver. I guessed that from the knees down his legs were probably birdlike. But from the way he carried himself in the robe, he would never look like a mess in clothes; there would be dignity and bearing to him.

His face was not as neat. His eyes were narrow, with a lot of lid and a bulge to them. Tiny blood vessels ran broken over his nose and cheeks. He looked like he might be a bottle-a-day man, yet he wasn't the type. I blamed the wear in his face on the sun. The wind played with the strands of white hair left on his head. He looked at the giant, who nodded again.

"Now," he said, looking at the girls, "what have we here? Four men, six girls. The odds are unfair." I was counting on his wanting to even them up.

"I'm shooting some film here," I said. "We didn't mean to intrude. Your man says this is a private island. We really didn't know."

"Not completely private," he said, still looking at the girls. "There are about a dozen estates at various parts of the island."

"Well, we'll be going in another hour."

"No, no," he said. "I will not hear of it. Please be my guests at lunch. We'll have it by the pool. I insist. Lutz, go and tell the cook." Lutz trundled off.

"I hope Lutz was not too rude," he said. "We are not used to visitors here. And . . ." He came up short. "Come, come, we will sit by the pool."

"Could we do some shooting there?" I bit my tongue.

"By all means. But no film of me, please," he said, pointing to his stomach. "Your name, sir?"

"Dean Selmier."

"You may call me Stossy," he said, winking at the girls. "All of you may call me Stossy," he said, laughing. "Is Mr. Selmier paying you well, girls?" His question was not aimless.

"Fifteen dollars," a girl from the States piped up. That figured.

"So little," he said, "for all these young beauties." He looked like he wanted to smack his lips, but he didn't. That would have knocked the hell out of his dignity and bearing.

"Go, girls," he said. "Go and play in the pool. The bar cart will be out soon." Off they went, and I sat down next to Stossy.

"These young people today, Mr. Selmier," he said, shaking his head. "Homeless, wandering. It wasn't like that in my time."

What time was that? I wondered. I brought him in at about seventy to seventy-five.

"I see them all the time on my rare trips to Ibiza. La Guardia Civil will chase them all soon."

He kept his eyes on their wet, shining little asses. I passed on the social commentary.

"Where are you from, Mr. Selmier?" he asked. A long shadow drifted over my shoulder. I didn't have to look around. I knew it was Lutz.

"Indiana," I said. "I just made my first film in Madrid. I didn't have much money, but I had to give it a try."

"Young men should take chances. After thirty, life has a way of creeping away, becoming pointless and sad."

"What keeps you busy out here by yourself?"

"Nothing. I just fish. And wait."

"Wait for what?"

"I am an old man, Mr. Selmier. What else do old men wait for?" I felt the adrenaline. I changed the subject.

"What kind of fish do you get here?"

"Many kinds. Game fish. When I feel I have the strength,

I try to test a big fish. But quickly they find out there is not much strength at all."

"I'd like to lean into a marlin," I said.

"You will not find the marlin here," he said. "They are open-water fish. But that would be some sight. Youth and a marlin. Have you ever hooked a marlin, Mr. Selmier?"

"Only once. When I was in the service. Took me three hours. After it was all over, my hands were raw and my back was nearly broken." Lutz brought a round of drinks.

"What is that around your neck?" the fat man asked, pointing.

"That's called a viewfinder," I said. "It frames the scene you are shooting." I bent forward, held the viewfinder close to his face, and framed him in it.

"Hey, you look great," I said, pulling back. "Stossy, you oughta be in pictures."

Lunch was served: lemon sole and cold white wine. Luis and I talked about nothing. The fat man was getting familiar with a Dutch girl with flowing corn-silk hair. Lutz stayed in the background. The Dutch girl was speaking to the fat man in German, but all I could make out was his name, Stossy. It was nearing four in the afternoon when I thought it time to make some sort of move.

"Well, it's time, girls," I said. "Back to Ibiza." They were up quickly, and running toward the steps leading to the boat and the beach.

"Such children," the fat man said, watching them go. "Here now, gone the next minute."

"Stossy," I said, "you've been very kind. I could stay here forever. I wonder if you wouldn't mind if I came back in a couple of weeks. I'd like to try a big fish again. It's been a long time."

I held my breath. There was no way to do it here today. If he refused, it was going to be a long and very risky job. I would have to wait for him in Ibiza, and who knows when he would show up there. Or I'd have to come back here at night. Either way, the viewfinder was out. I'd have to use a gun. And there would be no way to avoid the giant Lutz. Young men should take chances, but not this young man, not now. The fat man gave my request some thought as we walked toward the steps.

"I say this!" said Stossy. "Do not go back now. You stay and fish with me for a few days. It will be a change for me. I will not have to look at Lutz all the time."

"Tell me," I said quickly, before he could change his mind, "how'd it go with the Dutch girl? I thought you had her, the way she was smiling."

Walking back to the house and shaking his head, he said, "She told me sweetly that I was too old and fat." He kept walking up the steps and said, almost to himself, "The young can be very cruel."

Before the sun broke the next morning we were down by the pier, loading up his forty-five-foot cabin cruiser. The fat man was wearing a yachting cap and a light-blue jacket. We were all in the boat when Lutz sheepishly told Stossy that he had forgotten the beer.

"You drink too much beer," yelled Stossy. He motioned him to start the boat up, then relented. "Go ahead. Go back and get it!" Lutz moved out in double time. "All that beer he drinks," he said to me. "It gives him so much gas and it makes him sleepy."

"How long's he been with you?" I asked.

"Years. He's a dependable beast." He pointed to his head. "He hasn't been right since the army." I didn't have to guess what army. "He was the perfect German soldier."

Nothing happened that first day out in the Mediterranean. We just pirouetted here and there in the blue-green water, or stopped an hour in one place and then moved on to another. The fat man and I sat in two chairs equipped with straps and with holders for our rods, just waiting there in the blazing sun, trolling for long periods, breaking for a cold drink or a refreshing cold lunch or just the comfort of the cabin shade. Lutz sat in his chair up near the front of the cruiser, guiding the craft with one hand, a can of beer in the other. There were no fish. At three o'clock, with a wicked sun overhead, with the old man, now in a peaked cap, dozing in his chair, with Lutz napping up front, I began to get up slowly, moving around to the right of Stossy with my back to the giant. I started to bring my hands up to the viewfinder. Count to a hundred twenty, I thought. There was no wind. Then, suddenly, I heard the giant's hulk moving toward my back. I started to loosen the fishing rod from the holder.

"Too much sun," Lutz was saying. "I must take him out of the sun."

"That's a good idea," I said.

Two more days of the same thing, and the fat man was getting tired.

"Not a sign of a big fish," he said back at the house, as we sat by the pool at dinner. "I think it is best we stop."

"Let's give it one more try," I said.

"I don't know," he said. "My bones ache."

"How many big ones have you caught in your life?"

"Five," he said.

"Make it an even half dozen. Then you'll forget all about your bones."

"Once more, then," he said. "But we will rest a couple of days first." He didn't much believe that he'd latch on to one, but that wasn't why he had been going out each day, anyway. He wanted to see a young man whipped by a big fish.

"I shall tell you, Dean," Stossy said. "When you first came here, I thought you might be here to kill me." I looked for some words. "But I said to myself, Stoessel, what do you do with a man like that when you are not sure. Do you kill him first? Possibly. But if he was not here to kill you? There would be questions." He was wrong. Nobody would ask any questions about me. "No, I decided. Bring him into your house. Get to know him. Keep him close."

"And that leaves you where?" I asked. I rubbed the sweat in my palm with my fingers.

"With a nice young man. A young man who shoots films of tender little girls on beaches."

82

"But why would anyone want to kill you?"

"Oh, it's a story that will never end," he said. "It began a thousand years ago, it seems. The world is in blood. I was working for a certain company in Berlin. A certain colonel produces an order to my superior. The order says that a very specialized gas van should be designed and manufactured by the firm. My superior comes to me and tells me to design this gas van. I knew what it was for by the specifications. This was in 1942. One did not protest. But I asked anyway. They said it would be more humane than mass shootings above open graves.

"For years I heard the screams from those traveling execution vans. The colonel has since been hanged in Israel. I ended up living in South America and never designed anything again. I dealt in running guns and ammunition. Many enemies were made. I had to flee. Gas vans? Running guns? It comes down to the same thing: revenge; revenge, and then the blood."

"Are you still in the gun business?"

"In a small but effective way."

"But revenge? How could you know?"

"All animals know when they are being hunted. One hears the footsteps."

"I think you're wrong. If somebody wanted to kill you, a half-dozen men could storm this place and you're gone."

"Yes, perhaps, but not since the colonel was hanged after a world-famous trial. *Pianissimo*, Mr. Selmier. That is the word these days." He excused himself, and left the table.

Two days later we were bobbing and swaying under a noon sun. Stossy had caught a half-dozen groupers, but there had been no sign of any big fish. We broke for lunch, and then went back to trolling again, Lutz to his chair and his beer. The sun was like a branding iron on our necks, the sea like glass, only now and then a breaker of warm wind. We sat there talking, the fat man in his peaked cap and flowered sport shirt and I with a wet handkerchief around my head. He was going on about bass.

"Once, I fished for bass in America," he said. "I have never seen such a fish. He is a lonely, moody, unpredictable fish. I think he would eat his own children as soon as the other man's. He has no scruples whatsoever. I think he has a split personality, and suffers from delusions of persecution." We both laughed. He remained quiet for a few minutes, slowly working up to his nap. "But," he said, stirring, "I like where the bass lives. Near the cool, dark bottom, not even knowing that the world is going by."

He was snoring in ten minutes. I looked around for Lutz. He wasn't there. Where was he? I waited. Five minutes. Five minutes more. I got up from the chair quietly, and walked over to the cabin. Lutz had dropped anchor and was sleeping on one of the beds with his mouth open. The adrenaline started again. I walked back to the chairs. I waited again. Five minutes more. Silence fell around us like a waterfall. A slight wind blew across the deck. I went to the side of the boat and looked into the water. It had to be now. I looked into the fat man's face, sweating and red with those tiny blood vessels hooking through it like worms. I moved up close now, until the viewfinder was two inches under his nose. I listened for a moment. If a wind came now, the gas wouldn't even reach his nose. Count to a hundred twenty, I said. I took a deep breath, holding for fifteen seconds. Twooo minutes, Dean. I could hear Puffy's voice. I was ready. No wind. I pressed the middle button on the viewfinder. I didn't move. The gas curled up into his nose. I began counting, watching the fat man's face, listening for Lutz. Stossy's eyes never opened. His face twitched. Then, his entire body gave a single spasm, heaved, and collapsed. I finished counting as I walked over to the other side of the deck. I lay down and fell fast asleep in the sun.

I must have been there an hour when I heard Lutz move out of the cabin, and then his yell. I ran over to the chair. Lutz was shaking the fat man, and pleading with him to wake up. "Wake up, sir, wake up!" he kept screaming.

I pushed the giant away, and dragged the fat man out of

the chair and onto the deck. I began massaging his chest, then pounding it. I placed my mouth over his and tried to breathe the life back. Then, back to the pounding again. "Stop it!" Lutz said, flicking me off the body with his paw. "You will hurt him!"

"He's dead," I said to Lutz. "Can't you see that he's dead, you—"

"No! No!" he bellowed, cradling the fat man in his arms. He started to bawl but stopped himself and finally let go.

"Start the boat up, and let's get him back home," I said.

I looked at Stossy. He seemed to be sleeping like a baby. I pulled him onto one of the beds in the cabin, and put a sheet over him.

I walked to the bow. I took the viewfinder and aimed it at the open cabin, framing the cool darkness of the cabin and a high rise of white sheet. *Pianissimo*, fat man.

I was in the center of a dream.

PART THREE

PARIS, 1967

It was about ten in the morning, and all the world seemed to have me by the throat in this little dark and killing room, with its peeling wallpaper and the smell of black-market absinthe and Gauloises and final insult. The absinthe had worked itself over the years into the body of the room through the mouths of a long line of busted-out dreamers, all the leftover people in the Paris film business and those cheap distributors who either have no place to go or can't get out of the habit of trying to find gold at the bottom of the garbage can. Now the place was getting a new transfusion of that awful stuff from the projectionist sleeping next to me, his mouth opened like a drawbridge and his nose sounding like the L.A. freeway. The insults would be walking in the door in a half hour. I banged the projectionist on the side of his head with the palm of my hand and said, "Wake up." He thrashed in his seat like a crab on its back, and his startled breath made me turn my head.

"Here, have a mint," I said. "Have two of 'em. You can get the film ready now."

He passed on the mints, and just stared vacantly at me.

"What film?" he finally asked.

I looked at him, not knowing whether to laugh or to break his stringy neck. So it had come down to this—a tiny piss hole of a walk-up in the once smartly avant-garde section of Saint-Germain-des-Prés, down to a screening room that cost fifteen dollars for an hour and a half and a rummy projectionist who didn't know where he was and had me wondering the same thing about myself. This was the last stop, I thought, after six months of trying to convince distributors to move it, a process that can and often does knock the hell out of a man's spirit. I wished I was up in the mountains, or in the desert, in some shack, where there was no such thing as success or failure, or a label that said you were a mechanic or a tree surgeon or a chairman of the board. I didn't want to be anybody. But I knew that was a lie. I wanted to be in film, a part of film; I wanted to make pictures. It wasn't a romantic thing with me; it was something I needed, no less than those shells of bodies I used to see floating around Needle Park in Manhattan needed the powder that would quiet the howling inside them.

"Eh, monsieur?" the rummy asked, his head clearing.

"Look, it's this way," I said. "My name is Dean Selmier. The film is called *Maybe You Don't Like It.*" And many people didn't, I thought. The old man didn't bat an eye at the name, which put him in the company of a whole legion of people, from Hollywood to Rome.

"Remember, I gave you fifteen for the room?" I said. "Yesterday. Remember? Then another ten for you and the projector."

"*Ahh, oui, monsieur,*" he said, looking at the cans that I had moved over next to his leg.

"Okay, let's do it," I said, pointing to the booth at the back of the room. "And, Pop, don't fall asleep up there." I watched him walk away, a broken old man carrying two cans of thirty-five-millimeter film, one weighing thirty-five pounds, the other twenty-five. "Wait, I'll help you," I called out.

The screening room is a brutal place for a filmmaker, and when that picture goes up, it sometimes takes the shape of a mad dog tearing at your ego. My ego had been splattered throughout the world, even down to a little movie house on West Tenth Street in my hometown of Indianapolis. The owner there had said he would run it for three days. The film drew about thirty people the first two days. There would be bodies the next day, I promised. I drove out to a school for the deaf and mute, on the edge of town. The director looked at me oddly. I was wearing my usual clothes: black pants, black shirt, black cowboy boots. I gave her my best manners.

"But Mr. Selmier," she said, unable to figure out the proposition before her. "I mean, you know where you are. These kids—"

"Yes, ma'am," I said. "They can't hear and they can't talk."

"But why, Mr. Selmier? Why do you want them? Don't you realize how cruel that is?" The idea seemed to sicken her.

"Look at it this way, ma'am. I guarantee you they'll have fun. I'll provide the buses. There'll be a clown there to entertain them before the show. It's a funny picture. A spy comedy."

"Is there any . . . I mean, do they—"

"No, ma'am, there's no sex in it at all. I give you my word on that, ma'am."

"But why? Why are you doing this?"

"I just feel like I want to do something here in town. This film has made me a lot of money in Europe. I'm just trying to do somethin', ma'am. Besides, my brother was deaf and dumb, and I always used to take him to the movies. He loved 'em. He's dead now, though. Fell out of our tree house." I dropped my head slightly, all the while thinking of the chattering bastard and the day I did throw him out of the treehouse. He only broke his arm.

"Oh, I see," said the director. "I'm sorry. It's just that these children are so vulnerable. They are gentle and beautiful creatures. . . ."

"Can they come, ma'am?" I interrupted.

"Oh, I suppose so. It could be a nice treat for them."

The kids pulled up in four busloads the next afternoon, and the clown was waiting for them on the sidewalk; I was the clown. I had learned the makeup and some of the moves when I was a kid, having hooked up with a traveling circus down in Texas. As the kids passed by in line, I gave each of them an ice cream and a bag of popcorn, which I had made myself the night before in my mother's kitchen.

Once they were settled in, I went up in front and slopped through a routine: standing on my head and walking; a little Buster Keaton with a chair; and then I had a guy throw three pies in my face. The clapping was steady, intermingled with weird grunting, a sad sort of grunting that must have been their equivalent of a laugh.

Finished, I motioned upstairs for the film to begin. The house went dark. I walked to the back and stood there, breathing a little heavily, and waiting for what, I really didn't know. I ran a towel over my face. My stomach fluttered from the smell of the pie and the fact that this was my first full audience for the film. It was a long and crazy ninety minutes back there. No sound from the kids, no expressions that I could see the one time I tried to crawl down the aisle to look for some reaction on their faces, trying to see just one smile on a face. Suddenly the lights were on, and their reaction came: bags and popcorn flew up at the screen; hands waved at the drawing curtain in rejection. I could see the embarrassed director rushing about, obviously telling them in sign language to mind their manners. I turned away and went into the men's room. The clown's face was streaked with sweat. I picked a piece of lemon meringue off my eyebrow. I tasted it. Looking into the mirror, I tried to find some more.

The kids had probably been right, and by now, in Paris, I, too, was nearly convinced it was a bad film. But it was *my* film. The ragpickers of French distribution, six of them, trickled into their seats. Each sat alone, paying no attention to the others or to me when I turned to welcome them. I might as well have tried to hail a cab in Paris traffic in the rush hour. One of them did seem alive as he gnawed on a loaf of French bread and gulped coffee, letting the crumbs dribble down the front of a frayed dark suit with pinstripes.

Where was Puffy? I wondered. He was always prompt. I looked around again. The prospectors were getting impatient; the pinstripe, his bread almost gone, had begun to look like a sesame-seed dark-rye hamburger roll. At New York screenings I had never sat in the room. The filmmaker's presence makes the room too tense; I mean, they know it's your film; they *know* you're uptight and slyly trying to gauge some response. So you either go up with the projectionist or pace the empty hallways. But here, in this room, protocol was clearly out of place. Christ, what did I expect from these beggars? Even if they liked it, they would sooner part with their wives than come up with any front money. I looked around for Puffy again. He was finally here. I could hear him before I could see him, the sound being much like that of a big train sighing into a station.

"Come on, come on!" he was shouting back to the little mole who was with him. "Being late is a crime against manners, you little bastard." His whole life, his work, had been mounted on a simple code: do your job; be someone who can be counted on to be where he was supposed to be, to do what he has contracted to do. He was a diamond cutter with time, setting it up each day, measuring it precisely, and then tapping it for the results that he and you needed for the moment.

I motioned for the projectionist to roll the film. The room went black. Puffy and his friend sat next to me. The funnel of light from the projection booth shot through the blackness like a death ray, catching the dust particles and making them look like a million tiny bugs frantically swirling over one another.

"Goddamn Frenchmen," said Puffy, wheezing, gasping for air. "They'll bury me yet. I love 'em, but they don't know a thing about time. Now, do you, Monsieur Dick?"

The man nodded his head.

"Dean, this is Monsieur Dick," said Puffy. "That's not his name; but then again, I don't know anybody that's got a real name. Runs a little theater in Montparnasse. Can't speak a word of English. I don't think he can speak a word of French, either." Puffy unwrapped a candy bar and pushed the wrapper into his pocket. His pockets were always filled with wrappers. That's how you could tell how many movies he saw on a given day—by the wrappers. You could figure on six wrappers for a two-movie day, say about nine for a three-movie day. If Alain Delon and Jean Gabin were in town at different theaters, then there's no telling how many wrappers would be there. On opening day, he'd see each of their movies twice, and who knows how many times he'd be there after that. His loyalty and his passion were only for the movies and his work. Because of the movies and the candy bars, his teeth looked like the ruins of an ancient city. His passion for his work should have cost him his life a long time ago.

My film was rolling now. The Frenchman sat next to Puffy, and was rattling away in rather loud whispers to him. Between mouthfuls of candy, Puffy leaned over and said, "Monsieur Dick wants to know what you think of French filmmakers?" I looked back at the distributors. I could see only the outline of their forms. I thought of them as hooded monks preparing to bring excommunication down on me.

"Tell him," I said, turning back, "that the French eat shit and bark at the moon." I didn't mean that, but what else can you do with a question like that? A year of my life, the end of the line for my film, and Monsieur Dick wants to know about Claude Lelouch.

"He likes them," Puffy told him in French, but Monsieur Dick was right back at him.

"Be specific," Puffy said, leaning toward me. "You know how the French are." He winked.

"Hey, Puffy," I said, "what is this—a fuckin' quiz show?"

"My friend Dean," said Puffy, translating and gesturing with his hands, "he says they are made with love and a shoestring. A bit too metaphysical at times, though." Monsieur Dick nodded. Silence for a moment, and the scarecrow began pecking away again.

"Dick says that was quite true before the war. The French filmmaker was the voice of the country. He expressed the thought of France, the story of the defeat that was to come. He didn't make movies for the world box office then." I ignored him.

"Hell, Dean," Puffy added, "you know how the French are. They can't talk about the weather without turning it into a seminar."

"Yeah, and you love it. Tell me. What's he doing here?"

"He owes me a favor."

I turned toward the distributors again. The forms had gone; bedouins could not have moved out more quickly or silently. Without comment or the slightest bow to courtesy, they had come and left, leaving me behind to think hard—was it my face? my eyes? my ears?—about what it was they did not like. Back in Indiana, the kids at least had sense enough to throw things at the screen. That was fair comment.

I said to Puffy, "They're gone."

He didn't hear me, or didn't want to hear me. He kept chewing on his candy, and looking intently at the screen; Puffy was a gentleman. Next to him, my last chance, Monsieur Dick, started to buzz once more.

"Yes, what is it?" Puffy asked him, his eyes not leaving the screen.

Dick whispered into his ear. Maybe he was telling Puffy that he would take it for four or five days, that he saw something that appealed to his high sense of film art. I didn't care if he ran it in a phone booth.

"What's he saying, Puffy?" I asked anxiously.

"He wants to know . . . Well, he wants—"

"Yeah, out with it."

"Yes, well . . ." Puffy stalled some more, and then added, painfully, "Goddammit, Dean, he wants to know if there's any sex in the movie!"

The question cut my throat for a moment. "Sex!" I yelled. "Where's Renoir? Where's Lelouch? All that 'soul of the

95

country' bullshit? Get him outta here, for Chrissake. *Buttri-mit!*"

"Monsieur Dick," Puffy said, patting the little man's head, "my friend Dean says *'buttrimit.'*" Which means "to hell with you." "Stick it up your ass." "Go climb up your nose and jump off it!" I yelled back to the old drunk up in the booth to stop the film. Puffy guided Monsieur Dick up the aisle.

"I'm sorry," said Puffy. "I thought we had a chance with him. But with Frenchmen . . . well, they're just naturally contrary. Christ, they'd eat ice cream in a steam room." He hesitated, then said, "You wanna know what I think. It's satire. A spy satire."

"What the hell is satire? You're beginning to sound like that whack next to you."

"It's ridicule, poking fun. It's a dangerous form. It goes over people's heads a lot of times. Besides, they take spies seriously. A spy is romantic. They can't handle a comedy about spies," Puffy said. "I'm going now. You comin'?"

"No, I got to rewind the film. I'll see you later."

"Yeah," said Puffy, putting his battered and stained corn-cob between his teeth. "And, listen—buck up. You ever seen Kubrick's first film? It was a piece of—"

"Saw it. Tremendous. Called *The Killing.* Sterling Hayden was the star, and Elisha Cook, Jr., was in there somewhere. Lot of other good old pros."

"Can't con you a bit, can I?" said Puffy. "Just tryin' to put a Band-Aid on the cut. Should've known better. You haven't missed much on movies."

"Neither have you. But you're slippin'. Everybody thinks *The Killing* was his first film, but it wasn't. It was *Fear and Desire.* It was almost as bad as mine. Go on, get outta here, you old faker."

Puffy smiled widely, exposing the blight behind his lips. "Maybe this'll cheer ya up some. James called."

"Good. I'm ready for James now."

"When can we talk about it?"

"A couple of hours. By the hot-dog stand in the park on

the Champs-Élysées. It's too noisy around that stand near the Arc."

"But that guy around the Arc has better hot dogs."

"The park, Puffy. Okay? I wanna feel warm. I feel kinda cold inside today."

"Suit yourself," he said. "Come on, Dick. You and I have to have a little talk. A favor, Dick. You know what a favor is: it's . . ." His voice tailed off.

James, I thought, looking up at the empty screen.

I rewound my film, which is a long and aggravating job. In the screening rooms in New York they will do it for the big companies, but if you are a scuffling independent, you rewind it yourself. Here, in this room, with this projectionist, I didn't even feel slighted. I got the better of the deal. The film was still in one piece. The old man was sleeping, his head down on a sticky table, his arm dangling. I would have given a lot to see what all that absinthe had done to his brain. I stuck a ten-franc note up on the machine, and rushed outside—as much as you can rush with those big cans hanging from your arms—for air and sunshine.

It didn't take me long to decide. I walked a block, came to a public wastebasket, and then dropped twenty thousand dollars and months of dreams into it. It was not a hard decision. It was like a friend that you have to get rid of because he makes you feel things you don't want to feel, and if you don't cross him off, you'll start to be as fucked up as he is. It's selfish, but living hasn't been—and isn't done—any other way that I can see, unless you're a preacher or a priest, and I don't know what a vote on any of them would say, either. I had tried to give the film a life of its own; it couldn't make it. So send the horses around again, operator; I'll go around once more.

Besides, I never did like a year with a seven on the end of it. This one wasn't going to be any different. I still owed the bank in Indiana fifteen thousand, a loan which my mother cosigned so I could make the film. I also didn't like the feel of the world, there being a sense of a terrible sea ahead, like when a storm gathers in the middle of the ocean. For the first time, events seemed to be watching me, tracking me, and somehow I knew that something was turning over inside me, loosening the grip I always had on myself. That wasn't me. Maybe I was getting older. I always took the world as it was, and pissed on it if I had to. I didn't owe it a thing. It didn't owe me anything, either.

It was good to be rid of the film now, and I walked quickly across town. People stared at my boots, no doubt thinking I was from Texas or California, places that seemed to fascinate Parisians. Then, as their eyes moved up to the rest of my body—pale arms, pale face, brown hair, average height—they turned away sharply. Just another American. I don't know why I like Paris, I thought. It is more of a brain than a city, a thinking and talking place that never shuts up. In the cafés, the squares, in the parks, over *croissants,* they race from one subject to another: the daily rotgut Beaujolais, politics, crime, truth, Brigitte Bardot's ass; a woman's ass can never reach such a high level of comment as it does in Paris. So I was told. I didn't speak French. And I was told back in school that I couldn't think. I talk—reluctantly. Pass by me with Paris restaurants: I wouldn't know a salmon mousse from a can of tuna fish. Same thing for the city's monuments. I'd never set foot in the Louvre. Only one "monument" drew me to it: Notre-Dame. For me, this was Paris.

I could look at Notre-Dame for hours, watching the light and shadow play against it, or walk into its great womb and sit there, feeling the silence wash over me. And there the grainy film—*The Hunchback of Notre-Dame*—moved eerily through my mind in perfect detail. I could hear the voices of the mob:

"Oh, the horrid baboon!"

"As mischievous as he's ugly."

"It's the devil!"

"I've the misfortune to live near Notre-Dame, and at night I hear him scrambling in the gutter."

"With the cats."

"He's constantly upon our roofs."

"He casts spells at us down the chimneys."

"Oh, the shocking face of the hunchback!"

"Oh, the horrid creature!"

Walking, almost running, now, I heard the voices fade. They led me back to a face and a voice at a party the year before. I remembered the introduction made by Sandra, but most of all I remembered Garrotte's words, mainly because they first annoyed me, then disarmed me and left me strangely quiet with wonder.

I would see Garrotte again, I felt, as I came closer to the figure of Puffy next to the hot-dog stand. I started to jog, and I could see Puffy pulling out his pocket watch. I reached him as he took a hot dog from the vendor. He took a bite, sending the sauerkraut curling up into his mustache. He was wearing the same clothes he had on at the screening: rumpled seersucker suit, stained badly under the arms; an old button-down shirt frayed around the collar; a black tie with too many drops of wonton soup on it from those out-of-the-way Chinese restaurants he liked so much. The whole outfit was topped off with a dark-blue beret. In the cold weather, only two aspects of him changed: he added a big bright footballer scarf from England and changed his suit to one with big checks, both of which made him look like a huge and tired old neon sign.

"Damn cowboy," he said, as I came up on him. "Runnin' in this heat. I'm breathin' hard just eatin' a hot dog."

"Too much of that pig meat," I said.

"No, it's my fuckin' asthma," he said, wiping the sweat from his forehead with his sleeve. "It's a curse, I'll tell ya. I'd give anything to take a deep, pure, delicious breath."

"Yeah, we all have our crosses."

"Speakin' of crosses—where's yours?"

"It's a home-movie now. For some garbage picker."

We sat down on a bench in the shade of the park. There had not been rain for days now, and the big patch of green beyond the footpath in front of us started to give up slowly to brown. The park was empty, except for a wave of Japanese tourists making their way through the thickening haze, their cameras bouncing up and down on their chests. A bird sang in the tree in back of us. Puffy, his mouth full, shouted back to the bird to shut up.

"Can't stand the fuckers," said Puffy. "My granny used to have a canary back in Dothan, Alabama, where I grew up. My grandpa was dyin' then, and the racket from that bird used to drive him nuts. But he'd never say a word to her. Thought he was enough of a burden. So one day I went and chloroformed the fucker. Not grandpa. The bird. Then she got another, and I did the same thing. Settled a half dozen of 'em that year."

Puffy finished his hot dog, looked around for something to wipe his hands on. He decided on the inside of his seersucker. He always seemed to make an effort to prolong these meetings, I thought. I used to guess he did it because he was lonely; when I got to know him better, I could see that was wrong. Puffy knew how to sit in a room by himself. "Most men are bored," he once said. "They can't be alone with their minds, who they are. They can't leave things be. They meddle. They start wars. They swindle each other. They let politics run amok. They join the mob. Anything that comes along. All because they can't be by themselves. You I don't have a fix on yet. I know you run your own course. Me, I'm just a big old bullfrog sittin' on the edge of the swamp, listenin' to all the sounds, watchin' all the life patterns wriggle through it."

Puffy belched, then pulled out the Paris *Herald Tribune.* "Dean, ole buddy," he said, pointing to the paper, "I know ya don't read much, but somethin's going on in the world.

The world's startin' to pick up a crazy english to it. Especially in our country. It started with the Kennedy swat, and it's pickin' up speed."

"Yeah, I guess you're right," I said. "I got a letter from my mother the other day. She says for the first time in her life she's scared. She don't scare easy." I didn't want to tell him what I felt. My sense of time was going. I couldn't care less about politics or movements. I could only go by the visual, and by what my ears could hear. A new mob was on the loose, riding high on blazing electric-guitar chords and bitter, rallying lyrics that called for drugs. It was all foreign to me. Being twenty-eight, I guessed I could jump into it, but it wasn't mine. I wasn't going to follow music or drugs anywhere. The only music I ever cared for was some opera music, and you couldn't give me an aspirin. Besides, I'd been an outsider all my life. I didn't need company. Time and place would be back; I had my own game to run out.

"Can't blame your mom," said Puffy. "They set the prince down—Ali; he didn't deserve it. Newark's been nearly leveled. Detroit's in cinders. That shitkicker from Texas, Johnson, he and his napalm in Vietnam are gonna gut our whole country. He can't break that little old man in sandals—Ho. Look round you right here. That bat in the palace down the way is senile. He's fuckin' in Canadian affairs. He's given England the back of his hand on the Common Market for the second time. He's called the Jews a lot of names. . . ."

"Puffy," I said, "I know you think I'm uneducated, that I should know more, but right now I just wanna know what James has on his mind."

"Sure, Dean," he said, "but there's a point to what I'm saying. Bein' in Europe all these years you get a different picture of things in the U.S. and elsewhere. You get a feel. It's like bein' a lightnin' rod, I'll tell ya. The world hasn't felt like this since the thirties. You're gonna be a busy man, Dean. If you want."

"James. Okay, Puffy?" I said.

"Here it is," said Puffy, passing me a sheet.

The sheet was simple and to the point, with a picture attached. It read:

Name: Erich Paap
Age: 44
Marital status: Widower
Height: 5'11"
Weight: 178
Hair: Black
Occupation: Accountant
Nationality: Hungarian
Citizenship: German (for the last 6 years)
Residence: Vicinity Baden-Baden. Also keeps apartment in Munich (17 Rafstrasse)

"That's it?" I said.

"Forget about that thing," Puffy said. "That's what I'm here for. Two points. Marital status and residence. The hunkie lost his wife about seven months ago. She was twenty years younger than he is. A car got her. Accident? Uhh-uhh. . . . To everybody but Erich Paap. All of a sudden, you see, he couldn't add or subtract. He was doing the banking for all sorts of spidery revolutionary groups in Munich: the Serbs, the Arabs, the Croatians, the Ukrainian anti-Communists—who knows who he screwed? The wife got it. He loved her. He feels guilty. He's very jumpy."

I couldn't help but notice the change that always took place in Puffy at one of these sessions. The easy flow, the slop-hog laziness of his speech, would suddenly go. He became direct, precise, almost formal. The words were clear. He never smiled.

"They would have taken care of Paap, too, except he made sure the money turned up. A remarkable bit of common sense for a Hungarian; it must have been the German influence in his nature. Now, the apartment in Munich. Don't waste your time. He's on his farm all the time now. So what is Erich Paap doing that requires all of our attention? He's handling a lot of money for the

102

Russians. That in itself is all right. A man has to make a living. But Mr. Paap is the financial conduit for a big pot of trouble simmering in Paris, with students, with workers; all hell is going to break loose as soon as the French decide to begin living again after August. A young gentleman called Danny the Red visits Paap once a month, or his courier does. Red lives in Paris here. He also runs the students. We'd take him now, except they would grow another head overnight. Same thing will happen with Paap. But it won't be so easy for them to get someone else. The Russians are careful about who handles their money. Sure, they'll get someone else. In the meantime, we buy some time—to convince the French that real trouble is ahead, to make them ready."

"How long I got?" I asked.

"You got a month, maybe two," said Puffy.

"How much?" I asked.

"Ten thousand," he said.

"Kinda short, isn't it?"

"I don't make the prices, Dean."

"That's enough, I guess."

"I'm not going to ask you how."

"I don't know how."

"Just make it neat. A lot of people watchin' you on this one."

"It'll have to be up close—that's for sure."

"That's the only way for you."

"This is the last one for James," I said. "I won't go to the well for him anymore. This one will take care of my bill."

"You need anything else now?" Puffy asked.

"Not right now," I said. "I'll see you in about two weeks. Might need somethin' then."

Puffy looked at his watch. "Goddamn, I gotta go," he said. "That new movie by Resnais. Miss the beginning with him, and you've had it."

"Hey, Puffy," I called out to him as he was leaving. "Ya ever hear of a man by the name of Garrotte."

"Garrotte, Garrotte," he said, stopping and rolling the

name over. "Never heard of him. Why? Should I know him?"

"Naah," I said. "Only a strange man I met once."

I put a match to the sheet on Erich Paap. The haze was thicker now, the sun weaker. The park was lonely, so I stayed another hour. Thinking.

European trains always seem to make me feel like a Hitchcock character. They are full of mystery and sleek conversation, all of it primed for romance in the dining car across from a pale, blond lady in a big hat that shades her face. The crummy planet works, I thought, as I left the dining car— minus the lady—after a good lunch of well-made steak and fresh fruit. There was a poetry of order here. I have always loved ships and the sea, the sense of being apart from everything, but on the big liners I always feel trapped into a hard and plastic social caste, encircled by nosy guests and stewards, which is why if I travel by sea I try to go by freighter.

We were about three hours out of the Gare du Nord, in Paris, about five away from Munich. I sat alone in the first-class compartment, by the window, watching the richly green countryside, letting the sun beat on my head, which was tilted against the window. I was wearing a safari jacket, khaki pants, and a pair of desert boots. An expensive Nikon was around my neck and a big pair of field glasses rested next to me on the seat; I had a pair of rimless glasses with thick lenses in my top jacket pocket. My luggage was up on the rack: a small bag with odds and ends of clothing and a change of underwear, which was a jockstrap. My only other jockstrap I had on.

The train came to a smooth stop in Strasbourg and stayed

there awhile as the passport inspectors in gray-blue uniforms moved through it. I put on my glasses, for no reason; it was a reflex action. An inspector came into my compartment, and I fumbled for my passport. Handing it to him, I removed my glasses. He didn't give me a second look. He became concerned with the kid coming into the compartment, about twenty-two, with very long hair, dirty clothes, heavy walking boots, and a knapsack on his back. The inspector looked at him once, twice more, then muttered something in German and shook his head. The kid tried to move into the compartment sideways but his pack wouldn't fit; he kept trying.

"Here," I said, timidly getting up. "Can I help? You might be better off removing it out here."

"Good old Yankee ingenuity," he said. "Now, why didn't I think of that?" He stepped out into the corridor, freed himself of the pack, and then plopped himself into the seat across from me.

"You are a Yank, aren't you?" he asked.

"What . . . what's that?" I said.

"A Yank. An American."

"Yes. Oh, yes," I answered quickly. He began to take off his boots.

"First time in Europe?" he asked.

"Yeah, that's right," I said. The boots were off, and his long, bony feet, his stockings sticking to them, were stretched out over the knapsack in front of him. He reached forward and pulled a long sausage from the side of his pack.

"Let me see, now," he said, studying me. "I bet I can guess what you do for a living." His teeth tore at his sausage. A sour smell began to fill the compartment.

"A grade-school teacher?" he asked.

"No, no," I said.

"A civil servant?" I shook my head, smiling coyly. "A bank teller?" He appeared frustrated. "Blimey, I wish I were Holmes. He could give your whole history after a glance."

"An accountant," I said.

"About the same," he said, convincing himself that he

had been right. The compartment was smelling terrible. I looked at his feet.

"Where are you going? Munich?" he said. He still had halfway to go on the sausage. I told him he was correct. He said he had been living there about eight months. I became interested.

"I'm a dropout," he said. "From Oxford. One gets tired of Universitas Oxoniensis. The mirror of England, and all that." All that reached me was that one word: "dropout." I could understand that.

The conductor came into the compartment, checking for new passengers. He was one of the German crew who had just come aboard, starting a new shift. He hardly looked at me. His eyes were on Oxford, the hair, the sausage that was ragged at the ends, the pack that was blocking his way, and most of all the feet.

"Nein, nein," the conductor said to Oxford, waving his hand over the pack, and pointing to the sausage. He wasn't too crazy about the smell, either. He threw the pack up on the rack. Oxford offered him his ticket. The German looked at it, his face growing redder by the second.

"Out! Out!" he yelled at Oxford, going for the pack. "First class! First class!" the conductor kept saying.

"Let go of that, you bloody bulldog," Oxford said. The German went out, and came back with another conductor.

"This ticket . . . no good," said the new guy. "You do not belong here. This is second-class ticket." Oxford put up a lame defense, then started to gather himself up for the move. The kid could be useful, I figured. I looked at his feet again, started to change my mind, then thought, What the hell.

"What's the difference?" I asked the conductor. "I mean, how much more does he have to pay for first class?" The German said it would be forty marks. I peeled them off. They let the kid stay, and told him to get rid of the sausage. The first German left, muttering to himself, *"Englischer."*

"That's awfully decent of you, old man," said Oxford. "Just trying to use a touch of the old graft, you know what

106

I mean. Can't run a thing past these bloody Germans."

"That's all right," I said. "But you could do me one favor."
I hesitated, as if embarrassed. "Could you . . . I mean, would
it be too much to ask for you to put your boots on?"

"Not at all," he said. "My feet don't smell, but some people, I guess, don't like to see shoes off." I breathed deeply
and thanked him.

"Where are you staying in Munich?" Oxford asked.

"I'll find a *pensión,* I suppose."

"Look, you come with me," he said, eager to be helpful.
"I'll get you a room in my *pensión.* It's in Schwabing."

"Is it dangerous?"

"No, not really," he said. "It's a student enclave, mainly.
Lot of drug traffic. Dropouts. AWOL American soldiers. Professional opium smugglers from Turkey. Pimps from the
Vienna underworld. Peddlers of counterfeit paintings. The
place is the capital of the Munich subculture."

"No, I'm afraid not," I said, looking worried.

"Don't be silly," he said. "I insist." Oxford was no fool. He
knew a good thing when he saw it.

"Do you know anything about birds?" I asked.

"You mean women? Or the kind with the wings? I don't
know much about either."

"How about photography?"

"Quite a bit. . . . Hey, mate, you sound like you're shopping for a wife. I won't do. Don't let the hair fool you."

"Will you show me around Munich for a while? I don't
know how long it will be. I'll pay you."

"My pleasure," said Oxford, pulling his sausage out of his
back pocket. He left his shoes on.

Oxford will be worth the investment, I thought while washing my jockstrap that night down the hall in the bathroom.
I needed some eyes in Munich, needed to know the feel and
design of the place. I would have to *know* this town if anything went wrong. Puffy could have given me several contacts, but I always preferred to find my own. Made me feel
safer.

"It's the maddest city in a mad world," he said as we began our rounds. "A very emotional people, an eccentric people given to swift changes of mood. Not like the stiff-backed Prussians in the North. The town was built by the crazy Wittelsbachs. It's still crazy. Look at the names that found a home here: Hitler, Lenin, Lola Montez, Wagner. . . .

"Look over there," Oxford said, pointing to the Brauhaus covered with Coca-Cola signs, and saying that was where Hitler started his *Putsch,* only to flee with Göring, who had stopped and hid behind a stone lion, which was still there.

"Take a picture," Oxford advised. I clicked the camera.

For three days we wandered the streets of Munich, one scene after another spilling into my camera—so Oxford thought: the Deutsches Museum; the Alte Pinakothek; the Europa Espresso, once a popular haunt for every spy in postwar Europe, now only a trading place for drugs; the spike-helmeted stone generals around each turn of a corner; the endless loud beer halls.

"Get that one, Yank," Oxford would yell. "That fat German with the big mug up to his mouth. Look at the beer running down his jowls. What a picture!"

The days usually ended at an expensive restaurant with Oxford ordering the wine and the meal, and not batting an eye when the check came for fifty dollars. I would look at him, smile inside, pull out my thick glasses, and inspect the bill.

"It's a three-star," Oxford said. "Munich comes high." The kid had balls. I liked him.

But it was time to move. It began when Oxford entered my room on the third night. Now, what were we going to do tomorrow, he wanted to know. Stretched out on the bed, I remained silent.

"I know," he said, walking over to the dresser. "Let's start with getting the film developed. I know a guy who will do it quickly and cheaply. I'd like to see what we've got. It's the first time I've been a director." I stayed silent. He picked up the camera.

"Oxford," I said, "don't bother with the camera. I have a confession to make. There's been no film in it. I don't know the first thing about cameras." He looked at me with pity.

"Why didn't you tell me?" he asked.

"I was embarrassed," I said.

"You Americans and your toys," he said, as if he had finally found endorsement for a long-held conviction. "Buy now, learn later. Haven't the foggiest what to do with your money next."

"I'm sorry," I said. "I bought it at the last minute. Will you teach me?" He shook his head and walked toward me with the camera.

"Look," he said, as if he were talking to a little boy, "in case you don't know what you bought, this is a Nikon. It is . . ." He went on for more than two hours covering every detail about the Nikon and its lenses.

When he was finished, he said, "That's a Nikon. You're an expert now. But one thing: you need a shoulder stock or a tripod to shoot birds with the telephoto lens."

"Oxford," I said, "I hope you don't mind, but I'm not feeling at all well. I'm coming down with something. It must be all the moving about. I'm used to a certain routine."

He said he understood.

"Yes, but I have a problem," I said. "I promised my mother some bird pictures. I'm really not up to it. I want her to have the best. She frames them. Could you—"

"Take the pictures?" he said.

"And have them developed by tomorrow evening?" I said.

"You're an odd sort," he said, looking at me queerly. I handed him a one-hundred-dollar bill. He forgot how odd I was, took the camera, and left.

With Oxford occupied the next day, I went on some errands, first to buy a Thermos, some instant coffee, many cans of beans, tins of corned beef, then to a sporting-goods store for a backpack, a sleeping bag, and hiking boots. My next stop was a little shop on a side street off Maximilianstrasse;

we had passed it one day on one of our tours. The shop was filled with World War Two military remnants. I browsed for a long time before I called for the shopkeeper.

"Let me see that cap there," I said, pointing.

"Ah, the Luftwaffe cap," he said in heavily accented English. "Very rare. The only one I have." It was faded and tattered.

I fingered it, examined it closely, as if I knew what I was looking for. "Now, let me see those medals," I said. One was an Iron Cross. I couldn't make the others. "And, oh, yes, the bayonet." I held the bayonet, gauging its balance and weight in my hand. I never liked knife work.

"How much for all this?" I asked. He studied me, figured me for a collector. "The bayonet, as you know, is not much, but the rest . . ." I wanted only the bayonet.

"How much?"

He quoted a price equivalent to one hundred fifty dollars. It was robbery. I looked at the Iron Cross in my hand. But courage came cheap, I thought.

I paid up, and took a streetcar to a Honda shop in Schwabing. I picked out a bike, laid half the money down, and told the clerk he'd have the rest when I picked it up in the morning. Back at the *pensión,* I put all my gear under the bed and waited for Oxford. He showed up in the evening, eager to show me the pictures. Was I pleased, he wanted to know. Beautiful color, I said. They were birds, I thought. Just birds.

"Now," he said, "why don't I fix you up with a young lady?"

"What for?" I asked.

"Well, how 'bout a joint?" he said, reaching into his pocket.

"A what?"

"Never mind," he said. He would see me tomorrow. "You're a straight Yank," he added. I left the next morning. I never said good-bye to Oxford.

The journey from Munich to Baden-Baden, on the edge of the Black Forest, took about fourteen hours by motorbike, and when I pulled into the little spa, it was quiet and dark. I checked into a *pensión,* which took me a long time to find because this was not a town for the Oxfords of the world. Old, old money and a deep-stained grandeur had seeped into its facades and cornices and cobbled streets. I lounged about town the next day, getting my bearings. It was a town of the past; you could see that. It was full of old ladies wandering through gardens in felt hats and chiffon scarves. There was no noise. Only the peaceful sound of church bells and the laughing of bands of schoolgirls with white wool stockings and long blond hair. From the edge of town German hikers in short leather pants made their way into the darkly forested hills that rimmed the town.

The next morning, leaving my Honda in the tiny courtyard of the *pensión,* I put on my pack and headed for the hills. I had paid the lady who owned the *pensión* for the week, and told her, pointing to the Honda, that she could take a ride whenever she wanted. She giggled; it was not often an old widow was offered a ride on a Honda. Before starting my hike, I stopped and picked up a hiker's map from a tour agency. The area that I wanted was twenty miles south and five miles west. There was a footpath most of the way, but when I turned west, no path was shown on the map. I figured ten hours for the trip. I was an optimist. It took twenty-four. My feet double-crossed me.

Morning came on the fourth day, and the light shafting through the dark trees made me feel like I was in a cathedral. I had some coffee, took my field glasses and camera and shoulder stock, and started west again, leaving the rest of my stuff back in camp. It was a half mile or so before I came to a ridge, and there, another half mile below, was a farmhouse: a wide-eaved old wooden house with shingles like fish scales, fronted by a garden. Three hours passed and no one came out of the house; this is the real

111

work: waiting, waiting, sitting alone with your thoughts, nothing to distract you, I tried to think of old movies; ran through the whole part I had played Off-Broadway in *Escurial*. At last a figure was in my field glasses. It was Erich Paap, all right. He came out of the door with two German shepherds and a shotgun cradled in his right arm. He walked over toward the garden, picked some flowers, then started southwest, the dogs at his heels. He returned a couple of hours later.

Two more days passed. The same routine. Where the hell was he going? The next day I took his route, following him but giving him a lot of rope to the front and side, until he stopped a mile away at a cemetery with about a hundred gravestones and a few small mausoleums. Before going into the cemetery, he leashed the dogs to a tree outside the gate. He used a key to enter one of the mausoleums, leaving his shotgun standing against the outside door. He was there twenty minutes before he came out. His wife, I thought; this is where I would have to take him. The farmhouse was out, because of the dogs; I had nothing to handle them with. And he seldom seemed to sleep much at night, for I could often see his shadow up and down through the curtained windows. He would be easy for a rifle and scope, but when it came to a rifle, I couldn't hit a bull in the ass with a baseball bat. I resisted the skills of a rifle. Rifles are impersonal, like the distance men themselves. Distance men are technicians, have the smell of the manual about them, with all their wind gauges and elevations. They are like the people who can't look at a car without telling you about it right down to the smallest bolt. No, Paap would have to go here, with the bayonet. I'd give him a couple more days.

That night, having finished off another can of beans, I climbed into my sleeping bag next to the fire. I watched the fire, listened to the sounds of the forest, and went to sleep. I don't know how long I'd been sleeping before I heard the voice. I bolted up, looked about, but could not see anything. Coming out of the darkness amid the trees, the voice began again in German. I could see nothing there, except two low, thin streams of vapor. A man walked out from between the streams of vapor.

"What is it? What—?" I said excitedly.

"Do not move," the man said in careful and icy English. He walked closer, with the shotgun on his arm. He was wearing knickers over high boots. I said I was an American.

"What are you doing here?" he asked, raising the big blaster to my eye level from about three feet away. I rummaged for my glasses, the kind that made me feel like the actor Wally Cox—so hopelessly vulnerable.

"Where are my glasses . . . my glasses?" I screeched. "I can't see." He advised me not to move any more.

"What are you doing here?" he said again, this time impatiently.

"Looking for birds," I said. He studied me carefully. Then he turned and shouted something in German back at the two streams of vapor. In seconds, two gray and silver German shepherds were racing toward me. He gave another order in German, and they sat down next to me and didn't twitch a muscle.

"I need my glasses," I said. "Can I get them out of my pack?" I started to move. The dogs growled, then snarled, baring their wet teeth. It was just a tiny move, fellas; no need for all that, I thought. Ordered to be quiet, the dogs yawned nervously.

"I'm just spending a few days out here doing some bird photography," I said. He didn't say anything. He moved over to my pack, knelt down, the blaster still on me, and dumped all my stuff out on the ground: the Luftwaffe cap, the canned goods, the Iron Cross, my glasses, my passport, the camera, the bayonet, and a jockstrap, which he held up with two fingers as if fearing contamination. He then picked up the camera. The telephoto lens was still attached to it. He wanted to know why. I said I had forgotten to take it off.

"Very careless," he said. He handed me the camera. "Disassemble the camera." he said. I separated the telephoto lens, fifteen to sixteen inches long, from the body of the camera.

"Show me the object in it," he commanded. I showed him the glass lens. I knew what he was thinking. It could have easily been a weapon.

"What kind of film are you using?" he snapped.

"High-speed Ektachrome."

"What ASA?"

"Your basic one-sixty, but I'm boosting it to four hundred."

"What shutter speed?"

"A five hundredth of a second."

"What F stop?" He looked absently at the pictures of Oxford's birds.

"Average of F-eight, but sometimes five-point-six."

"I'm sorry," he said, lowering the shotgun. He looked at my passport again. "Herr Selmier, isn't it? You mustn't take offense. It is not often that one sees strangers in this far. And never an American."

"You can't take pictures of birds with people around," I said. "Back near Baden-Baden there are too many hikers in the area."

"Are you a professional?" he asked.

"No, just an amateur," I said. "I teach grade school. May I have my glasses?"

He gave me the glasses, and pulled out a flask. He took a long pull, and offered some to me. I refused. I put on my glasses slowly, as if trying to compose myself; now I really couldn't see a thing. I wondered how I must have looked to him. Did he see me the same way as Oxford did: as a bumbling, self-conscious type of American; a shy, lonely man for whom every day was the same; a man who had no friends and each night took his meals alone and went to sleep with a secret and unknown dread that maybe tomorrow would not be the same as today?

"You mustn't be alarmed, Herr Selmier," he said, taking another pull at his flask. I looked over at the bayonet. A few more of those, Herr Paap, I thought, and it will be your turn to be alarmed. The dogs were resting on their bellies now. The bayonet was about five feet away. I'd worry about the dogs later. It wouldn't be neat, though. It was wishful thinking.

"I've saved for this trip for three years," I said. "I didn't expect anything like this. In America, yes. Not here."

"I am fond of photography," he said. "I used to take pictures of deer and birds. My wife . . ." He fell silent. The booze was working on him. "Yes, my wife. Hundreds of pictures, a woman as pure and serene as this forest. Dead too soon."

His face turned toward me. The light from the fire played on the lines left by the company he had kept for so many years. He was a tired man, with circles under his eyes and a true weariness of soul. "Man is insane," he said, measuring each word. He wasn't excluding himself, I guessed.

"We used to go to Baden-Baden often," he said. "For the waters. The casinos. The cream cakes." He smiled, perhaps remembering a scene. "A very civilized way of life. But still not like it once was, filled with grand dukes and fine-plumed ladies. And music . . . music from the masters of the world." He rubbed the head of one of the dogs. "I wish I could have lived then," he said.

"Is all this your land?" I asked, trying to change the subject.

"No, no," he said. "You can stay as long as you like." He looked over at my gear on the ground. "Are you a fan of the Nazi military? I see the German air cap, the Iron Cross."

"No," I said. "I bought them to exhibit in my class back in the States."

"Do not teach children about war and politics," he said. "Let them be children." He got up, worked on the flask again, and said, "I must leave you now. Please accept my apology."

He started to walk away with his dogs, then turned and said, "Be careful, Herr Selmier. This is an evil forest, with strange legends of ghosts and giants." He paused. "And bizarre murder!" He laughed loudly, a chilling shriek that seemed to put eyes in the big dark trees overhead. And then he was gone.

"Buttrimit!" I muttered, berating myself.

I couldn't take him now. I took my glasses off, and threw them far into the black. I packed up my things, pissed on what was left of the fire, and began the long hike back. I would take him. Yes, I would.

I whipped the Honda back to Paris with meanness, cursing Puffy all the way for not telling me about the dogs and that equalizer always cradled in Paap's arm, feeling stupid for having been made by him and being too artful in my thinking. A bayonet, for Chrissake. If I had had a gun, Paap and his two hounds would have been stiff by now. Yeah, dummy, that's all the Hungarian had to see: a gun and a silencer. Bang! Yeah, but I wouldn't have left the gun in the pack; it would have been in my sleeping bag. That's the way my brain was turning over the whole trip to Paris. I made up my mind to talk it over with Puffy. I didn't want to spook him, to shake his respect and confidence in me; miss once, and the word goes out. But I also didn't want to spook myself. I didn't need another failure. I needed a success. The scars, I had to admit, were still pink from the film I had made.

I went straight to David's clinic. I walked into the old mansion, started upstairs to where some of the classrooms were. I passed a sign on the wall, painted in big, uneven letters: LA SYMPATHIE NE VIT PAS ICI. I could hear Sandra singing in the room at the top of the stairs. The song was in French. I stood in the doorway, wearing my Luftwaffe cap, and the Iron Cross dangled from my neck. I watched her for several minutes, running over her features as if I were discovering them for the first time: a long nose, long dark hair, an ample pair of breasts, and a solid ass. But most of all there was the strength that radiated from her. Out of her childlike eyes. Her sometimes fluid, mannish gait. Her crisp, swift words. She was not beautiful. She was a woman who had lived, who seemed to have been to hell and back and wasn't talking. Always, though, I came back to her eyes: forever moving between softness and hardness and an unspoken pain. She could be cruel, I thought, and never look back.

I finally moved into her line of vision, and waved to her to join me. She stopped the singing, and told the kids to draw the snowman that was on the blackboard as she moved my way.

One of the boys got up and grabbed her around the legs. His eyes were lifeless sockets; spit bubbled from his mouth; his lips tried to form words, but he could come up with only a tortured, deep groan. She picked him up off the floor, and said slowly, "Not now, Claude. We will go and play later." She guided the boy, his limbs moving in many directions at once, back to his desk, and put a crayon in his hand.

We were hardly out the door when she turned on me, ripping the Iron Cross from my neck and taking the cap off my head.

"What's that for?" I said, slightly annoyed. She reached into her bag, took out a lighter, and put it to the hat.

"I thought you'd get a kick out of it," I said.

"You can be a cruel bastard," she said.

"That's funny. I was just thinking the same about you." She didn't say a word, and now I remembered. I said I was sorry.

"Sorry for what?" she said. "Because I'm Israeli? Because you have the taste of a hog? I didn't do that because I'm an Israeli. I did it because I'm a human being. That Nazi nostalgia is sick."

"Look, come on over here," I said. "I bought you something, only slightly used." She looked at the Honda, and kissed me softly on the cheek. She sat on the bike; the child suddenly came back in her eyes.

"I'll buy you a new hat," she said. "A beret. So you'll look like one of those French film directors." We began walking, and she hummed to herself.

"What's that?" I asked.

"Just the song I was singing with the kids. In English it goes like this." She smiled and sang softly:

> Do, a deer, a female deer
> Re, a drop of golden sun

Mi, a name I call myself
Fa, a long long way to run. . . .

"Oh, David wants to see you," she said. "He said he had to have a talk with you."

"I can't now. I'm too busy. Where is he?"

"In Paris, looking for money. . . . Oh, and you know who I saw the other night. Monsieur Garrotte. He asked about you." She imitated his voice, saying, " 'My dear Sandra, where is the bell ringer, that most entertaining friend of yours?' "

"Are you fuckin' him?" I asked.

"I could've. . . ."

"And have."

"But wouldn't!" she said.

"You're a good girl," I said.

"Don't count on it, smartass," she said, kissing me on the lips. "Look, I have to go back now. You'll be by tonight? I leave town in the morning for three weeks."

"Yeah, and when I get there, play some other record besides the goddamn Beatles."

"You don't know history when you hear it," she yelled back, her arms folded. And she jogged back to the mansion.

I rang Puffy and arranged to meet him for tea up in the Eiffel Tower in midafternoon. He was working on some *croissants* when I got there.

"Are congratulations in order?" he asked as I sat down.

"Are you kidding! Why didn't you tell me he had dogs, and carried a blaster with him everywhere he goes? A long trip for nothin'."

"I didn't know, Dean," he said, not knowing what to do with his hands. "The contact didn't tell me. He'll never work again."

"That's what I mean about contacts."

"What's your plan?"

"First things first. More money. Five thousand more. Dogs, the kind you don't know about, come high."

118

"I don't know, Dean," he said.

"Yes, you do," I said.

"I think they'll go along."

"He's gonna go," I said. "I don't know how. But he's gonna go."

We sat there in silence momentarily as Puffy slurped his tea. I could see Notre-Dame from our table; my eyes stayed on it.

"This tower is tiltin' all the time," said Puffy. "One day it's gonna fall right into de Gaulle's bedroom. Bam! So long to the Fifth Republic." I could see Quasimodo hugging one of the gargoyles on top of the cathedral, saying sadly, "Why was I not made of stone, like thee?" My mind circled back to David's clinic, to the eyes of the boy, the spittle running from his mouth.

"I know how he's gonna go," I said, getting up. "I'll be on my way in three days."

"You need anything?" he asked.

"Yeah. Money, and a twenty-two with a silencer. Did you tell James this is it for him?"

"Yeah. He said fine. He said you won't quit."

"I didn't say I was quitting."

Sandra was gone when I awoke the next morning, having left a note that read "I am glad you never ask where or why. You are not a cruel bastard. Love." The sun streamed through the window, and I put some Beethoven on the record player. I plotted the day, making a list of things I needed and the stops I had to make. First, I went to a secondhand-clothing store and bought some old and baggy gray pants and a shirt. A studio across town was next; I had a French acquaintance who was an assistant makeup man there. He let me talk him out of an old dusty wig that should have been thrown away.

"Now you can make some money," I said. "I need a skin-colored hunch. Rubber. Waterproof. Can you do it?"

"Sure, let me make a fit," he said. "I can have it to you in about five days."

"I need it in two," I said. I gave him a couple of hundred. "You got a mold I can have, and some latex?"

"I can do a piece for you, too," he said.

"I can handle it," I said. "I think."

On the way home, I stopped off and bought a Polaroid camera and a small cassette recorder. Christ, Erich Paap was becoming expensive. But it wasn't off my end. That night I began to build a rubber piece for the side of my face, with special attention to the eyes and the nose. I wanted an eye that protruded, one that was lifeless and with the lid half closed; it took me six hours to make the piece. I pressed the piece next to the eye for a fitting, taking pictures of my face up close each time as I tried laboriously to perfect it; I couldn't get it right. Still, it wasn't what Lon Chaney once went through, I thought. Trying to create an illusion of a blind eye, he had taken the white membrane from the inside of an egg and put the film of it directly against his eyeball. I winced at the pain he must have felt. Hours later I had the eye I wanted. It was monstrous, maybe too obvious. But then, Paap would be my only critic. And if I was wrong, there wouldn't be another show.

The next morning I began working into the tape recorder, trying to capture the boy Claude's efforts at speaking. I put a small wet sponge in my mouth to create spittle. Satisfied, I concentrated on the walk, which developed from a bad spastic to a pitiful dragging of my left foot. Was I ready? I'd try it on the streets of Paris. I walked for hours, slobbering and pulling that foot after me like an iron ingot. Few eyes could stay on me, and when I went up to one man, trying to form words, he nearly kicked me away in disgust. With the hunch, I would be even more grotesque. I thought of Claude; his was a tough hand to be holding.

Three days later I was back in Baden-Baden. This time I found a *pensión* on the edge of town. As night fell, I started to put myself together. I glued the piece into place with spirit gum, blended and sealed the edge with liquid latex, and, when it was dry, added a coat of sealer. Finished, I slipped into the hunch. I stood in front of the mirror, putting on the dirty old clothes and the wig. I was satisfied. I checked Puffy's gun. Then I got out of the hunch, assembled my pack quietly, and left my room about midnight; I had to leave the face piece on because there would be no way to get it back properly in the forest. The long walk began.

Once in the area, I did not bother with the farmhouse. I went straight to the cemetery, and made camp in a glen near it. I couldn't chance a fire, so I slept there in the dark, thinking of what a pathetic tableau it was, that head of mine sticking out of the sleeping bag. By morning I was at the gate of the cemetery with flowers in my hand—and the .22 tucked inside the breast part of my hunch. I sat down, and waited. The sun grew hotter, making my back wet under the hunch. Old women wearing kerchiefs on their heads drifted in and out. Paap was late. I waited long into the afternoon; I had nowhere else to go. Where was he? Maybe he had killed himself? Guilt had nearly eaten up his heart and reason. Finally, I could see his figure down the long path that led to the gate. I got to my feet. He drew closer. Seeing me, he leashed his dogs. He was at the gate now. He walked over to the tree, and tied his dogs there as he had always done. He walked toward me. The dogs became wild now, growling and barking. They had sensed me; they knew my smell.

"Aaaagh, aagh," I said, slobbering, as he started through the gate. When he approached, I pushed up against him, extending the flowers. He moved me aside with his shotgun, and moved toward the mausoleum at the back of the cemetery. I watched him place the gun outside, and then saw the door close behind him. I let him get situated, then made my move. I silently opened the door; he was on his knees, with his back to me. A candle flickered, sending shadows over the walls. I was right behind him now as he turned around, with an angry expression on a face that had collapsed even more since I last saw him.

"Get out of here, you idiot!" he must have screamed in German. "What do you want here?" He started to rise.

"Just lookin' for birds," I said.

The bullet exploded up into his left eye, and came out the back of his head, sending bone fragments dancing in the air like flakes of dandruff. The eye looked like it had been picked on by a vulture as he lay almost fetuslike on the floor. I bent down and put a safety into his head.

Outside the window of the train, the green Bavarian landscape looked like a Christmas garden, with its ginger-cake houses of red slate roofs, the figures of people and cattle in the fields.

Alone in the compartment, exhausted, my head vibrating against the window. Lines from *Escurial* ran through my mind.

We are both great actors! Enough, the farce is over. Let us become ourselves again.

My good eye opened, catching the image of my hideous face in the window, with its popping, dangling eye, the grimy shock of hair, the hunch crawling over my shoulder.

Am I an actor? Or am I a killer?

Violence is so fast, I thought; it is over before you sense what has happened.

But does a clown ever recount his life?

Said the King to the Fool.

PART FOUR

There's a funny taste in my mouth. There's somebody funny in my body. My eyes are heavy—so heavy. They must weigh fifty pounds each. And they burn, feeling like somebody has poured something into them. I think of my hands. A movie? I look at my hands. They're not tied! They always tie your hands in a movie. If it isn't a movie, where am I? I'm sitting in a chair. I lift my hand in front of me, crack my eyes into slits. *Two bright lights.* I can't see anything else, and close them quickly. They don't burn anymore. They feel like a stone is in each of them. I put a limp hand to my face. I'm still clean shaven. I haven't been here too long. Or, did they shave me to confuse me? Who are *they?* I'm not in a movie! I wish I were in a movie. What's that? It's my body. I can hear it coming apart. Like the whining of a big ball of string being unwound by a machine. My body is going to sleep. I'm goin'! My tongue is thick. Give me back my tongue. Get up! That's it: walk it off. Where are my legs? You can't walk without legs. Get back to the chair! Here . . . I go. Break the fall with your arms. I don't have any arms. Here it comes. Here comes the floor. My face! I'm going to land on my face. I . . .

I am coming to, now. I remember. I feel my face. No blood. Nothing hurts. Two eyes. A nose. A mouth. I search the rest of my body while still lying there. I have my arms and legs back. The funny man is gone from my body. I open my eyes slowly, without trouble. They don't hurt anymore. It is now totally dark. Like a grave. I begin to move. Hey, wait a minute. I move my hands over my body. I'm naked! They took my clothes. I'm bare-ass naked. Who are *they?* I have a sense of the floor. It's warm, and feels like rubber. It's giving under the weight of my body. Get to your feet. Easy now. It's hard to stand up. The floor waves with each step. Ohhh! Shit! A wall. Falling. The floor again. I'm all right. The walls must be rubber, too. I feel my face. How long was I out? The hair on my face is a day or more long. Not much more. I begin to laugh to myself. Where am I going to shit and piss? They must be watching me. They got a lot of laughs comin'. Lookin' at a guy in a rubber room with no place to relieve himself. And no lights to see where the mess is when he does. Forgetting a pile here. Stepping on a pile there. I'm not laughing anymore. One thing must be done. Get to your feet. Find a wall. There. Now pace off this fuckin' rubber room. Get a sense of place. The floor sways beneath like a calm, dark sea. Bearings. Know where you are. You can handle this. Like the hole back in prison. My hands and feet slowly pick the room apart. It must be hell to be blind. I'd say the room's fifteen by fifteen. If they wanted a claustrophobia effect, I'd be in a four by four. What are they looking for? Who are *they?* There's no door of any kind. Ah, here's a hatch in a corner. If they feed me, the food'll be here. I'm tired. Go to another corner now. Go to sleep. Sleep.

I feel that I've been sleeping for a long time. Got to get outta this laziness. I do push-ups and sit-ups for hours, stopping only now and then to lie flat on my back in the middle of the room, or to walk around. I'm still banging into walls. But I'll soon have the number of steps down. I am hungry. If they're watching, they'll put food in when I'm sleeping. Why didn't they? I'm hungry. They probably have many ways to keep track of what I'm doing here. A one-way mirror from above. But how could they see through the dark.

Maybe they listen for their kicks. With a tape machine running to pick up sounds, or me talking to myself. But I haven't been talking; I must not talk! You want a sound, you bastards? Here you go! I strain. The fart is a whimper. How's that for a sound! Not much. I agree. The darkness swims over me. I want to cut it to shreds with a knife. The silence hurts my ears. How can silence hurt your ears! Get ahold of yourself, Selmier. Lie down again. I see a big clock in my mind. One of Thorstan's clocks. I listen to it tick. It's soothing. I go on the nod.

I haven't dozed long. Or have I? Who knows? I quickly crawl over to the corner. I reach out, feel with my hands. Ahh, here it is. A sandwich and a small carton of milk. I can't make out what's in the sandwich. Pâté? Maybe. Liverwurst? I hate them both. I eat like a hog. Have to watch that, next time. The milk dribbles over my beard. I wipe it off, and try to feel for time again. I don't get anywhere. Just a great feeling of absolutely nothing. Fuck time! Watch that. I almost spoke aloud. I must be kidding myself. The hair on my face is my only clock! Use your head. Why time? I'm here until they let me out. Maybe this is getting to me already. But there ain't no way I'm going to crack for them. Who is *them?* Do some more exercises. Keep fit. Oh-oh, here it comes. That milk must have passed through me like a train. I crawl to a corner. Make sure it's not the one with the hatch, for Chrissake! Your food! I get down like a Vietnamese in a rice field and give them back their sandwich and milk. I return to the middle of the floor. And sleep again.

But wait! I sit up straight. Wait! The dung over in the corner! I've been dreaming of it. Why doesn't it smell? I mean, in this room it would have to. And how am I getting air? Yeah, answer those questions, Selmier, and you get a free trip to Greenland. What an idiot I'm becoming! Back to the sit-ups. More sleep. I'm getting too much sleep. But what can I do? More food in the corner. A chicken leg and more milk. The milk has a chalky taste to it. Relieve myself again. But the corner is clean! They must have a hatch in all four corners. Whaddaya know? It's a game now. I'll test them.

Next time I have to go, I'm going to do it between the two corners. Then we'll see how clever they are. Brilliant! An egg sandwich gives me my chance. An egg sandwich? It's not morning. It's always midnight. There you go, with time again. Plunk! Right between the two walls. *Heeee, heeee!* Back in the center of the room, meditating on the shit. What a fool I am. If they don't remove it when I sleep, the smell will drive me outta here, and I got no way to get outta here. Sure enough. They ain't removing it. How long's it been there? Forty days. A day. I got to do something about this. Go over there. Put it in the corner for the dung collector. I'm laughing. I can barely control myself. You ever try to laugh and laugh without making a sound of laughter? Very hard. I'm thinking, What a job for someone to have to remove my dung. They must want something from me very bad if they're going through this day after day. The place smells horrible with the waste, mainly the piss that I step in as it rolls around the rubber floor when I walk.

Sleeping. Eating. Exercising. Relieving myself. Walking. But not often. I'm afraid I might step in my own shit. Always in fear that the dung collector will not collect. I mean, what's a guy pay taxes for? I began to think how bad it would be to have a woman in here with me. I smell myself. You smell yourself! Dummy! Whaddaya think you've been smelling the whole time? Somebody else? What would it be like with a woman in here with me? Oh-oh. Get off that subject. I lie back and look up, picking out stars in an imaginary sky. I feel my penis rise. With two of us, it would smell terrible. And what about the poor guy who has to haul out all that shit? Twice the job. No rest for the weary. Here I go again. Laughing. It hurts trying to hold it back. Damn, I'm hungry. My arms are like rocks; my stomach is like a blacktop. Those exercises. My mind turns back to the woman. I won't be able to hold back the laughter any longer. Sleep. Think of Thorstan's clock. That's all I can do: be still, shut up, and sleep. Now I'm biting my finger to keep from laughing. I'm shaking and so is the floor. What a picture! A room full of dung. Hers and mine. We can't even move around. There must be something I can think of. Anything. Eating? Hell, no! That leads right back to shitting. I've got to think of something on another track. That's what they'd need if the two of us were in here. A train track with a flatcar to get rid of the dung. Stop it! I can't stand it! I'm doubled up. Trying to muffle my barely stifled laughing. The entire room is laughing. Everything is shaking and laughing.

The smell wakes me up. Did I have a laughing fit? Or was it a dream I had? That's right. Push-ups. Push-ups. One, two, three. Keep doing them. Faster and faster. More and more. How many days now? How many months? Faster! Faster! Break your hump. I fall over on my back, and listen to my breathing. I try to make music out of it. I want music. A little Puccini, Maestro, please. I look for some more stars in my sky. . . . How do you get in a shit hole like this?

The faces: my mother, white as a church wafer, her gestures as textured and soft and compliant as a thin piece of veil; my father, his skin as burnished and grooved as his heavy boots, every move, every sudden turn of his eye, an act of restrained aggression; a lumberjack of a man with strength and vitality, but there are no more trees to fell. He runs his own linen-supply business in Indianapolis, and now, as on every Sunday, the only day he is home, he presides over midafternoon dinner. He surveys the ruins of the table, what is left after his four boys (I am the youngest) have rifled the fruits of the farm like clumsy pickpockets. He wraps his hand around a glass of bourbon, and now it is time for the field report from my mother, the tallying up of good versus bad, promise versus hopelessness, the final score for the week. Nobody ever talked during dinner, but there is always a score.

"Dean," says my mother, "is making great strides with the violin, Pop. You should hear him play that Hungarian tune. Play it for Pop, Son."

My father palms me back down to my seat. He is not fond of the violin, particularly when it is in my hands. There is silence now in the room, and it seems so heavy. My mother plays with her teaspoon. They are all waiting; only my father does not know for what he should be waiting.

"Pop . . ." my mother starts.

"I wanna go off, Pa," I say, wanting to spare her the responsibility.

"Go off . . . where?" he says.

"Anywhere, Pa," I say. "I wanna be on my own."

"Downright foolishness, I call it," says my mother.

"Foolish is what he's doin' now," says my father. "Can't learn in school. Or doesn't want to. He didn't take to the public school. He didn't take to the private schools. They kicked him out of that Admiral Farragut Academy."

"He's not a bad boy, Pop," says my mother.

"I know that," he says. "He just don't belong in school. Some people gotta go after life in their own way. By God, I did."

"Life isn't a picture show," says my mother. "Remember that teacher? Came here and said all Dean cares about, thinks about, are moving pictures."

"Maybe it is," says Pa. "Who knows, Mother? There used to be a time when the roads of this country were for boys to find themselves, to grow up on. Education ain't the only road."

"He's only fifteen," says my mother. "I won't stand for it. I won't. Do you hear me!" She jumps up, sending her teacup spilling over onto the tablecloth. She goes to her room.

"Go," says my father. We hear my mother crying in the bedroom. "It's the right thing for you. Always be right about yourself. I won't support you out there, but I won't let you starve, either. You know how to handle yourself. I'll be disappointed if you come back cryin' and whinin'."

"I won't, Pa. I promise you."

The next morning I walk with him to his car to begin the long ride to Indianapolis. He presses a hundred dollars into my hand. "Don't make a fuss about leavin'," he says. "Don't say good-bye. Just leave. For your mother's sake. And write her often." He shakes my hand, and says, "Don't run from the main chance, Son, but don't get caught by it, either. You

130

don't know what I mean, but you will." He looks at me oddly. "You're a strange boy. I hope you find . . . whatever . . . out there."

I don't want to leave. I want to stay there and see him every Sunday. I never see him again. The smell of bourbon and Sunday afternoons will always bring a picture of him to my mind. He dies while I am on Broadway, a bourbon-soaked and beaten man, destroyed by bloodsucking, mechanical men from the IRS who cripple his business. He sells the business but the money could never make up the loss. A man who still had a prairie for a heart but had settled for an office and a plant full of linen. When I hear of his death, I can hear him raging, and like to think the ground is rumbling when they put him under.

The road, out there, reality—whatever you want to call it —doesn't give up anything. What little there is for a fifteen-year-old you have to take with your hands. I use the scythe in Iowa, and the blisters on my hands annoy me. I use a broom in the men's room of a Nevada casino, but I never find a nickel on the floor. I pick up the litter in a park in Seattle, but they give me all the slopes and hills, and I can't even find a tree when it rains. There are beet fields in California. There are grapes in California. Anything a back can bend for, anything a hand can reach, is in California. Work my way, finally, to L.A., and here I am, smack in the middle of Hollywood, which is where I wanted to go in the first place. I look around. Where is Gary Cooper? Where is Burt Lancaster? Lemme see the teeth, Burt. Just once. Close up. Where is Clark Gable? Nobody. Nobody's home in Hollywood.

I shag tennis balls on the courts of an L.A. hotel. I clean out the stables at a dude ranch in Arizona. Where are all the stars? Where's the movie of the road? Where's adventure? Move next door to Texas and am helper to a helper on a coffee wagon in an oil field. Once more on the Greyhound, heading southeast, to Florida. The bus is the bloodstream of hope on the road. The bad breath. The twitching bodies.

The eyes of always one someone, young and old, strong and weak, going somewhere—away from something. In Sarasota I catch a circus ready to leave in a few days for its tour of rural towns.

"I can work the trapeze," I say to the boss. "I'm a flier."

"Where've you flown?" says the boss.

"Places," I say.

"All right, I'll take a look," he says. "Go up with him, Giambelli."

I dress up, and work my way up to the perch.

"Are you ready to throw a bird's nest to me?" says Giambelli.

"Sure. I'm a flier," I say.

"Get ready," says Giambelli.

I look below, look at the swinging trapeze. Oh, hell!

"Wait a minute," I say. "What's a bird's nest?" Giambelli drops down to the net below, laughing all the way.

"Get the hell down from there, kid," shouts the boss.

I drop down into the net, but come up fighting. "Well, I don't know everything," I say.

"You sure don't," says the boss, "but you got guts, kid. You'll try anything, won't you? You can go with us as a roustabout. Whaddaya say?"

I join up, stay awhile, learn a little, and move on.

I head south, to Key West, where I wash dishes in a restaurant. The kitchen faces the Gulf. I see the big ships passing through the steamy window.

Ahhh, that's where they are, Cooper and Gable and Lancaster and all the rest.

They're at sea.

I don't like the past. I like the future. The past is now, my dear Selmier. The past? Fuck the past. No, no, you got it all wrong. The past is fucking you. I think I'm going mad. Crawford! Crawford! That's a man out there. You can't kill a man. Maybe the wind'll come and blow him away, Dean. You're a dumb fuck, Crawford. Where are you, Crawford? You are here to learn how to kill. And to survive. Any ques-

132

tions? Yeah, you cocksucker. Whadda you gonna do for me? Leave me high and dry? Pigs never leave home, men. Somebody call the medics. Leave the teeth there. That's evidence! You've done it now, Selmier. Creep motherfuckers. Whadda you looking at, Selmier? The plants, sir. You're a fresh kid. Dismissed. Fuck you and your plants, sir. I hate the rain. The plumbago? *Hellllp!* Fuck the plumbago. Grow, you motherfuckers, grow! You're a necrophile, Selmier. What's that? I didn't say it. They said it. Fuck them! They oughta know. They taught me all I know. I want to be an actor. Maybe I'm acting with you. Foolish boy. Nooo, please, I don't wanna stay here fourteen years. *Hellllllp!* Hey, what's your name? James. Come with me, Selmier. Where are we going? We'll spend the night at the Holiday Inn. Can you climb? You're not afraid of heights. I'll climb anything you got in New York. Go to this acting class, Dean. Maybe you're right, Melanie. I got an earache. And death came very quickly, for death is never far from the places which he shares with madness. Fine piece of work, Mr. Selmier. Thank you, Mr. Robbins. What's a dwarf doing under my feet? You got stuck, Dean. Teacher didn't teach you much. Go jump off a curbstone and break your neck. You're on, Selmier. Fuck you and all your trumpets, James. Mom, can you spare fifteen thousand dollars? I wanna make a movie. You take orders from me when you're in Paris. A settler. What's a settler? But you eat too many hot dogs, Puffy. David. Who's the broad, David? I love you, Sandra; goddammit I love you. What you doin' with a gun in your glove compartment? I know. I know. Put the money in your bank, David. You can't? Yes, you will. I see. No, you don't. You don't owe me anything. Where's it say I need twenty-one men? Here, have some fish, Elorito. Get us some girls, Luis. Ibiza. Won't be long. Have to find some bass. In the big white house. Pass the wine, fat man. The viewfinder. I'll be damned. It works. Have to go to America. My film? What's wrong with my film? Fuck you! Kids, you wanna watch a film? Oh, you can't hear. Have some popcorn. Fuck you all! Back to Paris. *Hellllp!* I'm a failure. No, I'm not. 1967. What a bad fuckin' year. James called, Dean. Good. Why didn't you tell me he had dogs, Puffy? Whadda you doing here? Looking for birds. There are ghosts in this forest. Yeah, we're all crazy. You're through, James. Here, take your trumpets with you. I'm working for Garrotte. He cares about me. Shooo, they're watching. Who are *they?* Why doesn't somebody help me? Please! The past is now . . . now . . . now . . . nowwww . . . the stars are gone.

"Monsieur Selmier, can you hear me?" a voice says quietly, but it still hurts my ears. "Are you awake? Can you hear me?" I'm not talking.

Music begins to play softly. "You have been in here twelve days," the same voice says. "We are bringing you out now." I take the back of my hand and wipe some tears from my eyes.

"Do you know this music?" the voice asked.

Don't say anything. It's a trick. I listen to the music.

"We are not trying to deceive you, Monsieur Selmier," he says.

I know that voice. It's Garrotte.

"The music?"

"Second act. *La Traviata,* "I said in a gravel voice, sounding like an old man. I'm speaking. It seems strange.

"Can you tell me what part of the opera?"

It takes me a while to form the words, to match them up to my memory. "The aria . . . between the . . . father and the whore. I don't recall her name."

"Splendid, my dear Selmier," Garrotte says. He seems glad. "Now we are going to come and get you out of the room. Do not open your eyes. The light will hurt them."

I hear movement. Two men have me, one by each arm, and one of them is saying, "Steady, now."

"You'd better hold your nose," I tell him.

"You're right there," one of them says.

"How long I been here?" I ask.

"Twelve days." I try to walk, but my legs drag. I ponder the time. It is an eternity. It is a minute. I have no idea.

134

"Ahhh, there you are," I hear Garrotte say. "Don't open your eyes. Try not to talk." A blanket is put around me. I can feel the light on my eyes. "These two men and a nurse will now take you to a shower. I daresay you are curious about many things. Later." They put dark glasses on my eyes. "When you are through, you will be taken to a hotel. You will rest there until you have your strength back. The nurse will stay with you for the first few days." He tells the nurse to get me a haircut and a shave.

"Yeah," I say, "and plenty of cologne."

Three days later Garrotte turned up at my room. He was wearing an expensive-looking light-tan safari jacket. He shook my hand warmly, and then went to the phone and ordered up a couple of bottles of Dom Pérignon. He snipped off the end of one of his cigars, and dropped down on the sofa. He seemed relaxed. The distant formality was gone from his voice. By now, I was back in one piece, and the disjointed parts of my mind had fallen into place as if someone had picked a scrambled puzzle off the floor and put it together again. I was looking for some answers. He dueled with some small talk until the champagne came; he wasn't good at small talk. The waiter left.

"You were in a warehouse," he said, pressing his ashes into a tray. "With a rubber room in the middle. Of course, you know that. The room is often useful to us."

"One thing I got to know right now," I said. "Who was the guy who had to clean my dung out?" I had never seen him laugh. He was laughing now.

"There are people," he said, catching his breath. "He was paid well."

"I'm glad to hear that," I said.

"You look fine," he said. "You may have lost fifteen pounds, but you look fine."

"How did I look when I came out?"

"Like one of my gargoyles. And that might be a bit generous."

"Okay, why? You didn't trust me?"

"Nonsense. I feel toward you like I feel about Sandra, my dear Selmier."

"Was it a test?"

"Possibly. But not a test of trust or loyalty. Or a test to confirm a suspicion." I thought of the twelve days. My mind breaking apart. I was getting angry. But Garrotte was not a man that you pushed; you didn't get angry with a man like Garrotte.

"It was simply for a bet that I had made," he said, looking over his champagne glass. "And we wanted also to test the limits of the room's effectiveness. Could the right man break the room? That was the question."

"It was still standing up when I left."

"But it didn't break you! Perhaps in another two days you would have been begging to get out. I think so. But I did not want to see that. No more than one wants to see a thoroughbred shot. Twelve days! Superb."

"You should've let me in on the action. I have to get that loan off my mother's back. She went to the bank for me to make my movie."

"Don't trouble yourself with that. James was the one who arranged for the loan. It's been taken care of between him and me."

"How do you know James? I thought he was the most anonymous man in the world."

"Everybody knows everybody else in this business. Let's say my payment of the loan was part of a gentlemen's agreement. If we must be crude, a sale price. You have no obligation to James anymore."

"I didn't have any after Munich."

"Ah, but there you are wrong. They always have a way to hold on. But back to the bet," he continued. "One: I said that you would last longer than five days. Two: I said that you would not talk, or show any signs that you were coming apart. Three: I said that your mind would function immediately upon release. That was the reason for the opera question."

"You almost blew that one. I wasn't going to say anything,

but I recognized your voice. How long has anyone been able to stay in there?"

"Five days," he said. "He was a courier from Bombay. Part Indian and part English. I thought the Indian part would give us trouble. But the Western half of his blood and mind failed him. We found out what we wanted to know."

"I'm fit again. I think I'll leave here today."

"Are you ready to work?"

"I guess so."

"Well, take a few weeks off. Go to the Hilton in London. You'll find Sandra in suite Ten-fourteen. Play some." He gave me an envelope. "If you get bored, look this man up." He passed me a card with an odd mark on the back of it. The man's name was Quishn.

"Are you kidding?" I said. "After twelve days in that grave, I'll never get bored again in my life."

LONDON, MAY 1968

A message was waiting for me on my arrival at the Hilton in London. Sandra had decided to switch from the Hilton to a small hotel in Belgravia called the Cadogan. The Cadogan looked like a comfortable place, sort of out of the way, with a rich fray to it. Thick rugs. Heavy drapes. Dim lights from big chandeliers. Quiet dining room. Where the people talk in whispers. Where the waiters in elegant but worn-out livery flit from table to table quickly and silently, like birds finding their branches. The whole place was tired, but it worked, and not too many things were working in London. At first, I couldn't add up Sandra's switch in hotels, to this kind of place, where one might expect to see Noel Coward sipping afternoon tea and examining a finger sandwich. But

Sandra was not a Hilton person. The aloofness, the slightly musty air, as in an offbeat museum, would suit her. I rang her room. Nothing. I had her paged. She appeared suddenly out of a small room as if a wall had opened up.

"You're already checked in with me," she said, kissing me on the cheek. "Come and have a drink." I followed her into a little room, a tiny bar with a young Italian behind it and an ornate painting of a woman. Sandra ordered a bottle of Perrier water for herself, and I went to a glass of wine.

"You are now sitting in the Lillie Langtry Room," she said, as if she had made a discovery. She never liked to tour a city formally; she liked to bump into things. "She was the Victorian Marilyn Monroe. It was here in this room that Oscar Wilde was picked up and taken to jail. For homosexuality."

"Oscar Wilde?" I said, trying to remember the name.

"You must have heard of him," she said.

"Wilde, Wilde. Yeah, I got him now. They did some scenes from a novel of his in our acting class. The man with a pretty face who did so many bad things that his portrait began to look like the things he did."

"*The Picture of Dorian Gray,*" she said. She studied me through her glass. "You look fine," she said.

"Everybody says that," I said. "Did you know?"

"Yes. Garrotte promised me that he wouldn't let anything happen to you. He couldn't resist the temptation. I trust him. Besides, I knew he was quite fond of you."

"I got something out of it. I beat it, in a sense. Besides, it was a million laughs." I began to smile.

"What was so funny about it?"

"Don't get me going on that. This is not the place for it. Lillie wouldn't like it."

"Dean, let's have a ball here," she said, putting her hand on mine and grinning. "Let's walk and walk. Let's see things. Let's be silly. Let's be together."

"Lady, you point the way and I'll follow."

It felt good to walk aimlessly for hours in the sun, with her on my arm, listening to the jangle of the chain around her neck, the rustle of her quiet but richly embroidered caftan, watching the sun from a pewter sky on her happy face. Walking through the scrubbed white of Marylebone, through the green laziness of Hyde Park, and through her favorite, Chelsea, where she would turn off to inspect a shop window, or go inside and try one funky hat on after another and never buy any of them. She would kid with the shop clerks, saying to one of them, in a jeans place, "All right, where's the pot? I'm with the CID. I can smell it all over the place."

The clerk looked her straight face. "No, no, not me. I've never touched it in my life." She looked at him and then broke up. "Thought you might be, Miss. The coppers are always hasslin' us young chaps with long hair."

She loved the freedom of Chelsea's Kings Road, blazing with colors and camp, the eye-popping clothes in a boutique called Granny Takes a Trip, featuring a mammoth blowup photo of Low Dog, a Sioux brave. Her eyes never tired of the parade, young people wearing remnants of the Confederate Army, a girl in a granny dress, another in baggy Charlie Chaplin clothes, and always the stream of psychedelic colors painted on fences and cars by art students. Walking. Walking. Her face.

In another section of London she pulled me by the arm, and we were suddenly in another world of soft light and figures with wax faces and dress of other times. It was, she said, Madame Tussaud's.

"I know that," I said. "I'm not that blank."

I took to the place right off. It had a cinemalike quality to it. You could almost hear the rattle of Holmes's carriage through the fog, the *whish* of the slaughtering blades of kings and queens, the sound of violence everywhere. We had skipped the Grand Hall, with all its muttonchopped diplomats, stopped now and then in the Hall of Tableaux, looking at Lord Nelson, who looked as if he had just been carried, dying, from his ship. Sandra stared for a long time at a figure called Sleeping Beauty, almost breathing under a wrap as thin and bewitching as the wing of a green lacewing. "She was Madame St. Amaranthe," said Sandra.

"Guillotined by Robespierre because she rejected him."

We ended up in the Chamber of Horrors, with all the replicas of torture designed by man, the white waxen faces of men like Burke and Hare, who were body snatchers.

"Could you spend a night here alone?" asked Sandra.

"Why? You making an offer?"

"Madame Tussaud once did."

"Any takers?"

"No."

"I can't blame them. I'll take the rubber room."

At night, we taxied from one club to another: the Talk of the Town, the lavish and gauche supper club where for ten dollars you could have dinner and see a revue and a head-liner from 1900 sing "Coming to the End of a Lollipop"; or the Astor Club, with its garish orange lighting over the dance floor and its dusty artificial flowers. The second time we went to the Astor, Sandra wore a World War Two dress she had bought, and we danced in the bright orange to the thin sound of the band playing "Always" and "Now Is the Hour." Girls in pussycat costumes, with black tails dangling from their little asses, tripped out for the show, and Sandra said, as if she were listening for an air-raid siren, "The Nazis are at it again. Let's find a shelter."

Then we would go back to the hotel, and she would change into a gown, and we were off on the rounds of the gambling clubs, like Crockford's or the Pair of Shoes, or the Colony, which George Raft ran. I never took to gambling. She did. She liked to send out the dice. The Arabs, who were all over London, liked to watch her. They kept giving her their dice. They also kept looking down at the hills of braless white pushing up out of her gown.

"The Arabs are crazy about you," I said one night, back in the room.

"I'm crazy about them, too," she said. "I'd like to get them all one night when nobody's around, and pull a machine gun out of my purse."

London was beautiful.

A message under my door made it real.

140

Could you please see me at Crockford's tomorrow night.
—Quishn

Crockford's is a four-story town house with yellow walls, wine-dark paneling, red carpets, and what seem like tiers of crystal chandeliers. A picture of Queen Elizabeth, on horseback and very queenly, looked down on the players, the jumping cards and spinning wheels. The queen seemed to be following the action from table to table. I asked a guy who looked like Sir Cedric Hardwicke if there was a Mr. Quishn in sight. He said he didn't see him, but if I stayed over there—he pointed to a roulette table—he would surely be there soon. He never missed a night. That was his favorite table. I killed an hour around the table, watching the ebb and flow, mostly the ebb of drops of oil from one Arab and a contribution from Hong Kong corruption made by a daintily appointed Chinese.

"Ahhh, Mr. Quishn," I heard the croupier at the table finally say. "You are late."

I sized him up. He was an Arab. He had big ears. He had perfectly sculpted hands, with clean fingernails. I don't know, I thought. All Arabs look like Omar Sharif to me. He was with someone, a smaller Arab with nerves all over his face, dark circles under his eyes, and a receding chin. He had an attaché case in his hand. I picked him out as a bureaucrat, maybe an embassy official. I watched the two of them for a while. Quishn was putting chips onto the table with both hands. The one with the chin did not play. He made me think of a mosquito in my bedroom on a summer night. He made me nervous, with his eyes roaming all over the room and his hand pinching at his cheek. I decided to get Quishn's eye. He picked me out, and started to walk toward the men's room. I followed, but kept an eye on the other Arabs back at the table.

"I got your message," I said to Quishn, while he examined his teeth in the mirror. I passed him the card that Garrotte had given me, the one with the odd mark on the back of it.

He looked at the mark. "You are a difficult man to find.

141

You were expected to be at the Hilton. Your friend in Paris finally gave me your change of address. We are behind schedule."

"What's on your mind?" I asked, as he went back to his teeth to pick at an incisor.

"You must be in Kuwait in three days," he said. I wished he would take his finger out of his mouth. I couldn't hear him too well. "But first, *he* is on my mind."

"Who?"

He motioned back to the room with his head. "The man who is with me."

"So?"

"Have you noticed his attaché case?" he said. "I want that case. He is a blackmailer."

"That's not my line," I said. "You can get a thousand cockneys from the East End to bop him on the head and take the case. But I like the sound of Kuwait. As soon as you tell me what I'm supposed to do in Kuwait."

"The case is chained to his wrist," he said. "Paris has given me permission to use you. Paris is involved."

"So how am I going to get the case?" I said. "Chop off his hand?"

He didn't smile.

"The case will be in his house tomorrow night. He takes a long bath every evening at eight o'clock. The bathtub is downstairs in the back. He does not take a bath with his case. The stairs are in the front of the house. He will not hear you."

"Does he have a gun?" I asked, thinking, Does a rabbit hear the snap of a twig? This guy was so nervous he would hear a penny drop on foam rubber.

"Nooo," Quishn said. "His kind don't carry guns."

"How do I get in the front door? I told you, this isn't my line."

"Here's a key. The house is at Groom Place, in Belgravia. A black and red front at the end of a mews. It's only about five minutes from your hotel by cab."

I took the key. He said, "Bring the case to me immediately

at this address." He wrote it down on the back of his card. "And we will talk about Kuwait."

I walked through the alley that led into the mews. A pub called the Horse and Groom was at the front of the mews. I paused in front of the pub, and looked at my watch. It was two minutes to eight. I looked down toward the end of the mews—two houses, the fronts of which were facing me. There were about four houses on each side. I kept my eyes on the red and black one as I walked toward it, listening to the echo of my boots over the cobblestone. There were no lights on in the house, so far as I could see. But that didn't mean nobody was there; there were probably many rooms in the back, one of which now contained Quishn's Arab in a bathtub. I turned the key carefully in the heavy door, and pulled a small flashlight out of my pocket. Inside the house, I did not move. I listened for running water. I listened for a splash. There was none.

To find your way through a mews house in the dark requires a delicate step, and even then, you're more than likely to knock over a vase or bang into something. These seemed to be intricate little homes, with many small rooms erratically cutting into one another. There are a lot of doors that squeak in these kinds of homes, and the stairs are noisy, too. I turned my flash on the place. I was in a foyer, and off to the left was a room, maybe a sitting room, with its door half open. I spotted the stairwell at the end of the foyer. I listened again. Nothing, except the whole place was creaking as if it were a yawing old sailing ship. I worked my way toward the stairs, feeling the steps give under me. Two sharp turns on the stairs, and I was on the second floor. I tried a door. It was a bathroom, one with a big tub in it. Another door. It was the master bedroom. I moved my light around, catching a picture of a fox hunt on the wall; the house was no doubt a furnished rental. I went to the curtained window and looked out. You could see the whole mews, the alley that led to it, and the light from the pub. It was quiet and dark.

Quickly, I started to sack the room. I didn't care about

being neat. I had got a break, in his not being in the tub. I couldn't find that attaché case. I broke a sweat. The tub? I heard a click in my head. If the Arab wasn't in the tub, then he had the case with him. Lemme get out of here! Fuck-ups! Garrotte would hear about this. I had started for the bedroom door when I heard fast, choppy footsteps in the mews; then a key turned in the front door downstairs. I stood there, in the dark of the bedroom, like a pointer. I tried a window, knowing that I could hang down and make it easily to the mews. He was on the stairs now. The windows were locked. My hands searched for the lock on the unfamiliar and ancient English window. I was still by the window when the door opened. I heard the light switch. The light blinded my eyes for a second, and I heard a short sound. *Thwick!* I got my eyes back. He was nearly on me, his eyes flashing, his attaché case rattling from the chain on his wrist, and, up in front of his face, a five-inch switchblade in his right hand, poised to swipe. He was four feet away. The point of my hard boot did not have to travel far; he wasn't tall. The boot caught him flush on his windpipe, leaving him with both hands at his throat and gasping for breath. He dropped to both knees, and then tilted onto his side. Going down the stairs, I could still hear him sucking for breath. The bottom of my right leg felt as if it were bruised. I probed on the run with my hand. The cuff of my pants had been slashed, and I could feel a deep cut in the top of my boot; the knife had not made it through the leather. I listened. There were no more gasps. He was dead. Or would be soon. I took my boots off, and walked quickly through the dark, quiet mews.

Back in Paris the next morning, I dropped Sandra off at her apartment and took the taxi straight to Garrotte's château outside the city. He might call me impetuous. I'd say I was slightly off temper, afflicted by a case of galloping curiosity. Like, why isn't a guy taking a bath when he's supposed to be taking one? Like, why am I suddenly turned into a common sneak thief, and not a very good one at that? I had left the case behind. I wasn't going to cut off his arm. All right, so I blew it. But so did you, my dear Garrotte. You sent the wrong man at the wrong time to do the wrong job.

The butler showed me to Garrotte's study. He was seated at his antiseptic desk, the sunlight beaming over his shoulder. He was not alone. A familiar, fleshy hand held a delicate teacup.

"Surprises, one after another," I said. "Look in the Cracker Jack box and you get a tin whistle. But you never know what you find in some boxes, do you? Whadda you doin' here, Puffy? Gettin' some country air?" He looked at me sheepishly.

"Monsieur Puffy," said Garrotte, "is an old and valuable colleague. I am also privileged to call him my friend."

"I make it twenty years," said Puffy, looking into his little teacup.

"He is my eyes on the street," said Garrotte.

"You must have a fortune in your bank account," I said to Puffy. "James. Now here. I was worrying you'd die broke." I was kidding him now; my surprise was gone. I didn't have to know all his business.

"Monsieur Puffy works for no one . . . and everyone," said Garrotte. "They say a truly wise man is one who knows the civilization in which he lives, and then lives his life accordingly. Here is a truly wise man."

"Thanks, monsieur," said Puffy. I thought I noticed an exaggerated lift to Puffy's chin.

"And speaking of bank accounts," I said, "I hope I see something in mine after this fuckin' trip to London. I might have blown it all. I didn't get any case. I didn't go to Kuwait. I didn't do anything. Except nearly get killed. Add it up and all there is . . . is a nervous Arab with a crushed windpipe."

"Well, I'd better be going," said Puffy.

"No, no, no," said Garrotte, motioning with his hand for Puffy to sit down. "I think Monsieur Selmier is here for a lesson. He should have his lesson."

"Yeah, you might say I have some questions," I said. "I don't like to fail. Even when I don't know how to do what I'm supposed to do. Like stealing."

"Not so, my dear Selmier," said Garrotte. "You did not fail. Your bank account will show that."

I was starting to get the message. "There were no papers in the case? You just wanted him dead?"

"That is precise."

"Then why go about it this way? Why not my usual way?"

"Some people write a verse in a day. Others take years to write an epic poem. You, my dear Selmier, like epic poems. You are slow. Even tedious. But thorough and complete. Yet there are times when one wants to hear only a verse. A quick and satisfying verse."

"But why this way . . . and who was—"

"You have no right to know the answers to those questions," said Garrotte. Puffy coughed, and moved in his seat.

"Who am I working for?" I shot back.

"You know better than to ask that, ol' Dean," said Puffy.

Garrotte moved out from behind his desk, pulled a cigar from a drawer, and began to pace slowly in front of the garden window.

"Once," said Garrotte, flaming his cigar while looking into the garden, the smoke wreathing about his head. "Only once. I will give you a sketch. A minor sketch because you do not need much more, and because the artist himself does not fully comprehend what must be in the sketch."

He drew the drapes, and began to walk about the room.

"Consider a sphere, the earth," he said. "In the center of it is a vast, round space of emptiness. But there are ripples from this space. How can these ripples come from emptiness? The ripples? They are war, depression, assassination, and all the other violence of doing business. Who, what, is creating these ripples? Governments? Politicians? No. Some of them may perceive to a degree, but largely they are willing vassals, or in some cases helpless in the tide that sweeps out from the center of the sphere. Yet it is empty there. To most eyes. To men and women who vote, and still believe that leaders can miraculously change their lives. To editorial writers, who still harangue about issues, who lustily

146

enjoy government and politics as a game while ignoring the roots of power.

"Real power is not seen. Real power is the center of the sphere. This world cares not a whit for the needs, the hopes, of the individuals. This world is arranged for those with power. Within the center of the sphere there are three forces. Call them A, B, and C, each of them sending out ripples, often the size of waves. This decade alone illustrates well. Sometimes a leader emerges who causes waves not at all compatible with the center of the sphere. Jack Kennedy, for example. Now, only recently, Dr. King in Memphis. It is not over. One more will fall. I know nothing about why. I do not approve. But A does not interfere with B and B does not quarrel with C. The forces coexist, until such time as a balance is severely jarred. The assassination of one man, whoever he may be, does not represent a seismic disturbance to those who have real power. They are not concerned with injustice. Only disorder as they perceive it. One may see how wrong a powerful position is, but does one rush at its throat? Of course not. But some do, and then they find nothing or no one. Only the implements of power standing ready to separate them from whatever they believe, or, if need be, from their own extremely mortal bodies."

He sat down behind his desk.

"As simple as my face, Dean," said Puffy. "Things ain't what they seem to be." I was still entranced.

"You mean it's like the Cosa Nostra?" I said.

"Somewhat," said Garrotte. "In a remote way. Not as simplistic or as brazen. The stakes are much higher. Oil. Whole economies of nations. The balance of arms. Always a balance in everything. That is the word: balance."

"I think I understand," I said. "But who?

"Monsieur Selmier," said Garrotte, "it is the power of the boardroom. There is no 'who.' Only the empty space in the center of the sphere. And the ripples of man trying to survive while doing business. Balance and business."

"And me?" I felt like I had just tried to drink up an ocean.

"Power flows from the barrel of a gun," said Garrotte.

"Those are the words of Mao. He is right. But the gun in societies that we know is concealed behind three forces of power: A, B, C. Imperceptible, but always there. It has no history." He paused. "You are a gun, my dear Selmier."

"And you?" I said, thinking of this château of his, his manner, his own obvious power. "You must be right up there."

"Nooo, dear fellow," said Garrotte. "I am only a colonel. A marching colonel."

PART FIVE

PARIS, AUGUST 1968

Paris was empty, and so was I.

Like walruses that will suddenly leave land for water at a wrong sound, the Parisians heard and felt August and they were gone. The city was left to the old monuments and the heat that drains the glimmer and dignity from its fine buildings. It was left to the Germans, Americans, and Swedes, men wearing short-sleeved shirts of grand Hawaiian design or men still wrapped in business suits that seemed tired and lifeless, all of them with women hanging on their arms as if to branches of a big tree, the women full of wonder and enthusiasm that they would never be able to transfer to the faces of their men.

If you were not Parisian, it was good to watch this quiet, ordinary current of life flow over you, to see it still there, flowing as always, during a year in which the broken nerves of the world were dangling all over the place. But if you were a Parisian who had been caught behind the lines, who could not get away—and there weren't many—it was not your city anymore. It was a city of foreigners pointing at maps, of Japanese traveling in packs, of eyes puzzled by menus, of shaggy kids sprawled on backpacks in front of the

151

American Express office, a city of airplane tickets and traveler's checks and bad food and people gawking from the Café de la Paix, looking for a familiar face from Düsseldorf or Omaha. All that was left of Paris was the old monuments, the brittle, aging side-street whores with too much makeup, the snoozing clerks in the dark, quiet lobbies of run-down hotels, and the African and Spanish kitchen help who work like slaves in the bowels of large hotels and seldom see daylight.

The days were leaning on me. Sandra was off somewhere in the South of France. Garrotte was in Rome. David was always too busy at the clinic. The Dwarf was back in the States, by now resigned to the fact that he had not won the Academy Award; that was a long time ago, but the Dwarf does not go down easy.

Only Puffy, sweaty and reliable, remained in Paris. He hadn't set foot out of Europe in more than a decade. I once asked him why he never went home.

"Home's only a state of mind," said Puffy. "I went home, and I began to feel like a police dog in the middle of a Quaker picnic. Weren't nothin' there worth a sniff for me. Only two things I could do there with my bent of mind: make corn, or be a revenoo agent chasin' the corn. The first is a dyin' calling, would be like retirement; and bein' an agent —well, I might as well be dead, because where I come from there ain't nothin' lower than a revenoo man. Go back to Washington and take a desk job with the outfit? That'd be like puttin' a mule in a parade of Lippizaners. I'm good at what I do, but I don't fit. I don't fit anywhere back there. I'd probably end up like one of those old geezers in *Man*hattan, the kind you see in those funny-lit places like Horn and Hardart, all of them with pale and scared faces bent over hot tea and a corn muffin at midnight. Home's a word, and it ain't mine."

So the two of us would walk through the emptiness of Paris, or I'd go jogging along the Seine, and maybe later I'd join Puffy in an air-conditioned movie house, nearly empty at midafternoon. He would be sitting in third row center, easy to spot because of his heavy, wide back, his unmistakable wheeze, and his erect posture. Film was a serious business with Puffy. If I was on time, the credits would be rolling, and he'd have just begun to forage through a bag of popcorn, his starter before his entrée, of countless Almond Joys.

After the movie, his pockets bulging with candy wrappers, he would cut up the film in critical pieces. And if there are no ugly women for some men, there were no bad pictures for Puffy. Later, we would have dinner at some ghostly old café, where the waiter might seem disturbed at the arrival of a customer, and then we would part on some quiet, dark street. He would go back to his office, his summer quarters where he said it was always cool, and I would go back to Sandra's apartment in Le Marais, where I would lie in bed long into the morning, sensing her absence and my own emptiness. The days were long. The nights were long.

I missed Sandra, all right, but more than anything I felt I was losing touch with myself, with what I was about: acting and films. It seemed like I couldn't get off a dime. And yet I could see any career I hoped to have moving farther and farther away. Where had I been in film? Nowhere. Crawling down a dark aisle of a little movie house back home looking for a smile or for a pair of eager eyes on some deaf-and-dumb kid to tell me that I was good. What a bust, I thought, remembering the clown face that came apart in the aisle from my sweat. All I had were some stage credits, and the praise for *Escurial.* But nobody even knew I was in film. I hadn't worked at it, hadn't given it all I had.

The work for James, and now for Garrotte, had somehow become a substitute for me, satisfying the same emotions that I got from acting and giving me a feeling of some odd identity. Garrotte could count on me. I was good. I belonged. But where, to whom, to what? There would have to be a change. I would have to walk soon. Garrotte would understand. Maybe it was Paris in August; maybe it was Sandra's absence; maybe it was the hard fact that I had betrayed myself, that feeling that turned around inside me like an electric fan, chopping up my stomach and cutting off the blood to my brain, leaving me staring blankly, like a dead man, in the blackness of Sandra's bedroom. I was in a mood. Puffy knew.

"What's eatin' you, Dean?" asked Puffy one night. "The girl gone—that it?"

"More than that," I said. "I got this trapped feelin'."

"Why don'tcha leave town for a while?" said Puffy. "Get a new venue. Nothin's comin' up that I can see."

"I'm not doin' a thing in films," I said. "I'm losing the trail."

We walked slowly past a club with a large doorman who looked like he was out of *Captain from Castile.* We could hear violin music coming from inside.

"You wanna drink?" I asked Puffy.

"Oh, I don't know," said Puffy. "These places . . ."

I started past the captain. He looked at me, then at Puffy. He hooked me by the arm, and said, in bad English, "Club is full. No enter." I pushed his arm away. He moved in front of me. "Move aside," I said.

"Come on, Dean," said Puffy. "We don't want any trouble." I tried to move around the doorman. His hands came down on my shoulders. I turned quickly and knocked his plumed helmet off his head. He started inside for some help. Puffy called to him, picked the helmet up, gave it a couple of brushes with his jacket sleeve, and straightened the plume.

"Here you are, Cap," said Puffy. "Good as new." He placed it on the doorman's head at a crooked angle.

"Come on," said Puffy. "We don't need this."

"I was just stickin' up for you," I said, cooling down. "He didn't like the way you dress. Figured you don't have penny one."

"Yeah, well, you don't look like Adolphe Menjou yourself."

"Where'd you come up with that one?" I said.

"Who? Adolphe? You remember him. *Paths of Glory* . . . a hundred films. He *dressed.* I mean, he could wear clothes like Ronald Colman talked."

"You're right there."

"I'm also right now," said Puffy. "Listen to me, Dean. Pack it in. Get out. You're free and clear of James. The old man won't mind. Garrotte's already gotten his money's worth. You got enough money. You can turn around and never look back."

"It was never really the money," I said.

"I don't care what it was," he said. "You don't have a hold on yourself. You're splitting right down the middle. That's all right. I've seen it before."

"Like what?"

"Losin' control. First. Then nerves. The sweaty kind of nerves like you see on a horse in the paddock. Some guys are only good for one or two, maybe three or four. Stay around much longer, and it's only a matter of time. You either settle yourself or somebody settles you. A lot of turnover in this business."

"You're still here."

"I'm a relic. From a simple time. The early fifties. Before that, the OSS. Things were neat then. Russians. Americans. The risks were lower. So were the killin's. There were subtle ways to get what you wanted. Blackmail. Bribery. Kidnapping. Nice things like that. Slow but effective. Now, it's only this." He ran a finger across his blubbery neck. "The age of instant results." He flexed his shoulders jokingly. "Makes a man cold just thinkin' about it."

"You're unpatriotic," I said, kidding. "Like James used to say—can't ya hear the trumpets?"

"Yeah, there're so many goddamn trumpets now you can't tell one from the other. You can't count on your own anymore. You can't even count on who *they* are anymore. Ain't like the old days. Black and white. The map's full of gray. Special interests all over the place."

"It doesn't matter to me."

"It should. It should. It's Dodge City. And you're walkin' right down the middle of the main drag."

"I'll handle myself."

"Go tell it on the mountain. Word travels."

"What can I tell you?"

"Tell me you're gonna get out. Or tell me to get lost."

"I don't know what I'm gonna do. Why all this over a doorman's bonnet? Nothin's wrong with my nerves."

"Maybe not, but there's somethin'. Guys like you ain't supposed to have somethin'. You don't have girls. You don't have wives. You don't have addresses. You don't have anything you care about. Carin' means problems. Problems mean nerves. And nerves mean . . . well, I don't have to spell it out. Besides, Garrotte won't bet on sweaty horses."

"We're close. I can tell that."

"You're still a horse."

"Oh, hell, it's just movie work on my mind."

"Fine. But love it or leave it. You can't have it both ways."

"I only want the one," I said. "That's all I ever wanted."

Puffy smiled.

I hailed a cab, dropped Puffy off, and went back to the apartment. Sandra was home. She wasn't alone.

They were sitting on the big floor pillows in her living room, both of them eating Chinese food and reminding me of a pair of house birds working on a cuttlebone.

The guy looked out of place, sitting there in a loose yoga position, his knees sticking out like doorknobs, one of them propping up a plate along with his hand. He stood up, nearly knocking over his plate. He looked as if he had got his clothes in the wrong section of town. The shoes were pointy, brown and white, and ventilated. I hadn't seen a pair of those since my father used to take me to the barber shop. I bet they squeak, I thought. His pants, gray with stripes, were too tight, and his socks, thin and black with a red arrow on each ankle, got very little of the white of his legs. His cheap turtleneck, once a rich cream, looked tight across a heavy chest. It looked itchy, too. I noticed a black leather coat folded on the back of a chair. That wouldn't fit, either. He wouldn't care; clothes had probably always been a nuisance, if he ever stopped to think about them. He was a well-built man, say forty-eight, shaped like the business side of a hammer. He looked tired. I couldn't guess what he thought of me.

"This is an old friend of mine, Dean," said Sandra. "From Israel." He put out his hand.

"Hello," I said, shaking his hand. "Does your friend have a name?"

"That's not important," said Sandra.

"When did you get in?"

"Late this afternoon," she said. "I wasn't in an hour before he called. He said he's been calling for the last four days. Weren't you picking up?"

"Sure, but every time I did, there was a click on the other end. Silence, then a click."

We all sat down. Her friend snatched a particle of leftover shrimp off his mustache. I studied him some, trying to locate his position in her life. An old lover? Possibly. He looked to be man enough. She didn't like pretty men. He was hard of mind. You could tell that by his eyes. They were watchful. They said that you would have to get up early to beat him. He could handle women, I thought. Some women. Not Sandra. He wouldn't give a bit in the wind of a strong presence.

Sandra cleared away the dinner. I joined her in the kitchen. "What's all this about?" I asked. "He keeps looking at me like I'm going to lift his wallet any minute."

"That's just his way," she said.

"Who is he?"

"He's from the Secret Service," she said. I didn't like the sound of those words.

"You in trouble?"

"No. How could I be? I have nothing to do with them."

"What's he want?"

"Help. Israelis are like most phone calls. I mean, they always want something. They're not calling to *give* you something. Let's go back and hear what he wants."

"You mean he hasn't told you yet?"

"We talked around it. I told him I didn't want to hear it all until you came home." Right then, I wished that I was someplace else.

We each dropped down on a pillow. Her friend began to pace the room, and when his eyes came down from the walls and the ceiling, with him talking the whole time, he let them fall on Sandra, who sat there watching him as if he were a big fly and she were waiting for him to light somewhere. He had been talking passionately about the Six-Day War, until Sandra finally saw her opening and came down on him with a swat.

"It was great," she said. "It was fantastic. All that and more. Save it for the bond buyers back in New York. Give it to us straight."

He looked at her like a husband might look at a wife who had just said something to embarrass him. He plopped down on a pillow, exposing the red arrows on his black anklets. "You have been away too long," he said. "You have lost your identity. You do not know who you are anymore."

Sandra didn't back off. "You won't get anywhere that way," she said. "I know who *I* . . . am. And it's not what *you* think I should be. I don't exist for you. Or Israel."

"You don't know what it was like."

"How many times have I heard that?"

"You are an ungrateful woman."

"What's any woman got to be grateful for in Israel?"

"These times are bad for all."

"These times have been forever. Living. That's what I want to do. Not surviving. I can't love a state."

They were in a valley, two rams sending echoes through it with the cracking of their heads.

"Can we get down to business?" I said. I knew I shouldn't have said that; I had a feeling I might regret it.

"That *is* the business," said Sandra, still looking as if she'd like another go at him. "Israel."

He went over to his leather jacket, and came back with a

158

packet. He spread it on the floor. It was an aerial map. "Israel," he said, clamping his tongue on the name and pointing at a position on the map, "wants this place destroyed."

"See what I mean," said Sandra. "See the attitude. It's like a command from God."

"Sandra," I said, gesturing to her. "Let him live, will ya."

"We do not want this place to exist," he continued.

"Yeah, well, I got a place in California I don't much like either," I said. "Maybe we can make a trade." He wasn't listening.

"It must be destroyed."

"So destroy it. You wrecked five nations in six days. All you got to do is spit on this village."

"It's not a village," he said. "It's a small encampment. A training area in Africa. The Arab nations have been sending men there for special training. From there they come back and keep up steady raids on our villages. These people are trained in grotesque forms of terrorism. They do horrible damage. We also believe that these sweeps are the first beginnings of a counterattack by the Arabs."

"So take it. What do you want from her?"

"All we want from Sandra is for her to make arrangements. She is connected with . . . shall we say, people who can do this kind of work."

"That still doesn't explain why you guys in the black leather coats can't do it."

"It is too sensitive politically. We cannot, you see, be the aggressor, be offensive. In the eyes of the world and the UN we are entitled to defend as we see fit. But never can we attack, or we shall lose the sentiment of the underdog."

"It's the David-and-Goliath condition," said Sandra. "One little nation, a lot of big nations. It's almost the country's whole stock in trade. It's more important than fighter planes from America."

"We were allowed to attack in 1967," said the friend, "because it was seen as defensive, not offensive. But here our hands are tied. It is much like your Vietnam. We are in

159

a war, but there are strange rules. Political considerations. We are in a funny war."

"Aren't they all?" I said.

"They train fifty men at a time here," he said, tapping his forefinger on the *X* on the map. "Four weeks for each group. There is a week's interval before the next group. So far, they have produced six groups. A new one has just begun. It will end in four weeks. Three Japanese do the training."

"The way I see it," I said, "that's a job that's going to be expensive. Whoever does it, it is going to come high."

"No, it won't," said Sandra.

"Are you kidding? Half a dozen men. Weapons. Transportation. Explosives. And all that pay."

"Ask him," she said. I turned to the friend.

"There is no pay," he said. "There is no money. Just the expenses. The government would not at this time listen to such a plan. This is a private act by the Service. With the help of a private source. A check will be sent to Sandra. She has only to call this number and ask, 'Do you have package tours to Africa?' "

"Economy, I presume," I said. "Look, it's none of my business, but you couldn't get Spanky and Our Gang to do a job like this for no money."

"Sandra?" he said, looking at her. She was thinking. She must be crazy, I thought. Where would she go to assemble a strike group? Ahhh, Garrotte. Hell, he'd never permit it.

"Give me a week," she said. "I'll let you know then."

"Thank you," he said, putting on his leather coat. It didn't fit. This whole thing didn't fit.

"*Shalom,*" he said at the door.

"*Shalom,* yourself," said Sandra. Then, suddenly, she embraced him hard and warmly. He left. I could hear his shoes squeaking down the hall.

"Well, what do you think?" asked Sandra.

"I don't," I said. "I'm wondering what's on your mind. That's a strange thing you got up there on your shoulders. First you're ready to claw the guy to pieces, then you hug him like he's your brother?"

160

"No, he was my mother's lover," she said, then quickly changed the subject. "Could I count on you?"

"Nope," I said. "I'll buy a bond instead."

"I'm serious."

"So am I. I'm getting out of all this. I'm going to Spain day after tomorrow. I'm going to get myself in a film."

"Shouldn't you talk to Garrotte first?"

"I will. When I come back."

"He won't stop you?"

"Why, Sandra? Why get involved?"

"I have to," she said. "You should be able to understand that. You have to go back to films. I have to go back to my country."

MADRID

Luis was waiting for me at the bar of the Hilton in Madrid, where we had first met, more than two years before. I had been back only once since then, for a short holiday when I drank too much vodka and spent too much money on Amparo's women, who were very nice to me because she and I had become good friends. Amparo was in her early thirties, dark, and always wore a butterfly. She was officially retired to all but a few hand-picked clients. But all of the johns seemed to be amused by an American whore's having such a love for Spain—with her take, who wouldn't?—that she affected an accent.

I had met her while making my film and had given her a walk-on by having her stroll past a sidewalk café, wearing a white dress and holding a white parasol over her head. There, in that white dress, with the sun bouncing off it, she looked as free from vice as a nun in the tropics. She saw

161

herself in the dailies, and couldn't believe the image of icy beauty. I don't know why, but no woman ever looked better in a white dress than she did. The day after she saw herself on film, she went out and bought a white Mercedes and a sheep dog to carry around in it; she never did anything halfway.

Luis looked healthy, like a plump olive. Things were going well for him, he said. Now more than ever, producers from all over the world were using Spanish locations, equipment, and technicians. He said he no longer needed his Uncle Elorito, whose sleight of hand in business had never pleased him. The two of them, he said, had fallen out over my film. Elorito had blamed him for his losing involvement with me, when in fact Uncle was the one who had had him —Luis—scouring the lounges and cafés, like a pimp in search of prospects like me. Luis said now he did not care anymore. He avoided his uncle. He would let him eat his fish like the greedy old man that he was, and he would let him die alone. Work was everywhere in Spain.

"I'm sorry," I said. "I kept my end of the agreement. I gave your uncle a dupe negative and one print."

"No, no, Señor Dean," he said, "it was not your fault. Uncle played the film on one circuit. They did not like it."

"That's one more circuit than I had in America. I drew a blank over there."

It felt good to be back in the world of film again, to be sitting next to Luis and talking about who was doing what —and to whom. I forgot about the wasteland of Paris, my own barren spirit. I forgot about the man in the leather coat in Sandra's apartment, yet couldn't get rid of Sandra's desire for what was sure to be suicide somewhere in Africa. I was curious about how my film had looked in the Spanish version. Luis said he had a print at his home. His uncle had thrown the reels at him one day when they had been arguing. We picked up the print and we took it to a lab and looked at it on the movieola.

"Damn," I said, staring at the small viewing box, "it's awful. It sounds so hollow." It was strange listening to the dubbed Spanish matched to my lip movements. Where's the music, the sound effects?"

"You forgot the M and E, the music-and-effects track, Señor Dean."

I'm not perfect, I thought. Luis also thought I might have been negligent.

"The film on Ibiza," he said. "Why did you not add that to the film in editing? I was disappointed; I thought it would be good *cinéma vérité,* with the big Señor Stoessel and all those young girls. Too bad."

"Oh, I felt sorry for the old man. You know, he died. Of a heart attack." I shut off the movieola. "Christ, it's worse than the American version. Let's open the windows, or get out of here."

"Think of the experience only," said Luis.

"Any work around?" I asked.

"What have you been doing, Señor Dean?"

"Nothing. That's why I'm here. I need work."

He thought for a moment. "They will be having readings for a film called *The Challenges* tomorrow. It's for one of the leads. They already have Francisco Rabal for the other lead. It is a serious film. It has a good script."

"What kind of budget? Low?"

"High low."

"I'm not going to read for anyone. I don't believe in it. I won't go out on cattle calls."

"You have to read for him," said Luis.

"Arrange for me to meet the producer privately. Then I'll read for him."

"I don't know."

"Sure you do. You can do it."

Nights in Madrid were dull, if you listened to some of the natives. They blamed the nights on General Franco, who closed the sidewalks at two in the morning, his theory being that people would be at their best at work in the morning. The *paseo* on the Gran Vía in the gut of town was one of the great visuals in Europe, right up there with the faces and characters that streamed by on the Via Veneto in Rome. The procession of humanity may have stopped after two on the Gran Vía, but Franco's law didn't do much good that I could see. The Spanish were still working the nights hard, beginning with long and leisurely dinners at places like the Jockey Club and then beginning again near midnight in the nightclubs.

Amparo owned three nightclubs in Madrid, dark and modestly elegant places full of guitar music and flamenco dancers, decorous places that served as rivers to her house of expensive hookers on the edge of town.

The ornate house was a magnet to the elite of Madrid, from Franco's court to the powerful of the Opus Dei, a not-so-secret society of great influence. Amparo always knew who, where, when, and why, and nobody ever bothered her, because, to her customers, she had no ears and could not talk. I was fond of her. She was one of those people who make a difference when you are near them. She did not fawn. She did not pretend. She simply *existed,* in the best sense of the word, and if you were her friend, you always felt better for having known her, and if you were one of her girls, they said, you never got hooked on drugs and you never ended up like a common, lost scrub on the Gran Vía, with an empty purse and a collapsing face. Her women, they said, graduated to husbands of position and money, which proves to me that although men always insist they would never marry a whore, they often do. "My house," she once said, "is like a finishing school. They make very good wives, my girls."

Amparo was in an office at the second of her two clubs that I tried. Her maître d' led me through the club, then down a long hall. I opened the door. She was at an abacus, her long earrings dancing as her fingers flew back and forth across the colored beads.

"Why don't you get an accountant to do that?" I said.

She turned and said, "Ahh, my favorite director. The director who takes pictures of me that I never see on the screen."

"Nobody else did either," I said, kissing her on the cheek.

"It does not matter," she said. "I have the picture in my mind forever." Her fingers never stopped moving.

"How's business?" I asked.

"Business . . . it is beautiful. It would be beautiful when it is not beautiful." She poured a drink for me. "You look older," she said.

"I am."

"You come to Madrid to work again, Dean?"

"If I can find any. I'm trying to see a producer now. I want to see him alone. I don't want to be in a parade. It's like one of your girls filing past a customer, and he finally picks one."

"I do not parade my girls."

"I know. I'm talking about producers. They don't have feelings."

"Who is this producer?"

"Querejeta. Luis is going to talk to him."

She looked into a book, then began to write on a note pad. She handed me an address. "Be there tomorrow afternoon. He will see you. The rest is up to you. My great directors do not belong in parades."

PARIS

"So Madame Amparo got me my shot," I was telling Sandra. She glided lazily on a swing in front of David's clinic. "And—"

"Bless her decadent heart," said Sandra. She let her feet drag the grass.

"As I was going to say," I continued, "the lead was there in the producer's office. Rabal. He was off to the side of the office. The producer was curt. It went like this:

" 'The first time a whore ever sent me an actor,' he says.

" 'She's no whore,' I say quietly. 'Don't call her that. Not that the word matters to me, or her, for that matter. It's just a word. Except when you say it.'

" 'Whore,' he says again.

" 'Part or no part,' I say, walking over to him, 'I'm gonna throw your ass right out that window.'

" 'Fine!' shouts Rabal. 'He will be fine.'

" 'No offense,' says the producer. 'It is only a test. Luis told me to do it this way. He told me not to let you read. You would be better natural. That we should get you angry. We looked at some scenes from your film this morning. The part is yours. But you won't get rich.'

" 'I don't care,' I say. 'When do we start?'

" 'We need now only a director,' the producer says. 'And as always some more money. Say two months.' "

By this time, Sandra was soaring in the swing. I had been shouting, unaware of my voice. I don't think she heard a word I was saying. She came to a stop only when David came out and motioned us to come inside the clinic.

"Two months!" I said. "How you like that for a draw in luck?"

"Two months what?" she asked.

"I got the part, but they're not starting the movie for two months."

She brightened up some. She'd get me to go to Africa now, she was probably thinking. She was. "When do we leave for Nairobi?" she said. "Garrotte will think better of it if you go."

"What was his reaction?"

"Cool."

"Can't say that I blame him," I said. "He feels like a father to you. Fathers don't let daughters do things like that."

"He lets me do—"

"That's different. The odds are much better. And I know he doesn't put you in over your head."

"Can I count on you? This is the last time I'm asking."

"No. I told you: I'm getting out." Silence. "Look, you know

166

what I think of you. You know what I feel for you. I even have good feelings for your country. But that's none of my affair in Africa. And I won't chase the stick for any woman, no matter what I feel toward her."

We joined David in his office. He had company. He introduced the two, one of them a woman, as experts in abnormal child psychology. They were both in white smocks. I was confused. I never thought anyone was better in his field than David. The two doctors excused themselves, and said they would look in on Jean.

"Since when do you need consultants?" I asked.

"They've been here a couple of days," said David. "Frankly, I had begun to feel that I was falling behind. It seemed that I had been spending all my time being swamped by the practical side of the clinic: raising money, begging for grants, that kind of thing. I thought that some exposure to other minds might help me catch up."

Sandra rolled her eyes. "That's an expensive indulgence," she said, "for someone who knows more than both of them put together."

"Not true," said David. "I don't." He looked over at me. "We haven't seen much of each other lately, Dean, but I wanted you to see where some of your money is going."

"You don't have to show me," I said. "You always do the right thing."

The doctors came back, and the woman had a painting in her hand. She placed it in front of David, and the three of them began to study it. The painting was by Jean. There was a tree, a big sun, and a house and four children.

"He used all of the space," said David. "Look at that!" The doctors remained quiet.

"And that sun!" said David. "It's so big and beautiful."

"Yes, but here we have a serious contradiction," said the woman. "The colors are only brown and black."

"Latent depression," said the other doctor. "Unmistakable, Dr. Goldman."

"I don't understand," said David. "He was making such

excellent progress. Is he nearly finished with the second painting?"

"Yes," the woman said.

"Bring it when he's done. I'm anxious to see it. I can't believe this." He turned to Sandra. "He used all the space. Didn't put figures into just one corner. And that sun. Look at it! I don't know. Latent depression? That's an iron door between us now."

It wasn't long before the doctors were back again. The three of them studied the painting. It was similar to the first except everything was larger. "Brown and black again. But the sun is so big," said David.

"And brown," said the woman.

"What's he doing now?"

"Another painting," said the woman.

"Let's go down there."

Jean had just begun. He had a black tube in his hand. David looked at the boy's paint tray.

"Who gave him the paints?" David asked.

"I did," said the male doctor.

"This is a new set of paints," said David.

"No, it isn't," said the doctor. "The black and—" He stopped as if remembering something.

"And brown had been used before?"

"I'm afraid so."

"No wonder. All of these paints should have been opened. They are hard to open. He tried. And then quit. They get discouraged easily." He opened the tube of yellow, and handed it to Jean. The boy dropped the tube of black. David gave him new paper. He began on the sun, and then asked for the green.

"You don't have to catch up to anybody, David," said Sandra.

"Yeah, stop wasting my money," I said, joking.

The sun became big and yellow. The trees became green. The kid even had yellow smoke waving out of the house's chimney. He didn't want anything to do with black.

I felt the same way.

168

✝

Garrotte was in his study, the Roman sun still on his face. It was midafternoon. The curtains were drawn because he was watching television. I started to speak, but he motioned with his hand for me to wait. The television was a portable, sitting on his desk, along with that ivory pen-and-pencil set and a long-stemmed glass of Chablis. There was nothing else. There was never anything else. Like his mind, I thought. Quiet. Secret. Ordered. Mathematical. It would be hard to leave him. He had even given my own life a sense of light order. No, it wasn't mathematical. Rational. That was the word. How could I tell him that I was leaving? Would he be angry? Hurt? No. He never showed emotion. Besides, guys like me were a dime a dozen. Or were they? I don't know. I'm not a killer. I'm an actor.

I walked around to the back of his desk and looked over his shoulder. It was a French news special.

. "What's this about?" I asked.

"Love and beauty in your Chicago," he said. There were screams. There were nightsticks coming down on the heads of kids. "One of your fine American rites," he said. "The Democrats are selecting a presidential candidate."

The pictures were coming from a hall now. A fat man was raising his fist at a speaker. Then the camera cut to a room full of injured young people. Garrotte turned the set off.

"Enough," he said. "This is only the play. The script is more interesting. The writing and staging has taken a long time." He reeled off a series of events of this year alone: the assassination of Dr. King, the decision of President Johnson not to seek reelection, the presence of a half-million men in Vietnam, the assassination of Bobby Kennedy, the rising black militancy. "It is the oldest script in the world," he said.

"I don't recall a year like this one," I said.

"Perhaps you were not looking," he said. "The world, the human race, has always been like an animal with a bullet in its insides, forever trying to eat away the pain."

"How was Rome?"

He smiled. "Italy is always a relief. It is usually the howler monkey of the world. They swing and screech from tree to tree, making threats. But they seldom act. Have you ever watched how the Romans react in a traffic accident. The people gather, and look in wonder, may even become involved. They have seen hundreds of accidents, but the ritual always seems as fresh as if it were the first time. The drivers stomp, emote, cajole, reason. It goes on forever. But never violence. It is purely an exercise in semantics and theatrics."

"I guess you know why I'm here," I said.

"I know of one reason," he said, "but only sense another." He poured me a glass of wine, and we went to his couch near an empty fireplace in the middle of his study. "So what is this thing I sense?" he said.

"I think you do more than sense it. Puffy probably told you. And I'm sure Sandra did. I want to leave."

"Nerves?"

"You know better."

"You tell me. Even the best lose their nerve and mettle. I have lost it. Regained it. Lost it again. Someday I may want to find it again."

"Well, there's no nerves about it. I want to get back to acting. Completely."

"You know I won't stop you. I have no use for a man who is not sure of himself, who is divided inside himself. Usually it is the conscience that divides. Do I hear that old, familiar sound: the supremacy of conscience?"

"The only conscience I have is about acting. Settling people hasn't bothered me a bit. If I had any conscience, I gave that up a long time ago when I was rotting in the slam and a good Samaritan named James and the U.S. government made it all seem like a good idea at the time."

"And now?"

"I don't mind the work. In fact, sometimes I think I love the drama and risk of it more than acting. It also pays well. And you must know what I think of you."

"But there is no more drama?"

"I don't say that. I only say that I have to give acting all I got. I can't do both. So I have to walk."

"So you shall," he said. "So you shall, but first . . ."

I should have guessed the coming cross block. He pulled a map out of his pocket. It was the aerial map that had belonged to the Israeli agent. He said it was worthless in the building of any stratagem. I said there wasn't going to be any stratagem. He told me to be quiet and listen. He said I owed him and Sandra that much. He said people and the world would be better off if they employed enlightened self-interest. As for himself, he said, he had none but a rooting interest in Israel. He admired the eloquence of Abba Eban on the United Nations floor, and the tactical brilliance of Moshe Dayan. Beyond that, it served no purpose for him or the group for which he worked to go in and meddle in Israeli-Arab affairs at this time. He and the group had meddled before, but only out of self-interest. That clearly was not the situation here.

In brief, his only interest was in Sandra. He suggested, as balm for Sandra's passion, that I take her and a cameraman to Africa and shoot film of the encampment. The film, if we were spotted, could always be explained as a documentary on Africa being shot for television. He assured me that this trip was only diversionary, something to placate Sandra's sudden and intense wish to help her country. She could give the films to the Israelis, and that would be the end of it.

"We shall tell her it is a feasibility study for us," he said.

"What the hell are my interests in all of this?" I asked.

"None," he said. "Except Sandra."

He was right. Goddammit, he was right. She would do something rash. She would find a way to get to that encampment without us.

"And then," he said, "you can, as you so quaintly put it, walk."

Sandra called the contact for her African-tour package, and soon we were in Nairobi along with Charles Tulle, a French cameraman. I had planned on only a couple of days in this white, gleaming town that had been pulled from the mosquitoes, carved out of the swamp, and then made into a railroad depot. Now it was one of the jewels of East Africa, in some ways a showcase for capitalism, and only five minutes away were yawning lions and leaping gazelles. I wanted to give Tulle time to get some footage of Nairobi, to satisfy his artistic temperament and to avoid a lot of questions from him later. Before I had given him the job, I had told him to shoot what he was told, at a hundred dollars a day plus expenses. I also had to hire a guide, rent a Land-Rover, and buy supplies for four days: coffee, tins of corned beef. Nothing much. This wasn't a company picnic.

We checked into the Norfolk Hotel, an old, colonial place on Harry Thiuku Road, opposite the National Theater and about a fifteen-minute walk from downtown. The next day, I shopped about for a guide. The clerk at the desk told me I could find all the guides I could pay around the downtown hotels. I began to walk, finally ending up at the Thorn Tree, a sidewalk café in front of the New Stanley Hotel. I could feel the sweat trickle down my neck. I didn't feel like I was in Africa. There were too many skyscrapers, the sense of city planning creeping all over me. I looked at the big thorn tree shooting up from the café's floor. It looked old and tough. I asked the waiter how old it was. He said that it was not too old. It was a replacement for the old one, which had been poisoned by a liquid they had used to clean the floor. Civilization, I thought. The pollution from the traffic in front of me would get this one, too. The waiter brought a tall iced tea.

"I'm looking to hire a guide," I said. "You got any around here?" He told me to wait. He was back in ten minutes with a long, black reed of a man, his face deeply creviced with age but still handsome, the kind of face, I thought, you might have seen thirty years ago peering out just above the high grass of a savannah.

"His name is Ati," said the waiter. "He speaks good English."

"Okay," I said to the waiter, pressing some money into his hand. "I'll talk to him." I told Ati to sit down, and I placed a map in front of him.

"You know this place?" I asked. "Near the Ethiopian bor-

172

der." He looked at the circle on the map. I studied his big white eyes, listening to the clank and growl of the insane traffic and smelling the cancerous waste.

"Mountains," he said. "Some desert. No people go there much."

"How many days away by Land-Rover?" I asked.

"Three day," he said.

"Can you take me there?" I said.

"How many day we be gone?" he asked.

"Three going. Three coming back. Two at the most there." I held up two fingers, and pointed at the map's circle. "I pay you twenty-five dollars a day, American. Starting now." I gave him two tens and a five. He looked at it in his palm, smiling widely. "Now let's go and get a Land-Rover and some supplies."

The Nairobi expressways took us quickly out into stretches of land that looked more like Africa, away from the tin shacks outside of town, away from the massive power transmitters jutting into the clear blue sky like objects from space, and then past one game park after another. Ati and I did the driving, while Sandra and Tulle sat in the back, with Tulle letting his camera eat up everything in sight. Thinking of the cost of the film he was using, I had to come down on him, saying, "Hey, Tulle, this isn't a Disney special."

We made good time over all types of roads—blacktop, some others badly paved, sand roads, corrugated surfaces —because if you slowed down, the vibration would rattle your teeth. But we kept on the pace, making about 290 miles a day in spite of the Masai herdsmen, the cyclists, the sheep, the dogs and antelope. Here and there we would come to a mud patch or a stream, and Ati would get out, look it over, and then probe it with a long stick to see how deep it was, or to see if there were any objects at the bottom of the stream that would flatten our tires.

At the start of each day I would give him his twenty-five dollars, and, like the sun coming up, there would be those teeth and that beautiful smile. He was worth it. He taught me words in Swahili, and listened intently as I stumbled over them: *ngapi* (how much?), *nataka tembo baridi* (I want a cold beer), *jambo* (hello), *leo* (today), *kesho* (tomorrow), *naweza kupiga mapicha* (may I take photos?). I learned that Africans often talk in proverbs. "An elephant does not regard his own trunk as a burden" (be self-reliant). "It's the big watermelon that has no seeds" (for a braggart). "You are an ant trying to roll a rock home" (for someone doing a useless thing). Yeah, Ati, that's me, I thought.

On the morning of the fourth day we were moving across a small area of desert, a short range of mountain outlined against the sky ahead in the half light. Ati pointed at them, saying, "The circle on the map."

Hidden somewhere in that mountain was the encampment. We would leave Ati behind with the Land-Rover. I figured a day up and in search of the camp, another day of filming, and back down the next morning. Tulle and Sandra, I thought, shouldn't have much trouble with the climbing. The gradients were good; we were not going up against the face of a Swiss alp. Sandra and Tulle looked up at the mountain.

"Can you make it?" I asked Sandra. Tulle was grumbling in French.

"Don't worry about me," she said. "Tulle doesn't like the idea much."

"What about it, Tulle?" I said.

"It is a mountain," he said.

"Yeah, that's right. Not a big mountain. But a mountain." He spoke again in French to Sandra.

"He says he's afraid of heights," said Sandra.

"You did not tell me about a mountain," he said.

"Stay here with Ati," I said. "Just load the camera. I'll do the shooting." I could see him falling—with the camera. Without the camera, the trip was doubly useless.

Quickly, Sandra and I put on t-shirts showing that we were from a French television network, took some supplies and blankets, and started toward the black-green humps, hoping to make some time in the morning cool.

174

We must have been about fifty stories up before we started to see the top of the mountain. The climb had gone well, except for the camera straps' cutting into my back; we had taken a break every hour. The breaks weren't for Sandra; we rested because of the camera straps. It took us about seven hours to reach the top, mostly because of the definition of the mountain, the easy climbing moves that could be made without rope or grapples. It had not been a technical climb, which was good; but it would take us much longer to come back down. There was not much cover on the top—only a couple of big rocks. No shade. The sun was weakening slowly.

"You ever see a kid use a magnifying glass, hold it in the sun and let it beam down on paper?" I said. "That's how we're going to feel tomorrow. Like burning paper."

Down below, well away in a clearing of dense foliage, I could see the specks of men and buildings, but I didn't raise my field glasses. I was thinking about tomorrow, looking for some shelter from the sun. I got my bearings. Far to the left, spilling out of the mountain, was a magnificent waterfall, a steady faraway roar that sounded the way a seashell does when you put it to your ear. I watched it for a long moment, the eerie spray and mist curling up from its base, which was part of the river that snaked through the valley. Over to the right of us, down about fifty yards, I could see an area of the mountain that would give us shade. Sandra had the field glasses to her eyes; she didn't care about shade.

"Three buildings," she said. "Two helicopters. A lot of men drilling. Look at them. They look like they're toys with keys in their backs."

"Let me look," I said. "Yeah. Like parts in a transistor. You gotta give it to the Japanese. They know how to soldier. They'll even make these ragtags look like elite troops."

I gave her the glasses. "You've seen it all," I said. "There ain't going to be any more. One building's a barracks for the men. The large one. The other's a mess hall. And the smallest one is the quarters of the Japanese. Oh, yeah, and let's not forget the barbed wire and floodlights around the camp. Just in case you think all you need is a key to get in."

"I don't know," she said. "How can Kenya allow this?"

"You can bet they're being paid heavily," I said. "Kenya can't line up with anyone. They take whenever they can, and from anyone that's giving. It's survival. They'd give the Israelis the same setup. Why not? Who does Kenya owe anything to?"

Night dropped on top of the mountain, and the sky was cross-stitched by a million stars; it was the kind of sky that you never see in New York, the kind of sky that makes you think you want to stay alive, forever. We picked at our tins of corned beef, and washed it down with water. The air was chilled, but we couldn't build a fire. I wrapped her and myself in blankets, put my arm around her, and we lay there looking up, silently, at the good clean sky.

"I don't understand it," I said. "You're not the patriot type."

"I'm not," she said. "But too much of me is back there. Words. Pictures. Memories. It has become personal. I never thought it would become that way with me. I left with hate in me. I hated the patronizing by the men there. It is a myth that women are different there. They want to protect us, they say. They didn't protect my mother. They used her. Garrotte found me when I was twenty-one, in Tel Aviv. I was in the Secret Service. No service. No secrets. I was sitting behind a desk."

She talked about her mother, Anna, who had emigrated to Israel from Poland and had given birth to Sandra in a kibbutz in Upper Galilee. "Only a few huts," she said, "and a watchtower. It was an underground headquarters. The Haganah made ammunition and stored it there. The place was called Chanita. The world war was going on, and one night my father left on a mission into Syria. He never came back. So I was told. I was always being told about the past. 'You will never know how it was,' they always said."

Later, she said, her mother brought her to Tel Aviv to live. Anna was now in the Secret Service. They had been close to each other, but always there was this wall of her mother's passion between them, this search for ex-Nazis. Her consuming interest was one Dr. Mengele, whom she called Doctor Death. She tracked his moves like a lioness, specifically from information sent from South America. "I remember her one day on a firing range," said Sandra. "She could shoot the eyes out of a rat with a handgun. She turned to me and said that she would be going off soon. That was the last I ever saw of her."

Paul, the Israeli agent who had visited Sandra in Paris, was the one who had told her about her mother. "He loved her," she said. "She was a fine-looking woman. She had gone to South America as a tourist. She learned of Mengele's estate in the Mato Grosso. She had a letter of introduction to a wealthy Brazilian family, who made it possible for her to mingle socially: dinners, parties, that sort of thing. Then, suddenly, she heard a loud laugh at a party. She knew who it was. She turned and saw his eyes. It was Mengele. That was all in her last report. She said she had been invited by Mengele to an outing. She was happy the chase was over. There were no more reports. Months later, they found her decomposed body hanging from a tree on a hillside near the Paraguay frontier."

Paul had told Sandra about her mother during a trip they took to Haifa. After dinner one evening they went to the harbor and watched the fishing boats, with their gas lamps, guide the immigrant ship *Moldeth* to harbor. Officials were there to greet them, and the old men and women came off the ship and bent down and kissed the cement under them. It was then that Paul pulled her head tightly to his chest and told her that Anna was dead.

"I beat his face with my fists," she said. " 'Why did you let her go?' I kept saying. 'Why! My father. Now my mother.'

"Paul held my fists and cried, and said, 'She was not your mother, my little darling. Anna had been sterilized by Dr. Mengele. Your mother died in childbirth. Anna raised you. And she loved you deeply.' "

She drew closer to me.

"Too many memories. Too many pictures. I will spit them out here."

PARIS

Sandra and Garrotte were talking in the study when I arrived with the film. Here it is, I thought. I held up my end. The game's over. Garrotte could come down on her now, and I'd be off the hook with her. She couldn't blame it all on me if he was negative. He was a rational, pragmatic man. No emotion with him. As with me, his only motivation could be Sandra. But that was emotional, and quite unsuitable to his professional style. I wondered why he had taken her out of Tel Aviv. He was not the sort to go around and recruit women. He might believe in their ability to perform, but I could see them making him very uncomfortable. Because he was a gentleman, a courtly man, women in hire would always make him feel concern. It was always hard for me to believe that he had put a gun in Sandra's hand. But he had. I set up the screen and the projector, and started the film. The room was tense, or maybe it was just that I was. The film opened with a pan of the whole valley.

"A beautiful place," I said. "Ranges of mountain surrounding the valley for as far as you can see. The one we're on is not that tough. A sloping hump. Very few sheer faces. We always could work around them."

"How did Sandra do?" Garrotte asked. "No sprained ankles? No exhaustion? The pretty face that can't go any farther?" Sandra tapped him lightly and affectionately on the head.

"Like a champ," I said. "Down below is nothing but thick forest except for the camp's clearing. They must have napalmed the whole area to make the clearing."

"What sort of work are they doing there?" he asked.

"Lots of hand-to-hand stuff. Lots of outdoor classroom sessions. They were working a lot with explosives."

"The Japanese should mind their own damn business," said Sandra.

"Nobody does," said Garrotte. "They are only doing what the Americans and Russians have always done. The Americans put a lot of money and time into training anti-Castro forces. A president was killed because of it. Your own military did most of the training, didn't they?"

"That's right," I said, above the whir of the projector. "It'll be a bitch going down that mountain to the camp. I learned a lot of things in the service—even how to climb a mountain. It would have to be done at night. You'd need good climbing boots, rope, slide rings. This side of the mountain fronting the camp is mostly face. You'd need a big moon."

"Move the film back to the falls," said Garrotte. I backed it up. "There. It looks like an easier descent near the falls. Not perfect, but accommodating."

"Yeah, call it a piece of cake," I said with sarcasm. It was easier to go up a mountain, but coming down would be where Sandra could get stuck; novices have trouble with descent. It was dangerous. It was crazy. Why the hell was Garrotte leading her on? Give her the film, and let her pass it on to the Israelis. End the joke.

"That descent," said Garrotte, "would put us right on the river. Let's take a look at the river." The river wrapped around the forest, and passed within eighty yards of the camp's barbed wire.

"Excellent position," said Garrotte.

"Sure," I said. "Probably full of crocodiles. You can find crocodiles in your bathtub in Africa. They're all over the place. Snakes. Puff adders. Pythons. All the snakes you ever heard of."

"We can use an inflatable rubber raft," he said. He sounded like he was going, I thought.

"So we get down," I said. "Don't get eaten by a crocodile.

Don't drown. How do we get out? Go back up the face of that mountain? She'll never make it. Wait around for the trainees? We can't be sure when they'll show up. We'd be cutting it close. That's a tough fifteen-hour climb back up that mountain in broad daylight. I mean, how do you get out of there, for Chrissake? Take the river out where someone'll be waiting for us right in the middle of Africa, saying 'Avis' or 'Hertz'?''

"I see your point," said Garrotte, "but there isn't any point. They have provided us with our way out. The helicopters. We'll blow one, and I'll take us out in the other."

"You're going, aren't you?" I said.

"I am."

I turned and looked at him. I stopped the projector. The room became dark, and his face was gone. Sandra switched on the lights. Garrotte was behind his desk. I walked toward him, feeling the force of his gaze.

"You know," I said, "I admire you. You're somebody that I could never be. I—"

"Self-interest, my dear Selmier," he said. "Enlightened self-interest. Sandra and I are going to be married."

The words felt like a bullet must when it hits you between the eyes. The whole room began to whirl. I wasn't dizzy. It was only this feeling of floating out of myself. I came down and landed back in front of his desk, and focused on his face. It wasn't apologetic; nor did it come at you with irony or cruelty. He looked like a man who had stated a fact, and the sudden, startling weight of the fact would carry the day against any emotional argument.

"Is that right?" I asked, turning to Sandra. She nodded.

"Can't you see she's using you?" I said, turning back to Garrotte. "She doesn't love you."

"Love is a word for bad poets," he said. "Don't behave like a schoolboy. Have you ever told her you loved her?"

"I didn't have to. It was there. You could reach out and touch it."

"Ha! You are a schoolboy. Only the moment counts. No

180

deep ties. Take the moment and be off. Correct. To use a phrase of today, 'Keep it cool.' Nobody gets hurt. Women seldom mean it even when they say they do."

He was wrong. I only wanted to be sure of myself, of her. "Maybe I love her more than you think," I said.

"Maybe! You cannot qualify love if, indeed, it is more than a word." He could twist a guy like me into a pretzel with his words. It was senseless to go on this way. I was only making a fool of myself. I couldn't impose my will on her. It was her choice. I hurt. I'd just have to go on hurting.

"I'll see you both around," I said.

"You will not go with us?" he asked.

"No. There's too much between us all now."

"I should think that would be even more of a reason to go. I was counting on you. I thought I knew you."

"Then that goes for both of us," I said.

"I thought you'd be more professional."

"Professional. There's nothing professional about this gig. One woman with guilt and conscience. And two men without a cause."

"She is my cause," said Garrotte.

"That leaves only one, then," I said. "The one who isn't going."

"As I see it," said Puffy, "the ballbreaker risk is coming down that mountain. Unless he gets a mountain-climber type. But that won't be easy. It's hard to find any kind of type anymore."

We were walking along the Boulevard Saint-Michel. I was looking for some answers from Puffy. He always had answers, and if he didn't, he'd make them up. He wasn't making any up today. He could cite chapter and verse of the tangle.

"I don't have to tell you," he said, "but Garrotte is not a foolish man. Yet, from the first, from the day he brought Sandra here, I knew he'd do something silly. He was ready for it."

We turned onto the Quai des Grands-Augustins, and ducked into a *tabac* for coffee. He took the cream, and poured until the coffee didn't look like coffee anymore. The cream flowed over the top of the cup, messing up the counter. I had seen him do the same thing a hundred times. He took a glance from the waiter. He mopped up the mess with some napkins, and then didn't seem to know what to do with his sticky fingers until they found his jacket.

"A shrink would have something to say about this," said Puffy. "I do the same thing at home." He was back to Garrotte. "Yep, I could see it coming," he said. "I know where he's coming from: loneliness. Look at his history."

He said he would put Garrotte in his mid-fifties, though he looked ten years younger. He also had a hunch that he was Belgian, and Puffy's hunches were usually educated. He was sure both of his parents were killed in the First World War. Garrotte eventually went to Paris, and took to the streets. He slept in parks during the summer, and he hired on as a dishwasher in a hotel so he could sleep in the kitchen during the winter. He joined the French army when he was eighteen, and was kicked out three years later for stealing guns, though it was never proved in the court-martial. He drifted, until he took the next small step: soldier for hire. Paris was full of them back then, men with nothing from nowhere looking for something somewhere. The old were just playing out the string. The younger ones, like Garrotte, were after adventure, the kind of adventure with whispers and moonlight and lush palm trees and blue seas and all the dark places where you waited for a Chinaman or a sheikh or a Haile Selassie to offer you a fortune and make the days count for something.

"So you head off to Ethiopia," said Puffy, taking a slurp of his coffee, "and when you get there, whattaya have? You eat eggs that make you hold your nose, and drink milk from a sick cow. The cook's got syphilis, and when you lift your eyes up from the plate, they fall on a leper. But it's adventure. And it's money. You stick it all in the Bank of Ethiopia. You still feel good. Then the Itali-

182

ans take Addis Ababa. No more bank. Desperation."

After that, said Puffy, the stops were Somaliland, Yemen, any old place that had a problem. So Garrotte bounced from one place to another, sleeping on the decks of freighters. And, being a sensitive man, he knew he was adrift and belonged to nobody. A woman wouldn't marry you. They just like to talk about adventure. All you have are the brothels. Your consulate looks upon you as a carrier of plague, a soldier for hire who means trouble, a lot of reports and ruined card games.

The end of every adventure, according to Puffy, was in some port that Garrotte could not get out of, in a room he couldn't pay the rent on, always alone with some pictures and a few medals, roach powder for talcum powder, and the ragged books that he used to read far into the night. He did some time in Spain for the Loyalists, then became a leader in the French underground, and after the war he wangled his way back into the army during the French-Indochinese war as a major.

"He's a scarred old fish," said Puffy. "Adventure ain't nothin' to him anymore. It's too many months of loneliness with tiny and rare splices of beauty. He's tired. He wants a seat in the human race. He wants the beauty now. To keep. That's why the girl."

"She can't love him," I said. "And how can he love her? Letting her work for him. Going on jobs. I saw the gun, the bullet crease in Sandra's shoulder."

"Oh, he loves her, all right," he said. "But she's an uncontrollable young lady. That happened early on in their relationship. I remember the time. She said she was going to leave if he didn't put her to work. He gave her something easy, but it almost backfired. He said he would never let it happen again. And it hasn't. Then this African thing came up. He had to bend for her on this. He did. With conditions: marriage."

"Would he hold her up like that?" I asked.

"Yeah, for three reasons," he said. "He loves her. He wants her out of the business. And he doesn't want the two of you to hook up. You're a knockabout like he was. He doesn't want that kind of life for her. He also figured the two of you were a fleeting thing. He likes you. He respects you. But you're still sleeping on the deck of a freighter and going nowhere, the way he sees it. You're still a knockabout."

"Great!" I said, laughing. "Class differences, in this fuckin' business."

"I'm givin' it to you straight, Dean," said Puffy. "Play with it all you want."

"She can't love him," I said.

"Don't be so sure," he said. "You never know what Sandra's thinking."

He pulled a slip of dirty paper out of his jacket pocket and looked it over with a pair of beat-up glasses I'd never seen before. He ran his finger over a list. "Got to get back and get going on this stuff," he said. "It's for Africa."

"What's he got?" I asked.

"Climbing shoes, ropes, half-dozen grenades, first-aid supplies, Kasmilkov automatics, rubber raft . . ."

"Christ, they're forgetting the wet suits."

"It's here. It's here. Lemme finish. . . . Wet suits, cans of gas, flak jackets, thirty-eights. They'll pick it all up in Nairobi."

"It's a load," I said. "Is he up to all of this? I mean, the climb down, with her. It'll be tough for her; it'll be tough for him."

"I wouldn't bet against him," he said. "I know he hasn't marched for a long time. But maybe that's what he wants to find out, too. If he's got it anymore. I don't know. He was good."

"How long you say you've known him?" I asked.

"Twenty years," he said. "We used to uncork a lot of bottles together. I hope he makes it." He gave me a funny look, and then his eyes dropped down as if he wanted to say something, but couldn't.

"What's that for?" I said.

"Oh, nothin'. Weren't nothin'."

We started back to the street. He said he had to take a taxi.

He pulled one over, and then paused with one leg in the cab. "You'd help matters," he said. "There's no denyin' that. But look. I don't blame you, Dean. You're doin' the right thing, gettin' out. It's the smart thing. There's nothin' in this African goose for you. No money. Not even the girl anymore. Garrotte will make it. You'll see."

And her? I thought.

"See ya in the movies, Dean," Puffy shouted out the window.

I went to the American Express for my mail, and headed back to the Hôtel Dragon, where I was now living, having left Sandra's apartment. Paris was alive again. The Renaults, the Citroëns, the buzzing little sports cars, screamed by like steel arrowheads, and the sound of grinding gears, screeching tires, and honking horns swore at anybody on two legs; the sound was that of a big, intricate homemade instrument of many parts. The people moved lively, once more with larceny on their faces. They had had their August. They would have to wait until Easter before they could jam the trains again and flee to Lyon or Arles. I thought of going to Madrid. But in Madrid, while waiting for the filming to start, there would be too many whores and too much drink and too many Spaniards bitching about Franco and never doing anything.

I threw my mail on the bed and began going through it. From my mother, a letter saying that her ladies' club was thinking about a trip to Paris next summer, saying that people don't seem to like one another much in America anymore. From Michael Dunn, saying that his legs were bothering him so much that he had to take pain-killers and booze to get through the day and night, and that he might be doing a picture with Elizabeth Taylor and Richard Burton. From Equity, the actors' union, a notice requesting dues. From the bank here in Paris, a statement of David's account. The only reason I got a duplicate statement was that I also had a signature on the account. After all, I had to cash checks myself.

I looked at the copies of the canceled checks: fifteen hundred dollars for the two doctors who didn't know how to open tubes of paint for a kid who even had trouble holding a brush; money for the kitchen help; money for materials; money for the mortgage; money for nurses; money and more money going, going, and going. I looked at the deposits. I hadn't put anything in for a while. There were checks from parents who could afford to pay. There was a thousand-dollar donation from a firm in Paris. There was twenty-five hundred deposited on the fifteenth of August. I wondered where that came from. Except for the money I gave him, David had requested that each deposit made should have its source. I walked over to the drawer, took the last two monthly statements out of a bag, and ran my finger down the columns. It stopped on the fifteenth of July: $2,500. And then again on the fifteenth of June: $2,500. Had David made peace with his father? No. Impossible. A rich girl friend? Maybe. Who knows? That's his business. Christ! What won't a restless mind do for relief? Looking at bank statements!

I lay back on the bed, feeling disconnected, like a plug that had been jerked out of a socket. If only that Spanish picture were starting. Why wasn't I going to Africa? I thought. Because of Sandra's betrayal? Yeah, Dean, that's a good, dramatic word. Betrayal! Bullshit! How could she have betrayed me? I never committed myself to anything. We were only a couple of kites in the wind. You can do better than that, Dean. We were a couple of leaves in the wind. Yeah, stick to acting, Dean. But I love her! So why didn't you tell her? They like to hear it. Garrotte was right. He's always right. I like him. He'll stick by you when nobody else will. He's got fire in his belly. He's staking himself out in the sun because he loves her. He's run the course. He needs her. Don't be a schoolboy! Go! They'll get hurt. Are you afraid? No. No. Only cautious. I got things to do. I got movies ahead of me. It would be a good scene, though. There in Africa. Drop down in there. Bang! Bang! I'll be able to watch her. She won't get hurt. They won't be able to say

I ran out on them like a schoolboy. You have some pride. Garrotte never moaned when you and Sandra were all over each other. Do the right thing, Dean. One more time. You love her. You always will. Leave her the right way. Leave her with something.

I rolled over and picked up the phone. It rang for a long while before his butler came on and turned me over to Garrotte.

"It's me," I said. "When you leaving?"

"Tomorrow night," he said.

"Got another ticket?"

"No place in the world like it," said Garrotte. He was behind the wheel of the Land-Rover and looking out to the front and left. A herd of gazelles were in flight, shrouded some by the spray of dust from their panicked yet balletic movement. Sandra was next to him, and I was by the window. I couldn't hear him too well because of the growling and bumping of the Land-Rover.

"What's that?" I yelled.

"The country!" he hollered. "No place like it in the world!" He looked at me with a flicker of excitement in his eyes. I nodded.

The trip had gone well so far. I was loose despite the strain among us. Sandra and I did not talk much. She had done what she had to do. The time was over for explanation. There was only a mountain over a valley now, and that was all that mattered for the moment. I wasn't going to leave *me* slumped over barbed wire in the middle of nowhere, or her in pieces at the bottom of a mountain. I tinkered with the thirty-eights near the fire. We had been out two days and had made camp near Lake Rudolf. Garrotte sat on the other side of the fire, breaking down one of the Kasmilkov automatics and cleaning it; watching his hands, you could tell he'd been there before, a hundred places that crawled away from his eyes and were caught and held by the weak glow of the fire.

"We're a little more than a day away," I said.

"It will go well," he said. "You will see."

"Sure it will," I said.

"You will use one of these, of course," he said, holding up the stock of the automatic.

"No. I'll stick to the handgun. Don't care much for those fancy things."

"Do you sense anything?" he asked. "A flow of juices?"

"Like what?"

"Being here in this country. The work ahead. If the great Leakey is right, man was born not far from here."

"I wouldn't brag about it."

"I forgot my fascination with Africa. I've known many a man to give it all up and stay here. It was the last free place on earth for a white man. I worked here for a spell. For a black potentate. I was his bodyguard. When he went to restaurants in London and Paris, I would have to call him 'Your Highness' loud enough to be heard. He knew how to spend money. But he was a hard man with salary. To make extra money, I'd have to sell him cheap jewelry. He had taste—women, wine—but not in jewelry."

"You were a knockabout," I said, unable to resist taking a nick at him. "Like me."

"Yes, a knockabout, as you say, my dear Selmier." He hesitated and didn't pursue my words. The silence seemed to let the years fill in the difference. He looked over at Sandra, who was sleeping.

"I won't forget," he said.

"You can. All of us are even after this."

With the hands of a surgeon, he slapped his automatic back in one piece.

We were up the mountain before nightfall, looking down on the camp with our field glasses. A mist started to settle in on the valley. I counted six men now, and when night fell, lights went on in both buildings, the barracks for the trainees and the quarters for the Japanese.

"What's your count?" I asked Garrotte.

"Six," he said.

"Same here," said Sandra.

"Early arrivals, I guess," I said. "They'll all be coming in soon. We've cut it close."

We slept that night in our wet suits because of the cold, and early the next morning, before sunrise, we started to make our way across the ridges of mountain to the falls, where I hoped the descent would be shorter and easier. It was a full day's hike under a hard sun, and there would be little sleep until we reached the bottom. We arrived at our spot with an hour of daylight to spare. I looked at Garrotte. He was worn some. The veneer of château life was gone from him. His beard was shooting out fast, and he looked gray around the sockets of his eyes. His pace, though, had been sure and strong. Sandra had struggled some of the way. She looked drowsy. I didn't think she'd be fit to handle the ropes going down. I didn't feel too well myself.

"I'd like another day up here," I said, "but we can't spare it."

I walked over and looked down the side of the mountain, studying it through my field glasses. I gauged it to be three thousand feet down, with only a couple of places to rest.

"We'll sleep for an hour or so," I said. "Then we'll have to go. We have to be at the bottom or close to it by sunup. If we aren't, they'll spot us sure as hell. Remember now, trust the ropes. And most of all yourselves. If you get in trouble, don't panic. Wait. And hold. For Chrissake, hold on."

The light of the moon was fair to good when we awoke. Here and there, there were clouds moving across it like tumbleweed. I took the lead down, with Sandra in the middle and Garrotte on the end. I cut a slow pace at first, letting them get the feel of it all, letting them build their confidence. Garrotte had done it before; I could see that. It was Sandra who bothered me. Her moves seemed halting, unsure. You have to attack a mountain, or else it will beat you. You can have all the strength, but it is in your head where you take a mountain and crumble it in your hand like stale bread. Go after it, honey, I could hear myself saying to her. Don't let it beat you. She got better. I picked up the pace some. I could hear Garrotte talking to her. "Fine, darling; you're doing fine." I listened for any unusual change in their breathing. I could feel the veins popping out of the old man's arms, the rivulets of sweat trickling down his fingers. We were halfway down when we came to our first rest stop. Sandra dropped down to her knees. Her face and hair were wet with sweat. She eased out of her pack, and took off her gloves. She sat there looking at her hands. They were badly scraped.

"Here, take these," said Garrotte, handing her his gloves. He took a shirt out of the pack, and ripped it in two. "I'll wrap my hands in this."

"Can you handle the rest?" I said. "You look like you've had it."

"I've never been so scared in my life," she said. "How long can we stay here?"

"Not long," I said. "We've got a good way to go, and only, say, five hours before daylight."

"You'll be fine," said Garrotte. "There's only about nine hundred tough feet to go. The rest will be easy."

"And keep your legs still," I said. "Don't waste motion or be rigid. Think of your body as being as light as cotton candy."

I looked up at the moon. It was still up there, good and strong. I didn't want anybody to steal it.

The rest of the way was slow, painfully slow. She didn't have much left. You could see she was coming apart. Her breathing started to come in gasps, and once in a while you could hear her moan. It took us nearly five hours to go the nine hundred feet. What was left of the mountain was only foothill, with the falls to our left sending up its white and gossamer spray. Garrotte and I took turns nearly dragging Sandra's half-limp body to a bank at the base of the falls. It had been a hell of a lot to ask of her. It had been a hell of a lot to ask of us all. By now, I had forgotten who had done the asking. My mind and body were exhausted, and I knew now how a marathon runner felt when he had to kick those last four hundred yards out of his heart and his mind, while the body rebelled and sanity seemed so awfully far away.

We slept. It was midafternoon when a jab of sunlight through the trees opened my eyes. Garrotte was already up. Sandra was still asleep. The color seemed to be coming back to his face. He was kneeling next to Sandra, holding one of her hands and dabbing it with a wet rag. The hand was cut across the bottom of her fingers. He laid her hand gently down next to her side, and covered her with a blanket. We walked to the edge of the narrow stream of water that a mile away would become the swift, eddying current of a river. I splashed my face with water.

"Well, we're here," I said. "Don't ask me how or why. But we're here. We'll go in tonight."

"Yes," he said. "Which do you want—the barracks or the Japanese?"

"You can handle the barracks with grenades. They won't know what hit 'em. When I hear the barracks go, I'll do the Japanese when they come out."

"I heard that," said Sandra, who was in back of us and mimicking the walk of an old woman. "What hit me?"

"Just a good-natured mountain," I said.

"Look," she said, "let me have the barracks. I wouldn't trust myself with that automatic backing you two up. You just touch it and it goes off."

"You got the barracks," I said. "I don't want a bullet in my back."

"Don't let her kid you," said Garrotte. "She has the touch of a harpist."

"Then it's settled," she said.

"Why not?" I said. I looked at Garrotte. He spread his hands in agreement.

"Now," said Garrotte, "once you are on the porch of the Japanese, count to twenty. The barracks should go up when you hit twenty. Get all three of them. If one gets away, all we will have is three tired people chasing one very good soldier in this forest. His forest. I would not like that prospect."

"What about the helicopter? You'll have it ready?"

"Don't worry about the helicopter," he said. "My first concern is for you two. I'll be backing both of you up. When the situation is in hand, we'll be out in minutes. We'll take the helicopter back to the Land-Rover on the other side of the mountain. It wouldn't do to take it back to Nairobi. We'll blow the copter and drive out in the Land-Rover."

We went back to sleep.

Night brought the mist again over the valley. Garrotte passed out the gear to each of us, and three grenades for Sandra. I inflated the raft, and we put on our wet suits. The moon was brighter than it was the night before. We climbed into the raft, the three of us linked by a rope in case we capsized. The camp was a good four miles. The river picked up speed quickly. We were using wooden paddles and made do as best we could. The current got too mean in the center, and we worked closer to the left bank where we could handle the raft with a bit more ease. I kept an eye out for crocodiles on the bank. There were none.

We were making good time when the raft hit something, rearing us up and out, the current carrying us like paper in a gutter after a rainstorm. I heard Garrotte shout in pain. We were helpless for a mile or so, and then the current slowed and we made our way to shore, the three of us still roped together.

"It's my eye," said Garrotte, gasping for breath. "Must have . . . been struck by . . . a sharp rock." I lit a match and cupped my hand around it and looked at his eye. There was a four-inch cut running from the inside corner up over his eyelid and to his forehead. There was no white to his eye. It was all blood. His eye could have been damaged. I didn't know.

"Keep it closed," I said. "It doesn't look good. Get me the kit, Sandra, and some cotton gauze with alcohol on it." I patted the gauze around his eye. The cut was deep. "Hand me that tape there, Sandra." I made a butterfly, the kind used on prizefighters; it pulls and holds the edges of a cut together. I looked around, trying to get our bearings. I could dimly see the floodlights of the camp one hundred yards down and another seventy-five yards inland.

"Are we near?" he asked.

"Not far," I said. "The bleeding should stop with these butterflies."

I worked on him for twenty minutes. Then he stood up. The swelling around the eye grew as you watched. He didn't look like the great wise man of Europe anymore, yet the eye seemed to fit another level of his character—long forgotten—that might once have served him well in the alleys of Marseille.

"Let's go," he said.

We made our way up to the fence. The perimeter of the camp was a dingy yellow from the lights. Garrotte worked on the fence with his wire cutters, and we crawled through. We moved out of the light on our bellies for fifty yards until we were facing the two buildings. It was dark and quiet. Garrotte motioned Sandra to move on toward the barracks. I bellied to the front of the door of the Japanese, held out my gun, steadying it with my elbow, my free hand holding my wrist for aim. I lay there like a rattler. I could see the brief flash of a match, and the pulsing brightness of a cigarette tip. I could hear the wind-bells tinkling on the porch. I started to count—one, two, three, four. She could handle herself— five, six, seven, eight. She beat the mountain and the river, didn't she?—twelve, thirteen, fourteen, fifteen. Do it, Sandra —sixteen, seventeen. . . . *Bam!*

The whole sky seemed to light up. The Japanese were out the front door, almost all at once. Firing with their automatics. Anywhere. I pumped five times on the thirty-eight. Bullets kicked up around me. I felt a sting on my back. I knew I got two of them. They were lying in front of me. Where was the third? I heard a burst from an automatic behind me. I turned quickly and was ready to fire when I heard his voice.

"Here is the third," said Garrotte, holding him up by his hair. He was still in his shorts. I don't know how he did it, but he had got behind me.

Sandra was back, panting, her eyes all lit up. We pulled back. Garrotte took a grenade and threw it through the window of the Japanese quarters. "How many you use on them?" I asked Sandra. "It sounded like a battery of howitzers over there."

"All three," she said. "I rolled them under the house and ran like hell. One of them made it outside of the house. I don't know how."

We passed him on the way to the helicopter. His body was smoking. His arm was off, and a leg was hanging by a thread. He was still alive. Garrotte touched his trigger, making him dead.

"How's the eye?" I asked.

"I feel like I have a cactus in it," he said, climbing into the helicopter. There was no fuel in it.

"Goddammit!" I said.

"Easy now," he said. "There's still another one. And look over there." He pointed to a storage shed. "I'm sure there's fuel in there."

We hopped into the second copter. In seconds Garrotte had the thing sounding like a symphony.

"Play, you fucker, play!" I shouted.

Garrotte smiled. His eye was closing fast, the blood crusting around his cut. We were up in the air. "Sandra," he said. "Give that shed a few shots."

She picked up the automatic, bent out the window, and gave the shed a touch of her harp as we veered sharply away. The shed went up in flames, taking the first helicopter with it. We hovered for a while, looking at the ruin of the night, the smoking debris below, the orange of the shed blending with the moonlight and green of the jungle, and I thought of how strange the pieces were: an Israeli in a Paris apartment who appeared like a ghost out of a girl's past; the decomposed body of a once-fine-looking woman who heard a laugh one night at a party in Brazil; and Garrotte here, who wanted a young woman and wanted to show her that above all he was still a man who could take a chance with life—and love.

194

"Look!" Garrotte shouted. "Take a good look, my friend! That's why you'll never leave. Excitement! The search for excitement. The run from boredom. The drama. That's why you came. It's the same thing that makes the rabble cheer when war breaks out. Excitement! You'll never leave it. Feel the juice flow!"

And then we were off.

I reached under my flak jacket, and touched where I had felt a sting. It was sore. The sting had been a bullet.

Like the walrus I could hear a wrong sound.

PART SIX

I didn't go back to Paris.

And it would be December before we started work on *The Challenges*. I had to dig in at a *pensión* on the Gran Vía; the Hilton days were over. It wasn't because of the money. I didn't feel like being around too many people. If I wanted company, I'd call Luis or go to the Hilton bar, where I would watch the brilliantined *machos*, who used to be the first to rage over a local girl's dress length, watch the *suecas*. The *suecas* had long legs. They had long blond hair and milky skin. They didn't give a damn. A *sueca* was a vacationing Swedish girl, but after a while it came to mean any girl from Holland, Germany, England, or America with a Nordic look and a game glint in her eyes. They had overrun Madrid, humbling the local men, who had battered their women for centuries with priestlike demands. The *mostachos*, the continentals, had to be a bit more nimble with words and attitudes—the *suecas* said what was on their minds—rather than rely on their peacock strutting and their clever facade of above-it-all superiority.

The Spanish women caught on quickly, and no longer fell over before custom and male thought, or dressed as if in a state of perpetual mourning. They saw the hypocrisy of their men with the *suecas*. Their climbing skirts told what they thought of it all. The once-puritan police were helpless in the face of so many, and had soon given up. They no longer came down on couples holding hands on the street, or kissing in the park. Even the mighty Church, though groaning, mellowed some, and gave up throwing women out of pews because their elbows showed. The sixties had finally made it to Madrid. It was a light town again.

But you can only watch social change for so long. I started to feel tense, could almost hear the nerves and muscles bunching up in my legs and on the back of my neck. I thought of Amparo's whores, but decided to go on a long hike through the Tagus Valley, near Aranjuez, about sixty miles from Madrid.

I was two days out in the Sierra de Ávila when I awoke one morning to find waves of men coming in my direction, carrying guns and sticks. I thought it must be a manhunt. There were at least five hundred of them, farmers and peasants from villages nearby. One of them wanted to know if I had seen any wolves. I hadn't. Wolves, even large packs of them, will go out of their way to avoid a man. The wolves, he said, had been killing their cattle and sheep, so they had decided on a battue. I asked if I could join them. He gave me a stick.

For three days we searched the slopes and woods, and I listened to them curse and beat their cans and shoot at shadows until mutiny seemed in the air. Eventually they gave up. The tally: one fox, which seemed to mock them with its smallness and its tiny death mask. I looked at the fox, being held up by its tail, and then I looked up at the silent, brooding slopes of the Sierra de Ávila and tried to get an image in my mind of all those wolves running silent and free.

Back in Madrid, I thought, you can never be free when you want something badly. What did I want? The movies? Sandra? They were probably making plans now for the wedding. Face it: she's gone. You had a shot, but you never even put a bullet in the chamber. It had been like a piano sonata between the two of us, I thought, while sitting in the sun near the fountains of Avenida José Antonio. You didn't expect a sonata to have an ending; it just melted into the whole of the composition, but it was always there and you could feel it. We didn't need marriage. Or did she? She liked good, solid endings after all, I guessed.

I began the mornings by the fountains, and then I would walk for hours through the warrens of Madrid, where the poverty of the city was so obvious. But you could not feel sorry for the poor, because, like all other Spaniards, being alive, having a tomorrow, was all that counted, and though they may shake their fists at fate and swear at the struggle, they are never numb with fear. Or so it seemed in the smelly, noisy, passionate streets of a thousand faces. Only the old, the very old, who had no more possibility of happiness, who might have been stung personally by the civil war and so many government repressions, could be counted as beaten; their faces belonged, Luis once said, in the Prado.

I began to use the mornings to run in Retiro Park. One morning I looked next to me and there was this hulk, sounding like the inside of a ship's engine room. He was snorting and grunting, sending snot sliding down his upper lip and spittle flying out of his mouth. He seemed to be laboring. He wasn't in good shape. His knees bumped against each other as they pumped up and down; his jabs and hooks flailed at the air with all the harmony of a kid's rattle. He stayed next to me, and I couldn't help but wonder how the two of us must have looked running side by side in this park, with all the statues of royalty around us, I and this great hulk of uncoordination bobbing up and down in a peaceful cutout of beauty and symmetry. The loafers, the lovers, in the park had to smile when we passed.

"*Boxeador,*" he said, panting. "Estrada." I didn't know if that was supposed to mean something.

"*Inglés,*" I said.

"Heavyweight boxer," he said.

"I didn't think you were a bullfighter," I said.

"Ah, the bullfighter," he said, the sweat racing down his

face, the words barely bouncing out of him. "The bullfighter
. . . all the people love the bullfighter. No love the boxer."

"How many fights you have?" I asked. That was a silly
question. His face told you where he had been. The scar
tissue around his eyes was in lumpish tiers. You could put
his nose in the Prado also. He spoke like all fighters who get
hit too much, but I've seen worse in the lobby of the old
Garden and at the bar of old Gilhooley's on Eighth Avenue;
things get old fast in New York. All in all, I'd say he belonged in another line of work. You can't tell that to fighters,
though. They dream more than actors. Even the lowest of
them can find more reasons to prolong a hundred-dollar-a-
fight career.

"I have . . . sixty fight," he said. I gave him forty; they all
pad their records. "I win. I lose. I geeve them some. They
geeve me some. Everybody happy."

"What you get for a six-rounder?" I asked.

"Only main event, señor," he said. "One thousand dollar,
American. In pesetas." He should have been an actor. He
hadn't been near a main event since his mother gave him
life. And the best fodder for the prelims comes cheap. I
didn't bother to ask him his age. He'd probably tell me he
was twenty.

"I am twenty-two," he said. "Many beeg fights coming.
You American. You take me to America for beeg fights. I
fight Cassius Clay."

"He doesn't like that name," I said. "Besides, the government retired him."

"How can . . . that be?" he asked.

"It's a free country," I said. "They can do what they want.
Don't you have a trainer?"

"He leave me," he said. "He go to Andalucía to work with
. . . a leetle one. A featherweight."

"No manager?"

"No manager. He leave me, too. He say I make hees eyes
sore. I do not . . . *comprendo*. I never heet heem." He gave
it some more thought, and then said, "You be my trainer,
señor."

"Ohhh no."

"I pay. We will make much money. We will go to America."

"When's your next fight?" I asked.

I could kill some time with this big slug. I knew some of the moves in a corner. You didn't have to be a genius. They are mostly fakers, the cornermen, full of trade secrets and vague magic that never works. The press eats it up; it sounds mysterious. I once saw the old elf, Charlie Goldman, who used to train Marciano, coming out of the Garden one night with his little bag in his hand, and I went up to him. I figured he had a lot of practice on Marciano. He seemed shocked. I guess he thought I was going to ask him for his autograph. I wanted to find out only if Crawford, who boxed in the amateurs, was right.

"How you stop a bad cut, Mr. Goldman?" I asked.

After making sure I wasn't from the press, he looked at me as if I were crazy. "I'll tell ya how, son," he said, motioning me down to his level as if he were passing a Pentagon secret. "Pray, son, pray."

After that, I made Charlie Goldman the best trainer who ever lived. The rest of them could only smear Vaseline, drown their fighters in buckets of water, or ruin fighters' eyes with razor blades to relieve swelling.

"When?" I asked again. I hadn't heard the date the first time.

"Two day," he said.

"What they call you?" I asked. "Your name."

"Estrada!" he shouted, as if I should have known. "Babeee Estrada!"

"Great!" I yelled. "Baby Estrada. A heavyweight called Baby!"

We stopped running in Retiro, and Baby took me to his gym. It was like all other gyms: a dirty cut. It smelled of liniment and sweat and stale dreams. Flies stuck to the walls as if the walls were slabs of sugar. The floor was full of spit and thin wet cigar ends dropped by bored managers with little slices for eyes; Gleason's, uptown Manhattan, was a palace in comparison. I used to go up there once a week, until I got tired of the Puerto Rican four-rounders bumming beer money off me. I had just started to climb buildings at the time for a living. I didn't have much beer money myself. But this place only looked like a gym. If you listened, you'd never know they trained for fights here. All the talk was about bullfighting. El Cordobés was the talk of Madrid. He was theatrical and dramatic, the rock star of the arena.

Nobody said hello to Baby. He got dressed. I watched him wrap his hands. He couldn't wrap a sandwich.

"Here, lemme help you," I said. I had to be better at it than he was. Crawford had taught me how to wrap hands when he used to get ready for fight programs at the base. He had also taught me how to handle a cut some. But you couldn't cut Crawford with an ax. Baby had to wait a long time for floor space. He was way down in the pecking order. So he ran in place for a long time, and he shadowboxed in front of a mirror. I thought of his former manager's sore eyes.

"Whaddaya reachin' down there for?" I said. "A shovel?"

He was dropping his left down to his knee for his left hook.

"*Sí, señor, sí,*" he shouted. He was earnest. And then he'd start looking for the shovel again. He finally got five minutes on the heavy bag, and when his turn came for ring time, they closed the gym, and then they kept shouting at him to hurry up and get dressed before the lights were turned out on him.

I tried to talk him out of the fight while he was waiting in the dressing room to go on. He was in a six-rounder. The dressing room was filthy, with green mold on the shower bottom and the stench of too many bodies next to too many other bodies. There was a kid gagging in the corner, a flyweight. He was throwing up, the vomit flecking his legs. It could have been his first time out; then again, he might have been one of those fighters who can never keep their nerves and fear locked up. Some try to talk it away. Some try to stare it down in a mirror. It had nothing to do with courage. It was natural. Baby was as cool as one of those apricot ices he liked to suck on. I wrapped his hands. His knuckles were in good shape for a heavyweight's. They had never hit anything but air, I thought. Some kid with pimples tucked his head in the door and yelled for Baby; it was time. I rubbed his face with Vaseline. His skin was like butter.

Baby jumped into his corner, with me following him. I was carrying a stool, a bucket of water, and a towel. Baby danced, and waved to the crowd. They didn't wave back. The bell rang. I hated to hear it. Baby moved out nicely. It would be his best move of the fight. Down went his left arm for that hook, for the shovel that was never there. *Whap! Whap!* The guy stepped back to admire his work. And then stepped back in again for some more. *Whap! Whap!* The blood spurted out of Baby's left eye, all over the other guy. I motioned for the ring doctor. He started up, while Baby was covering in a corner. He looked at the eye, and stopped the fight.

"I could have—" he said.

"Yeah," I said, cutting in. I wiped the blood from his chest. There wasn't any sweat.

"I weel be better in America," he said.

"Yeah," I said. The doctor took him back to the dressing room.

"How much you got coming?" He didn't say anything.

"Money. How much they owe you?"

"I not know," he said.

"I'll go see," I said.

I went to the promoter's office. He was counting money. What else do they do? I thought.

"Baby Estrada," I said. "What's he got comin'?" He didn't bother to look up. He shoved a little pile of money across the desk.

"Three thousand pesetas," he said. About fifty dollars.

"*Cinquenta* dollars," I said. "You're all heart." He looked up, and shrugged his shoulders.

"Look," I said. "Don't use him again. Ever."

"*No, no más,*" he said. "He ees bum."

"Not twenty-four hours a day," I said, having counted the

money and found it one hundred pesetas short. "Only when he puts his hands up." I wiggled my finger. "One hundred more pesetas," I said. He handed me bill across the desk.

I went back to the dressing room. The doc was just about finished with Baby; I've seen cheap baseballs sewn better. I looked at Baby's face. With all that scar tissue to close, the doc probably had a hard time knitting, and the *cerveza* on his breath hadn't improved his aim. The eyes didn't bother me. I was thinking of all that scar tissue on his brain, those tiny scars that build up and make you babble in the end. He was thirty-five if he was a day. He didn't have another punch.

"How many he take?" I asked the doc.

"Doce," he said, packing his bag.

"The last twelve," I said. "Get dressed, Baby. We're going to see a lady about a chauffeur.

Baby took his work seriously at the whorehouse. He drove the ladies on their shopping trips, and took Amparo from club to club in her white Mercedes. She bought him a couple of white suits, let him sleep in the back of one of the clubs, and paid him seventy dollars a week. Back at the house, late at night, he would massage her feet, and make her tea. She hadn't liked the idea at first, but slowly she grew fond of him. She even talked of getting his face fixed up, his nose straightened; you'd have to give the doc who could do that a Nobel.

Work began on *The Challenges* in early December. For a lot of actors, making a movie is tedious, except when they are young and unknown, and then they never want the days to end. Later on, when they are older and known, one hour is too long on a movie set.

I was young. I was unknown. The days were gold. This picture would be my exit; it would open the door to all the excitement I would ever need. I wasn't happy when shooting stopped for the holidays. Madrid had become an outdoor cathedral, and I got as far away as I could without leaving town. I spent Christmas Eve and Christmas in the whorehouse. The place was empty; there was only Amparo, Baby, and I, and a few stragglers, girls who had no place to go.

On Christmas Eve, Amparo put up a small tree and got Baby to carry a huge statue of the Virgin Mary from a closet. And before she went to bed that night, she dusted it off and lighted a candle beneath it. Christmas was a long but good day. We drank and laughed, and Amparo made a special dinner, fantastic veal parmigiana and lasagna. She could cook. And then we had a strong Spanish coffee with brandy in the living room, the three of us talking about nothing, until, a few minutes after midnight, she made her way to her room, content that she had made it through the day, and eager for the morning, when she would wrap the virgin in a sheet and put her back in the closet.

I was thinking a month ahead. The picture would be finished, and I didn't want to go back to Paris. I could go back up the Sierra de Ávila. But it seemed to be too busy up there, not far enough away. The Sierra de Gredos? No, too close to Madrid; I'd be tempted to come down. I turned to Baby, who was smoking a long, thin cigar and looking at the ceiling, at the fluttering of the candle in the dim, perfumed living room. He looked comfortable and secure.

"Where you from?" I asked Baby.

"Andalucía," he said.

"That's a big place. Where?"

"It is poor there, señor. My leetle village."

"Where?"

"On the back of Sierra Nevada. Nobody go there. Nobody like to stay there. I leave long ago."

"We get a map tomorrow. You show me how to get there?"

"I no want to go there, señor."

"You don't have to. Just show me. You stay here. You like it here?"

"Sí, señor. I like. Ambiente. Ask for my brother Rudolfo. He speak a leetle inglés."

He took a sip of brandy and, sighing, cradled the fat glass in his palm like a landowner.

24

SIERRA NEVADA, FEBRUARY 1969

Baby was right. This was the hind bone of Spain, a stretch of villages that laced through the foothills like a worn and broken string of worry beads. I had gone well beyond Guadix, where the houses are stuck into the mouths of rocky hills, a forlorn and miserable terrain that became even more desolate at Murcia and on into the villages. It was early evening, and the sky was the purplish red of a black eye when I reached Baby's town. It wasn't a town; it was a spot, a blemish, on the face of Spain. The main street was half a block long, enclosed by tiny houses of whitewashed mud that seemed to have been thrown at them. Smoke puffed up at the sky. The wind sent squalls of dust howling down the street. It was cold. It was a long way from anything, a place with no past or future, without one good reason why, if you were young and big, you shouldn't trade it in for a mess of scar tissue, a nicked-up brain, and fifty dollars a fight.

I knocked on a couple of doors, looked into mute and suspicious eyes, until I finally found the home of Rudolfo. He was Baby's oldest brother, bigger and wider than Baby but just as friendly once I told him who I was. He wore a black beret, a black coat, and a dirty white shirt buttoned up to the collar. An old woman wrapped in a black shawl rocked by a fire. The fire, along with some big candles, provided the only light in the room. Another woman, much younger, worked on a bowl of white flour. He sat me down by the fire. The earthen floor was barely covered by planks of wood and mangy skins. He poured me some harsh black coffee. He struggled with English.

"Babee . . ." he said, holding up an imaginary letter in front of him. "He tell me. You come."

"I stay here?" I asked. "Until the weather breaks. Then I go up to the mountains."

"*Sí, sí,*" he said, nodding his head, and pointing to a corner. "You sleep." The old woman kept rocking, staring into the fire.

"Madre?" I said, looking up at her.

"No, no," he said. *"Tía."* He motioned to his head. "Old, old aunt. That ees wife," he said, pointing at the woman at the flour bowl. He said something in Spanish, and she laughed.

We sat by the fire and ate flour fritters for supper, and it was a long time before I could go to sleep, owing to the grease and strong coffee mixing in my stomach. So I lay there in the corner in a half sleep, listening to the hard rain and wind outside and the snoring of the old woman by the fire, until I heard the crow of a cock and felt the wintry light of morning. I opened the door, and could see the snow-capped peaks of the Sierra Nevada, their majesty so far and yet so close to the coughing and smoke of the room behind me, the first stirrings before the groveling for the barest of lives.

Light did not help the town much. The sky was clear, as if an abscess had been cut out of it. The street was muddy, but it would cake soon under the bright, hot sun that gleamed off the whitewashed homes. There was a fountain at the end of the street—more of a basin—where the women washed clothes. I made a pass through the town. There wasn't much, except for a general store with a goat still dripping blood, hanging head down in the window and specked with flies. Across from the store was a café where the men went for wine and talk. The men were mostly dressed like Rudolfo. The women were in rags, or in dresses made out of old army greatcoats, their eyes big and expressionless as they came and went to the stream outside town with pitchers on their heads. I supposed there were times when they laughed, but I wondered when, and at what.

I spent most of the days up in the mountains, a five-hour walk up and five hours back. I was looking for natural shelter so that when the weather cracked I could spend all my time in the mountains. This was beautiful country: pine trees, crests of lavender and rose, streams. By the end of five days I had found a cave and no longer wanted to return to the village. But I went down for the last time to buy some blankets, to say good-bye, to have one more drink with Rudolfo in the dark and still café, where old men with grimy fingernails clenched their glasses of wine and their strange pipes and stared at me with watery, dead eyes. I bought the house a couple of rounds, hoping to loosen the old boys up. It didn't; the gesture didn't even produce a smile.

I left the next morning for the mountains. The weather was good, though still cold. Not far from the village I saw a man on horseback wave to me, one of the Guardia Civil. He was a good-natured cop, about fifty, friendly, just trying to do his job. He said he had seen me several times, and had known that I was staying with Rudolfo; there would be time later, he had thought then, for a talk. It was not often, he said, that one saw strangers in this region, and never a *norteamericano*. I handed him a tin of salmon and my *bote* of wine as we sat on a rock in the cold sun.

"The villagers, they think you crazy," he said. "Only a crazy *norteamericano* come here. Or—"

"No, I'm not runnin' from anything," I said. Except maybe from myself, I thought.

"That ees good," he said. "But the government must watch strangers. It ees very careful about Andalucía. Much trouble can start here."

"Why is that?" I asked.

"You see no church in the village. Is that right? You see no church in any of the villages here. We must watch Andalucía always. If there ees trouble, eet weel begin from the *ateístas* in Andalucía."

"I only saw old men and young boys," I said.

"That ees true. Many are gone. But Andalucía is a very beeg place, señor."

"Where do they go?"

"Madrid. Mostly Barcelona. The government always watches Barcelona. Some go to Germany to work. Like three of Rudolfo's brothers. They work on big stadium in Munich. The other is boxer. You know Babee?"

"Yeah. He's doin' fine."

"He's boxing now?" he asked.

"In his dreams only," I said. "How often you come through here?"

"Twice a month, and that ees too much. It is a sad place, señor. Many sad people. But do not mistake. They are bandits." He touched his heart. "They rob you if . . . you were not friend of Rudolfo. And no one—not even me—would know that you were here in thees village."

"When does hot weather come?"

"A month. Soon." He looked at my machete. "That will not bring you much food, señor. You need a bow. A spear. A gun."

"I won't be hunting much."

"Too bad. A boar is worth one thousand pesetas. So is a wolf. Watch always the boar. He is dangerous. A boar with even a spear in hees side has been known to rip a horse's throat, or tear hees saddle and upset hees rider."

"Rabbits?"

"¡Oh santo Dios! España is full of rabbits."

He took another squirt from the *bote,* and got back on his horse, wishing me well. He kept the tin of salmon.

Like much of my life, there was not much design or planning to my trip up here. I had only the clothes on my back, plus my pack of tinned food, the poncho and blankets, and the machete I had bought in the village. I had no idea what I wanted from these mountains, except that I wanted to be out of the run of things; maybe one of those shrinks back at the prison would have said I was looking for something spiritual. It seems clear now that what I wanted most of all was that charge, that exhilaration, that always comes when you know and feel that not a single human being who knows you is aware of where you are. I've always wanted to be a shadow, the kind that used to drift over a field back home on a fall day: there . . . and then gone. The desire, the feeling, seems so opposite to what is asked of you in acting. The conflict never seems to end. My ego, my dreams, have always wanted acting. The other side of me, whatever it is, wants the movement of the shadow.

I spent the first few weeks in a cave because of the cold. You have to be very careful in choosing a cave. You never know what you might find there, anything from bats to wolves. This was a small dry cave, a good place to work. I kindled a fire on rocks near the mouth, and began to work during the day on a lean-to and a bow and arrows. After the tins were gone, there would be nothing to eat. I could go down to the village to get a few things, but I figured what the mountain offered was better than what those poor devils had. Besides, I wanted it this way. If I wasn't lucky with the bow, then I would just have to go hungry. The thought didn't bother me; it's the thought that panics people. There is always something to eat.

I began to cut and trim a small poplar sapling ten feet long until I had the ridgepole. I placed the pole between the limbs of two trees, about four to five feet high, and started trimming more sapling to place at a forty-five-degree angle toward the back, crosshatching them with more sapling. I used soft boughs for the walls and roof and some birchbark for waterproofing. With a fire in front and browse for a bed, it would be a cozy little place. At night, back in the cave, I worked for hours on the bow and arrows. Not having made any since I was a kid, I found it was painstaking work. I tried and ruined several branches of well-seasoned birch before I got it right. Then, looking at it, I changed my mind. It was a sorry excuse for a bow and arrow, I thought. It looked lopsided. The feathers were made of wood chips, the arrowheads of chipped flint hardened by my fire. If I ever hit anything, which was doubtful, the arrow would surely bounce back and hit me between my dumb eyes. So I began to whittle a long branch into a spear. It was good to work with wood again, and the smell and feel of it seemed to touch off other days in my dreams.

"How ya use one of them, Mr. Jake?" I ask one day in the fields in back of our family's Indiana farm.

"Nothin' but mule's work," says Jake, "but there's a way to it if a man's fool enough to learn." I see the scythe flashing in the sun. He puts the scythe down, and takes the can of cold water from my hand. I see his callused hands, the water running down his chin.

"There's a way to it," he says. "Like a painter's way, or a music player. But not a way for a little fella like you to be learnin'."

"Lemme use it, Mr. Jake?"

"No, can't do that, boy. Your daddy, he'd ticket me right outta here. You'll cut yourself. Or me. You'll blunt the blade, or break it clean off. You'll make the earth bleed, too, by pullin' up dirt with the grass."

"Show me, then, Mr. Jake."

He rises, the dark hands once more gripping the scythe. "Well, it's like this," he says. "You stand straight and tall, and follow every swipe closely, all the time, you see, moving your left foot forward, and you let each swipe get away well and free. Scythe ain't a knife. It's a pen—pendulamm. It's a swing."

I hear the music of his scythe and his breathing, hypnotic in its effect.

"Ain't nothin' to it, really," he says. "It's like a song you sing over and over. You're not hearin' the words. You just keep singin'. Monotonous like. Usin' only half your mind. The peaceful half. Where you don't know what's goin' on and don't wanna know."

I offer him a piece of candy.

"That chewy stuff ain't good for my plate," he says, pointing to his teeth. "Yeah, it's all just timin' and monotony. You and the scythe just wait for the grass when it's in its prime and then . . ."

I see the blade, and then hear the swish of the scythe. I watch him for a long time in the silence of the hot fields.

The days were warm now, and I was living in the lean-to. The spear would drop a large animal, but it would be of little use for small game like squirrels and rabbits, so I began to construct deadfalls in the woods. A deadfall is a log or a slab of heavy wood that when triggered drops down on the back of the animal. You place sticks and branches over it, trigger it with a figure-four device, bait it, and hope that some of them will get nosy. I set up a dozen deadfalls and checked tham regularly; I wasn't working for those thieving boars and wolves. The wolves, I knew, were all over the mountain, and once I saw, thirty yards away, a long line of them, an outline of gray moving down the mountain like a procession of pallbearers, solemn and unhurried. A wolf knows how to mind its own business. A boar doesn't, though.

I first saw him out of a corner of my eye from inside the lean-to. He was ten feet away, directly in front of the shelter and the dead fire at its mouth. He was on his belly, and crunching what was left of the rabbit I had had for dinner the night before. I eased toward my spear. I was wearing only my jockstrap and boots. He caught a sound, and stood up, ruffled—like, say, Charles Laughton as Henry VIII being interrupted at dinner with a leg of mutton in his hand. I found out boars don't like to be messed with when they're eating; boars don't like to be messed with ever. I slipped out to the front of the lean-to, and crouched. He stared contemptuously, and then backed off. He was an ungodly-looking beast: six inches of tail; three hundred fifty pounds, maybe; three feet across his shoulders; about three feet high at the shoulder, with tusks about a foot long, all of it swirling into a mass of coarse gray-black hide.

"Don't go away, old boar," I said. "The eating's good here." I raised the spear. He turned his tail, and trotted off, his leisurely step telling me of his splendid lack of fear or concern.

I made the rounds of my deadfalls, hoping for something more than a rabbit. Too much lean meat, even for a couple days, worried me. It can give you diarrhea or a badly upset stomach. There was nothing, so I made do with some berries that night, even though there were a few tins left. I didn't need a full stomach every day. I spent the mornings policing the deadfalls, gathering up a bird here, a squirrel there, always a rabbit, and then cleaning them back at the lean-to. And then, in my jock and boots, I would go up to a slab of rock jutting out over the timberline, lie back, and let the sun brown my pale, civilized body.

Give a wild boar this much: they don't call them "brass-necks" for nothing. There he was again, back in front of my lean-to, snorting and pawing the ground as if I were a week behind in my rent. I threw a boot at him, and all he did was poke it about with his tusks. Picking up the spear, I bolted out of the lean-to and after him. He turned and ran for about five yards, then suddenly turned in a slow arc, like a two-decker London bus, turning up the dirt after him and heading for me. I backed toward the lean-to, waited until he was nearly on top of me, and turned to the side. His movement carried him into the lean-to. I could see him inside, kicking up the browse floor, ripping at the heavily boughed sides of the lean-to before falling still. I crouched in front of the shelter, listening to his breathing. He was in no hurry to come out; it seemed as if he had found a home.

"Come on outta there, you ugly fucker," I shouted, throwing a piece of dead firewood in at him.

He came out, squealing, and faster than anything I had ever seen over a six-yard distance. He was a cannon shot heading right for my belly, and quickly he swerved, catching my legs with his ass and knocking me ass over tin cups. He retreated to the fringe of the woods, and there, stolid and pleased, contemplated my idiocy. I chased him that day and many other times until we were both tired and would rest five yards apart, the two of us panting and looking at each other with animal blankness. It had become good exercise. Once, I heaved the spear at him, and it bounced off his thick back like a toothpick. The only way I could ever get him, it was clear, was to draw him so close that I could stick the spear into his throat.

But why? I thought one day, looking into those eyes that seem to go in different directions. Why should I kill you? You're ugly; that's for sure. You probably taste worse than horse meat. You ain't worth but sixteen dollars to bounty payers. You're a destructive bastard. But you are special; I gotta give you that. Forest drives, cats, civilization—none of it backs you up. And not even famine can break you. You'll eat anything. You're not like your relatives. Wallowing in mud. Victims. Laughed at. Fat as a pig. Lazy as a pig. Nobody likes a pig. Dirty like a pig. No respect for themselves. But you're lean and strong and don't give a damn. If they wanna make chopped ham out of you, they gotta come at you. With all their cheap tricks. I don't think you mind the ones who wait for the acorns to drop and for the moon to be full. You don't mind one on one, do you? That's what I'm gonna give you. One on one.

The boar got up and walked away.

I was on my way down to the village when I saw them in my field glasses. I drew closer to make certain of what I saw. No, no, it couldn't be. The sight was enough to get the villagers to build a church and never leave. There he was, Michael Dunn, gesturing with his hands, up on the shoulders of Baby, both of them looking down at this old man with a mule. There was a crowd around them, all of them looking up at Michael. He was wearing a white straw planter's hat and a white suit smudged with dirt; his shirt was open at the collar. It was hot and dusty, and the sun caromed brutally off the whitewash of the village. I drew up behind the two of them and the crowd. The people didn't know where to fix their eyes: on the Dwarf's head or on his little shoes dangling over the big chest of Baby. The Dwarf mopped his brow.

"Goddammit, Baby," he shouted. "Tell the fucker we only want to rent his fuckin' mule. Not eat it!"

I walked around to the front.

"Okay, Baby, take him over to the café," I said, "before he gets sunstroke."

"There!" he yelled. "There you are!" He slapped Baby on the head a few times. "Lemme down, ya big ape! Lemme down!"

"Christ, I can't even get lost from a dwarf," I said as we sat down at the café. The Dwarf sat on the table with his legs crossed. I could see the marks from Baby's big wet hands on the thighs of the Dwarf's pants. The local kids nearly fell over one another while looking through the open door.

"How in hell did you get here?" I asked.

"Amparo told me where you were," he said, "and she let me have Baby. We flew to Granada, took a bus from Gaudix, and got a bad car and driver to this." He waved at the town with his hand. "I must be nuts. I'm not even looking for Livingstone."

"How long you been here?"

"Got in last night." He poured down a big glass of wine. He wiped his mouth. "And leaving in the morning. With you, I hope. Can't spend another night in that house—Rudolfo's. I woke up this morning and that old woman, the one that never talks, was sitting next to me and stroking my hair. Cackling like hell."

"I thought you'd be makin' love to Elizabeth Taylor by now."

"Yeah, right. She couldn't keep her hands off me. Just like Inger Stevens when I made *Madigan* with Richard Widmark."

"What'd she do—flush you in the toilet every time you needed a shower? For real, what are you doing in Spain?"

"I was in Madrid on another picture deal. By the way, the word is going around the Spanish film industry that you're terrific in *The Challenges.* What happened? If you can make it, anybody can." He pulled his head back. "Don't hit me!"

"When's it being released?"

"Late spring. First screenings are next week. You coming down?"

"Not yet."

We killed the rest of the day in the café, and then, toward evening, we took some goat cheese, wine, and flour fritters and went up to a cool promontory looking down on the village. We sat there, the Dwarf nibbling at his goat cheese, and the sun dropped as if someone were slowly pulling a shade. He said he was going to sleep right there on the rock; there was no way, he said, he would sleep at Rudolfo's again.

"Whatever you say," I said. "Just don't go sleepwalkin'.

You fall over there, and not even the buzzards will find the pieces." He picked up his blanket and hobbled back to the rear of the rock.

"Your legs still bothering you?" I asked.

"Not much now." That black bile in the café must have been like a paralyzing bee sting. "Back in New York, they were killing me. Started up heavy on the booze again. But with pills this time. One week I didn't even leave the bed. Just stayed there reading paperbacks, and looking at game shows. Was becoming a fifth-a-day lush. It's odd. In a way, I've been alone all my life, and I still don't know how to be alone."

"You shouldn't've come up here, Michael," I said. "It wasn't an easy trip even for me."

"Baby was a big help," he said. "Where'd you find him?"

"Oh, I don't know. I always manage to find 'em."

"Come back with us in the morning, Dean. There's no percentage up here. You've been up here over two months now. Why?"

"You come up here to tell me that?"

"Yeah, that's right. A friend, a real friend, is supposed to worry about his friend. I don't have many friends. You know that. I've got to watch out for the ones I have."

"I'm all right," I said. "Nothin' to worry about. I'm just up here gettin' a bead on myself, doin' a think. It's been good for me. The last few years have had me reelin'. Everything's been so fast."

"Is it the girl—Sandra?"

"She's part of it. I've always had this wall up around me with women, but she got through . . . and then hung me out to dry. But I still love her. How you doin'?"

"Amorously, I'm the same old dud. All heart. No body. No legs. And nothing between my legs."

"Just another pretty face, right?"

"Yeah, they love the face and the voice."

"What's your next picture?"

"I don't know for sure. Nothing but junk offers. Horror pictures. I oughta do a remake of *Snow White and the*

218

Seven Dwarfs, and play all seven of those little bastards. How about that for a tour de force? I'd be brilliant. . . . Hey, that's an idea. I'm gonna look into it."

"I thought you were on your way after *Ship of Fools."*

"I hoped it would be that way. But it was just a moment. Like the ship itself. I'm boxed in a corner by my size. Looks like I'm gonna have to do a lot of television."

"It's a merciless fuckin' business, this acting."

"Yeah, even the top ones know it. I was out in Hollywood not long ago, and I had a couple of drinks with Michael Landon. He's a smash hit on a television horse opera, but don't let that fool you. The guy can act. He's got it all. I was tellin' him about my situation, and he said that all actors ultimately end up the same way. He said there are five planes to an actor's career: 'Who is Michael Landon?' 'I want Michael Landon.' 'I want someone like Michael Landon.' 'I want a young Michael Landon.' 'Who is Michael Landon?'

"The point is, Dean, get after it now, while you're young. Don't let it slide for all this wilderness shit. You can do it eventually. You got the hard ass for it. You can take the bumps." He gave a short sigh, and held the *bote* of wine up to his mouth. "I wish I were you physically. Nothing would stop me. As it is, I go to bed and sometimes I have this awful nightmare that I'm a dwarf. And I wake up, startled, and feel my body and I know . . . ohhh, how I know. So get your ass down from here and start taking the bumps."

They left the next morning at the first pale wash of sun. The old guide was at the reins of the mule, with Michael on its back, bobbing up and down like a cork on the sea, and Baby walking alongside him, and I watched them for a long time until all I could see was powdery dust in the distance.

When I returned to the camp, there was no camp. The lean-to had been leveled. The wrecker was at the edge of the woods, calculating the damage. I took the spear and the machete and walked slowly toward him. I'd hook him under the throat with the spear, and then hack him to pieces with the machete in my right hand. He deserved it, this godforsaken beast; he was making me part of a territorial dispute. I give him rabbit, I give him squirrel, I play with him, and this is what he does. Or maybe he sensed that I was only half playing, that I would have killed him if I had had the chance.

"Here you are, you . . . you overgrown rat," I said, waving the spear about three yards in front of his snout.

"It'll only feel like a fishbone in your throat," I said. He walked to the right, then to the left, and came back to his place directly in front of me.

"I don't—"

I didn't get a chance to finish. He was coming at me like a subway train blasting out of the underground into the sunlight. The spear caught him under the throat, and just when I was ready to chop down with the machete, he was gone. I couldn't believe it. The spear was in two pieces, one next to me, and the point, about a foot long, was lying a couple of yards away. There was no blood on the ground. There was no blood on him that I could see. He was standing ten yards away. I picked up the two pieces of spear and threw them at him in anger.

I started back toward the destroyed lean-to, and I began to laugh. I couldn't stop laughing. I was proud of him. He knew how to last. He was a finisher. The lean-to could be rebuilt. I would let him be from now on. Because, I thought, there was kinship here, and why—never mind how—would you want to kill such an animal, such a beast, which, like no others, would have the courage, the confidence, to drink at a water hole between two tigers?

I was becoming expert up here in the mountains. Expert at survival. I wasn't weary of life. Far from it. I felt close to that day in the field, watching Old Jake and his scythe with sort of a detached yet honest interest. I was comfortable with my surroundings up here in the Sierra Nevada. You never needed any money, or clothes or friends or love. Nothing suppressed you, or used you, up here, and the days were for laughing at yourself and all that was below. Maybe I had finally become that perfect superior buzzard that Michael Dunn once said I always wanted to be anyway. He told me that a writer once said that if he could be reincarnated, he would want to come back as a buzzard, and he could go anywhere and eat anything. He was superior to man because he knew nothing of time or ambition. A man can't eat eight hours a day, can't make love eight hours a day; all he can do is work eight hours a day, which is why he is so miserably unhappy.

If I wasn't exactly a buzzard, I wasn't unhappy, either. The trouble is that yesterday is never far behind. It tracks you everywhere you go because you are a man and have a memory and feelings.

She came up over a ridge, out of the shade of the poplars and pine, in blue jeans and boots and Western shirt and the kind of cap the young Jimmy Cagney used to wear. She was leading a mule. I dropped my field glasses, and my jaw went slack.

What the hell! How in hell! How did she— What's the use? You could never underestimate her if she wanted to do something badly enough. But why? I ran down to meet her, forgetting to put on my pants. I was of two minds. I was glad to see her, because you always had to be glad to see a woman like her, and for a second I felt the way I did when I first saw her, by the swings in front of David's clinic, first on all fours, then on her back, her eyes tilted back at me and her chest heaving at the Irish wool. But I wasn't glad to see her here, because she was an intruder now. Sandra was some of what I was trying to forget, and no matter what there had been between us, it could not be put together again with a splice of a kiss and words of regret.

I kissed her on the cheek, and pulled the floppy cap down over her eyes.

221

"What are you doin' here?" I asked. It sounded cold; I didn't mean it to be.

"You smell," she said.

"Yeah," I said. "Not washin' regularly will do it all the time." She looked me up and down. I must have been a pitiful sight to her. My weight was down. I was wearing only my jockstrap and boots. I hadn't shaved in months.

"Quite an outfit," she said.

"Good for the skin," I said. I led her and the mule up to the camp, and we talked along the way.

"All I can say is, when you drop out, you drop out, don't you?"

"Not far enough, it seems."

"You don't seem delirious with my presence, do you?"

"Let's say I'm just mixed up."

"It's not what it seems," she said.

"Nothing ever is . . . what it seems. Well, that's not good enough in our line, is it? It's not good in our line of love, either."

There it was, I thought. Why couldn't I resist the sudden bite, the flare that always flashed when I thought of her and Garrotte?

"Where is he?" I asked.

"In a hospital in Switzerland. For an operation on his eye. It's not good."

"Shouldn't you be with him?"

"I was. He knows I'm here. This is more important."

"You married yet?"

"No. Soon, though. But there's no hurry."

"I guess not," I said. Her answer took care of the brief rise of ego in me. She wasn't up here to mend any fences. I had underestimated her again. She never went back on her word.

"What the hell you got on the back of this mule?" I asked.

"Things to eat," she said. "Nuts. Cheese. Tins. And wine."

"No chicken soup?" I said.

"You know I hate the stuff." She laughed.

"How 'bout a nice rabbit for dinner?"

She gagged. "How can you? I mean, it's uncivilized."

"That's why they taste so good."

That night, after eating, we sat by the fire until we both ran out of small talk; neither one of us was good at it.

"Okay," I said. "You make the best nuts and cheese I ever tasted. Your company is a pleasure. Now, three questions: how? who? and why? Put a lot of accent on the 'why.'"

"Madame Butterfly," she said.

"Jesus Christ. I only wanted to use her place as a message drop, for possible film work. She turned it into a missing-persons bureau."

"Don't blame Amparo," she said. "She didn't want to tell me. I convinced her that she had to."

"Convince me, while you're at it."

She got up and walked over to her pack. She pulled out a gun, and tossed it to me. And then she walked toward me, waving the biggest hand knife I ever saw.

"You got a problem," she said, calmly.

"Not up here I don't. Not a problem in the world."

"There's also a couple of grenades in the pack."

"Hey, Franco's got the country. I don't want it."

"You'd better get serious." She reached into her jeans and pulled out a note.

"Read this, and then laugh if you want," she said.

The note was in longhand.

My Dear Selmier:

It is with great distress and concern that we have learned, through Puffy, that your life is in danger. We do not know how Puffy learned of this, but in a lifetime of association I have seldom found him to be in error during his day-to-day duties for me, or in other matters of such grave consequence. Were you in Paris, the matter would be merely academic. It would be handled. It would not be a serious test of you or the organisation. As it is, I have no idea where you are, but Sandra says she can find out. Needless to say, I prefer that Sandra not be involved and that you do all possible to dissuade her from her natural precociousness. Along with Puffy, I implore you to use every precaution.

Be careful, my friend,
Garrotte

"I'm still laughing," I said, handing her the note.

"What in hell is wrong with you, Dean?" she said, hammering each word. "Do you want to be killed? Have you lost your mind up here?"

"I was just thinking: whoever he is, he's sure had to do a lot of waiting. He was probably waiting in Paris. He was waiting in Madrid. He sure knows how to wait."

"You have any idea why?"

"Sandra, run that one at me again, will ya? I can think of several reasons. All of them dead. Especially three of them in a valley back in Africa."

"I meant . . . I thought you could remember a moment, a slip, you could tie it to."

"There weren't any slips."

It was bound to happen. Somebody gets a name. Looks at it. Looks a little longer. Drops a piece into the puzzle. Watches how it fits. Drops another piece. Presto. A target.

"Where's he waiting now? He might have given up," I said.

Why should he? I thought. He's on a per diem with a good fee and maybe a bonus. It's like going to the mill every day: it'll always be there. He's in no hurry. Or if he's Middle East, he's got a flag stuck up his ass. Then he's a fool. He's probably not all that ring wise. He's just a loyal trooper. Fanatic, though. Expendable. Ship him out and see how strong the breeze is. If he doesn't come back, then they'll put it in surer hands. If he does, they have the results without spending anything more than the cost of some flea-bitten hotel rooms and the plane fare. There's no point in guessing at his origin or caliber. Guessing is more dangerous than whoever it is that's trying to kill you. He's a man. He wants to kill me. It's that simple.

"I'd say he's probably in the village down below, from the way Amparo's been handing out my address to anyone who asks. Or he's on his way there. I don't really care where he is."

Sandra shook her head sadly at the fire. "You worry me, Dean. You're not in control anymore. You ever drive at night and catch an animal in your headlights? It just stands there. It doesn't move a muscle. It gives up. And you have to help him. You have to swerve, go around him."

"Just make sure nothing is in the other lane."

"I can't leave here with you like this."

"Like what? I never felt better in my life. And didn't you read the man's note. Keep your two cents out of this. It's none of your affair."

"Africa wasn't your affair, either."

"I had my reasons. Nothing very bright. But reasons. Anyway, you asked me. I'm not asking you for anything except to leave here and go get married."

"Dean, I . . . I love you. You must know that. Maybe that's why I came up here. To tell you. But I love him, too. For different reasons. Just as strong. He knows how I feel. He understands. Can you?"

"Yesterday, no. Right now, I think so. I know so. You're doing the right thing. I don't have much for you. Maybe not even love a year down the road. I don't want any explanations. We never went in much for explanations."

"Where do we sleep?" she asked.

"You sleep in the lean-to," I said.

She went inside, and I could hear the browse rustling as she took off her clothes. I sat cross-legged by the fire, my back to the lean-to.

"You got enough blankets?" I called out.

"No," she said.

Her voice was at my back, and now I could feel the soft ridges between her legs rubbing on the nape of my neck. I stood up and turned around, stunned as I always had been when looking at her naked. The soft light of a good sky fell on her, and she looked like one of those perfectly round white stones that you come across sometimes on the beach at night and you have to pick up. She kissed me and let her hand slide under my jockstrap. There was no gathering hardness. It had been there since I first saw her through my field glasses.

"Don't say anything," she said. "Not now."

"I'm no fool," I said.

When morning came, I eased out of her embrace and began to pack her things for her trip back down. She was still sleeping. Browse was snarled in her long hair. Finished, I went back into the lean-to, knelt down, and picked a strand off her eyelid. She jumped up, startled.

"Easy," I said. "It's only the milkman."

She got herself together, and we sat silently for a while over coffee. She was thinking. I didn't like it. I had seen that same look on her face when the Israeli agent had visited her apartment.

"Whatever you're thinking," I said, ". . . don't."

"I think I should stay up here with you," she said. "Just to be certain. The odds never hurt anyone."

"You don't have much respect for me, do you?"

"It's not that," she said. "You seem out of it, detached. I don't think you have a hold on the situation."

"Think whatever you want," I said, "but get your ass down there." I was too harsh. I pulled her head to my chest. "Look, it'll be all right. I can wait forever. He'll have to come up here. If he does, he's had it. The sounds, the woods—it all belongs to me up here. He could never get close enough. And if he's got a rifle, he'd better be Buffalo Bill. He'll only get one shot."

She walked over to the mule and went through her pack. I had put back the gun, and she tossed it to me again. Then she handed me the grenades.

"Keep them," she said. "For me."

She filled the mule with her backside like an old cavalry sergeant. She bent down, and I kissed her on the cheek.

"You're a helluva human being," I said, slapping the mule's ass.

And then she was gone.

I watched her funny cap drop out of sight below the ridge.

†

I waited a week, and three times a day I checked the sign points in the woods: footprints, disturbed thickets—anything that would reveal a man's presence. Nothing. I waited another week, and still there was nothing unusual. So I made my way down to the village. I couldn't stay up here the rest of my life. I wasn't restless; it was just the other side of me taking over. I wanted Madrid and work, movie work, again. But first the village. One stranger, one pair of eyes that didn't belong, and he's mine, I thought. I'll hang around a couple of days, give him his chance. Or maybe he'll wait for me to leave, try to get me on my way back to Madrid. If he's a technician, that's what he'll do. If he's a patriot, who knows? They don't think much. They just act. Like once-a-week gamblers who bet with their hearts.

I began to walk slowly toward the village. It looked like a bug caught on a dust web in the hot white corner of a window. I passed some kids, and they looked at me—and ran. Crazy kids, I thought; they had seen me before. I passed some women at the fountain, among them Rudolfo's wife. I waved to her, and she, with the rest of them, began to huddle together, all of them staring and pointing at me. The old men popped out of the dark café, their eyes big and empty. I stopped in front of Rudolfo's and rapped on the door. He opened it, and the color in his face began to drain away.

"Hey, Rudolfo," I said, "it's me. Remember?"

"I see," he said. "I see, but . . . no believe."

"No believe what?" I said.

"You, señor," he said. "You!" He crossed himself.

"I thought you were an atheist," I said.

"The devil is here. Nobody . . . nobody go out at night in the village."

"Have you seen a stranger lately?" I asked.

"Sí, señor."

"Where is he?"

"He is gone."

"How long?"

"Ten day."

"How long was he here?"

"Three week, señor. And then he go."

"What did he want?"

"He said he waiting for you. He say you owe him money. He say he will wait forever." He was a technician, I thought.

"Was a woman through here?"

"Sí, señor. The same woman who said she wanted to go up to you in the mountain. She come down. Stay for three day, and go."

"Where'd she stay?"

"She stay with me. She drink in the café till late at night. She the only one. All alone. She geeve me thees." He reached into his pocket, and pulled out some money.

He grabbed my arm. "Come, señor! Come with me!"

"Where? What the hell's wrong with you, Rudolfo!"

"Come! Come!"

I followed him out of the doorway of his house. He was at a half gallop. A crowd formed in back of us: the kids, the women with their baskets of clothes, the men from the café. They were a cloud of dust behind us. And then they stopped, as Rudolfo and I began to make our way up a small hill. I looked back at them, and they were all crossing themselves. And when I turned around, I could see why.

I don't shock easy. I can remember only two other times: once, when I was a kid, when I watched and listened to a couple making love in a Greyhound bus; and a second time when I saw Crawford pull that trigger on his rifle in the desert. I was shocked now. More, a chill of horror went through me like a gash of lightning.

He was naked, and propped up against a tree.

The blood was caked on his arms and body, and the flies buzzed around the open hole on his shoulders.

He didn't have a head.

"How long's he been here?" I asked.

"Eight day," said Rudolfo. "Maybe nine day." He hesitated, and then crossed himself again. "We theenk it ees you, señor. He ees your color and size."

"That was probably the idea," I said.

"Where ees hees head?"

"Close by, I'd say." I looked at some shallow dirt. "Go get a shovel. We'll bury him."

I didn't have to dig long. I lifted the head up on my shovel. His throat looked as if it had been cut three quarters of the way around, and what was left was either pulled off by hands or ripped off by a knife.

I saw my own head on the end of the shovel.

PART SEVEN

MADRID, SUMMER/FALL 1969

Never is the sense of the macabre, the eerie, the unknown, sharper in Spain than at the hour of twilight. The sky, melting into one violent color after another, is a hallucinogen that can send one's mind, like a dog, after its tail. Whether you are on a mountain, a burning Castilian plain, or in an alley in Madrid, you are always in a castle in a country of castles, listening for a bony tap on the window or the echo of a distant shriek. Look down at it from the air, see the vast sprawl of mountains everywhere, jutting up like towers, and there is no escaping what Garrotte, who once fought there, had said about it: "It is a land of ominous portent."

I didn't understand him then, maybe still don't, but there is something in an actor's mind that, though he can't break it down, can grasp and feel it emotionally. What is it, I thought on the plane to Madrid, that makes me stick close to this country, that makes me feel one with it?

I was sitting next to a briefcase on the plane. He could have been American or German, maybe Swiss. I didn't care. I don't like to talk to people on planes, for several reasons: I don't wish to intrude; I don't want to answer a lot of censuslike questions; and, most of all, a plane trip is a risk, and I am always unconsciously studying the risk.

He didn't interest me. It was his briefcase, a rich sleek leather, and its contents that held my eye. He had a gin and tonic on his tray, perilously close to his frantic left hand—which held a ballpoint—and my lap. I would never have figured him for a left-hander. I like lefties—any boxer, pitcher, or thinker who comes at you from the wrong side. I'd vote for a left-handed president, if I voted. It's a pet theory, that's all. I always think a lefty, whether he is behind a paper for a bank loan or the banker making the loan, will give you an even break. You never find any real left-handers in American embassies, and you'll never find a slumlord among them. I have a habit of asking the stewardess on a plane about whether the pilot is right- or left-handed. If he's lefty, then I know he won't crack; he's got staying power: try as they surely did, they couldn't take his left hand away from him in grade school.

Not an ounce of reason, but there it is. Besides, I didn't think the briefcase next to me made much sense, either. There he was, scribbling down figures, tiny viruses that would surely mean the business or the actual funeral for someone, maybe himself. There he was, tracing his pink finger up one hill of graph and down another, and with each swing of his finger I could hear a door opening or slamming shut in his brain; somebody would pay for the down side. How many Cokes were not sold? Whose figures didn't balance? Whose company was vulnerable? He tore at the contents as if they were little bits of meat, oblivious of the terrible beauty of Spain below.

It was odd, I thought, how a man's life sometimes can come down to an obscure symbol like a briefcase. The whole Western world, especially America, was briefcase crazy. Before, it was the lunch pail; now it was the case, all shapes, all sizes. Where have all the lunch pails gone? The case had become the great exterior prop, the identity card for the lowliest insurance man, the minor clerk, even the scruffy newspapermen who are the last to conform; it used to belong only to bankers, lawyers, and train conductors.

Nothing comes out of a briefcase except trouble: Vietnam, oppressive law, confusion, the petty power and intimidation that eats at the spirit in a million ways.

He finally knocked the gin and tonic over on his case, and half of it landed in my lap. It had been full. He hadn't touched it, and we were nearly at Madrid. His hands leaped at the case. He rubbed it with a napkin as if it were a baby's head. He didn't give me, or my wet pants, a glance; he didn't care. I didn't care, either. I was a lucky bastard. I didn't have to travel through life in a briefcase. Oh, sure, I can be a slave to list-making; I'm peculiar, too peculiar and impractical sometimes, I think. But this poor devil—he was in a thousand pieces, none of which he would recognize if he could stop and look honestly at them. And if he did put them together, thinking of when he was young, he would be a stranger to himself.

"My pants are wet," I said. "But if you don't mind, could you tell me one thing? Do you like your work?"

"Work? Work?" he said. "My work is money. Do you know money?"

"Do I look like it?"

"To know money is to know everything," he said.

"I guess you're right," I said.

"No, I do not like my work," he said. "It is not necessary to like my work."

"That's a nice briefcase you got there," I said.

"Very expensive," he said, fingering it.

Yeah, it sure was.

Money counts in movies—the money behind you, the money you can demand. It is the obvious sign of success. But for the few who have caught the freak lightning, there are hundreds of others who never really know what film success is. There is something invisible about it even when it is right before you for a flashing moment, something that creeps by on silent feet. And then it is gone. And all you have left in your mind is the marquee for the picture, the ads in the papers with your name in them, the posters with your picture in the theater windows. I couldn't sense success as I stood across the street and looked at the marquee for *The Challenges*. The movie was making money. It was playing all the circuits in Spain. It was a success. But was I? The answer came quickly.

The only part I could land in Spain was the lead in a movie called *The Ring*. It was about a blind boxer. You would have had to be blind to enjoy it. It was completely worthless, even as film education. My real awakening began a few months later when I ran into Franklin Schaffner at the Hilton in Madrid. He was directing *Patton*, with George C. Scott. He had done most of the exterior work outside town, but now he was in Madrid for interior scenes. I knew Schaffner from the time I had worked for him on a segment of *The Defenders*, a television series back in the States. I knew Scott from *The Ballad of the Sad Café*, back on Broadway. His wife at the time, Colleen Dewhurst, and Michael Dunn were the stars. *Patton* was the biggest production ever to hit Spain.

"You too big to play a small part?" Schaffner asked, after failing to recognize me at first.

"Big?" I said. "You gotta be kidding."

"You're all over the place in *The Challenges.*"

"Looks can fool you," I said.

What a sound stage for a big movie most resembles is a termite castle. The work being done there is not evident to the eye, and whatever can be seen is slow, ponderous, on the edge of disorder. If you were to film, say, an eight-hour shooting session, and speed it up so that it was only a five-minute film, the director would seem to be all over and some people would seem never to move. The director is the chief termite, the food source for the whole production, the food being derived from an unspoken interaction between the director and the workers. The food is movement, another scene, another step toward the end of the picture. The director moves, everybody moves.

The chain of command, the pecking order, is exact. The

236

director rarely talks to anyone except his script girl, the director of photography, and the actors. Everybody else waits for the setup, the scene that is to be shot. They wait. And they wait. And they gossip, usually about the stars; it's the perfect rumor mill. Then they wait some more. By now, the director has huddled with the director of photography, and they have settled on a visual approach to the scene, camera angles, tone—its soul. The head of photography then confers with his first, second, third, and fourth cameramen, few of whom care about being the future Renoir; it's a job. The head man seldom touches the camera.

Slowly, the setup takes shape. The cameras are wheeled into place, the sound men move in, and then the prop men. All of them are fussy, temperamental, ever alert for invasion of their domain. It is the survival of the wariest, from the cameraman on down to the grips, the mules of the set, and the "best boy," who is the top gofer.

Up to now, you haven't seen an actor. If they are stars, they are in their trailers, reading their lines, working on crossword puzzles, or practicing meditation. Scott—he probably wouldn't be doing anything. He'd be sleeping. He's a natural. He no doubt had the scene clamped shut in his head days ago. His stand-in is on the set now. He is the same height and the same complexion as Scott. He will be used for light readings and camera position. The job is a plum. When Scott does come out, he reminds me of a sand crab. He is there, kicks up some sand, and vanishes into his trailer.

The script girl thrusts my lines in my hand. I am a grubby private in Africa. Scott, as Patton, has just taken over command in Africa, after a humiliating defeat. The Arabs have been stealing the clothes off our dead. The command is in shambles. He's going to shape it up. Scott comes out on the set. He sees me, and stops.

"I've seen you before, haven't I?"

"Sure you have," I say. He's thinking.

"Ahh. *Ballad of the Sad Café.* I didn't recognize you. I was used to seeing you with little Michael."

"All right, let's rehearse it," shouts Schaffner.

I begin to move an object on a desk. Suddenly a prop man bolts down on me, fluttering like a bird locked in a car. He's screaming, "Don't do that! Don't do that!" I had violated, desanctified, his work, his fireplug.

"What're you going to do?" says Scott, crooking his neck with resignation.

The scene takes two days to shoot. Patton comes into a building where I am sleeping. He looks around, waving his riding crop, and locates me behind a desk. He kicks me in the ass. I jump to my feet and snap to attention.

"What are you doing here, soldier?" he asks.

"Sleeping, sir," I say.

"Go back to sleep," he says. "You're the only sonuva-bitch who knows what the hell they're doing around here."

End of scene.

After the shooting I began to talk to a cameraman. We watched the set being torn apart, each group dismantling its little fireplugs. The whole process would begin again in the morning.

"This one's gonna make millions," said the cameraman. "Millions, I tell ya. Millions! The ink will flow."

"You like this movie work?" I asked.

"Hell no!" he said. "The pay's good, though. That's what counts."

I *was* in a briefcase.

"You mean, you don't get any excitement out of it?" I said.

"Excitement?" he said. "You gotta be crazy."

Yeah, I sure was.

The Challenges wouldn't quit on me. It stayed healthy on the circuits of Spain and began returning money to its backers; at least I was a part of a success on the ledgers. I had been the unifying force in the picture. It was a picture with three separate episodes, all with a common theme: death and love, with an undercurrent of Spanish gothic running throughout. There were three different directors, who changed actors and actresses, but I shared the lead in each of the segments. I was a prankish U.S. Air Force major in the first; a footloose, game-playing draft dodger in the second; and an impotent, sensitive, and damaged war veteran in the third. I ended up dead in all three. The picture wasn't that good. I'd give it two and a half stars for sincerity and effort; it had its moments.

But for me, there wasn't any cream for all my leanin' and dreamin', I thought. That feeling of success was still so very far away for me, until suddenly *The Challenges* was chosen as the official Spanish entry at the San Sebastián Film Festival. And there I was, arriving at the airport for the first of ten lunatic days, the kind of days when you stop and think, try to match the things said, the people, the atmosphere, with yourself. Everything seems out of focus. It is hard to move out of the corner, away from the wall, and grope toward the center of the ballroom where all the eyes are. You have to adjust. I didn't get a chance. You couldn't move through the crowd of fans, press, official greeters. The festival was a big event in San Sebastián. Cameras clicked, people were shouting, the press closed in on me, and television people led me away to a little room, with klieg lights blinding me and people pushing me. I thought I was being arrested.

"Some film, señor?" somebody behind a camera hollered.

"Go ahead," I said. I sat there sweating. The room went quiet. I listened to the camera. It didn't sound right. They kept it running and trained on me. Still it didn't sound right.

"Ahhh, that is fine, señor," the voice shouted again. *"Gracias."* I got up, and started to leave.

"Hey," I said to the voice. "You sure there was film in the camera?" He looked at me sheepishly.

"You didn't have any film in the camera, right?" I said.

He stumbled some, and then said, "Please forgive, señor. We thought you were a star. Everybody here, they all wait for stars. At festival time, they scream at anybody comes off plane."

That's more like it, I thought: no film in the camera. Some things never change.

I checked into the Villa Navarra, a hotel on a tree-shaded street in the town where they wait for heroes once a year. San Sebastián is in the province of Guipúzcoa, tucked up in a corner of the north, near the French border on the Bay of Biscay. I gave it a look. The place had bells on its feet. Glasses of lifted wine sparkled in the sunlight. Guitar music floated out of cafés. And beautiful women, black, brown, and golden, strolled in and out of sidewalk cafés, leaving behind their scents, and checks for someone else to pay. Big posters, in clashing colors, were on everything that could hold paste or a nail. And from the north of town the Sacred Heart statue atop Mt. Urgull gazed down stoically. He'd seen it all before. It would pass.

There were long lines in front of every regular movie house, where many of the exploitation films would be shown, namely the horror and sex films, and occasionally a diamond of beauty, ambition, and thought. The films would run in these houses twenty-four hours a day. The trick was to get a critic or a distributor to go and see your movie at three A.M., to see a film made by an unknown. The town was full of unknowns of one sort or another. Frances Ford Coppola was there, with *The Rain People,* starring Robert Duvall and James Caan. Nobody knew their names then. Like *The Challenges,* Coppola's film was an official entry and would be shown in the beautiful new auditorium, to a large audience. The rest had to struggle for attention. If you were a young director, you might end up with a three-A.M. slot, with nobody watching, or with a merciless gang of cutthroats for an audience.

Look at the lines of people waiting for tickets at the auditorium, and there was one common link among them: their intense secrecy and solemnity. They were of all nationalities. Some wore capes and big floppy hats; some looked like graduate students, some like eccentrics who make a career out of film festivals. They stood there patiently, reading books; one was pondering the mysteries of *Film Sense* by Eisenstein. They never talked to one another, or laughed. They waited for their moment at the ticket window, where they would often buy tickets for many films. Some would see all the official entries; the total would be, say, twenty-four films in ten days. But you couldn't ask them what film they were buying tickets for. They would react as if they had been asked to disclose a sexual kink to a stranger. Once at the window, they blocked the entire area off with their backs and arms, and whispered their choices so nobody would hear. I don't know why. Maybe they thought they were critics, say a would-be Rex Reed, powerful and important, sought after, someone who could bring a modest film to prominence. Maybe they understood the aura of a film festival, could sense the hopes and dreams that always gather, the power and politics that always feed on hopes and dreams. Somehow, maybe, they could feel it all, get caught up in it, and become the stars, the festival itself, little clearinghouses of opinion, judgment, and damnation. The less serious side of them could be found at the airport, outside the hotels, in the cafés, as they watched for the stars and shaped the rumors that are sent through town on a conveyor belt. They were a funny blend of sobriety and hysteria. The film buff, the kind at these festivals, is fascinating, and now I can understand why a man or woman might spend a lifetime studying the ways of a minor, odd insect that nobody ever heard of.

The San Sebastián Festival was a circus, with three themes: art, glamour, and business. And there were four kinds of films in town: the Hollywood "nervous" film, a film that nobody knows what to do with; the low-budget art film, a film looking for serious comment and recognition; the independent film, a film looking for a peg—a Balkan distributor, anything—on which to hang a sale; and the big, big production, a movie entered in the "out-of-competition" category, seeking to get publicity without risking failure among the judges. *The Lion in Winter* was here this year. They had all entered this nightmare alley with one thing: great expectations.

Art was rabid in town. The talk was of Truffaut and Godard; one of their films might be on the way. "Oh, my God, I can hardly wait"—that kind of talk, the heady talk of art in film. The endless speculation. Would it be here, that born-again silent film by some long-dead Russian director who, if he were alive, would sound like all other Russian directors? Or was it true they were going to show the six-hour—or was it sixteen?—uncut version of Erich von Stroheim's *Greed*? It was like being at a fashion show. This year's neorealism was next year's hand-held camera. What happened to surrealism? Where is *nouvelle vague?* They could chew on this stuff for hours and ignore the only question that ever matters, before a killing or a movie: will it work? does it work?

Glamour, that unordinary presence of moment and people, the whiff of something in the air, that illusion of sex, was just as visible as art. Glamour had many parts. There were the hordes of starlets, with their see-through blouses and their come-on eyes. There were the two-to-three-hour interviews in rooms where the cold water in pitchers was always warm, and the translations caved in under the stress of overworked, baffled translators. There were the costumed freaks, on the far side of everything, straining for notice, certain to try to be outrageous even in the act of lifting a drink at one of the many parties. And always the upstaging going on—an actress with her miniskirt up to her crotch, an actor laughing loudly—while you were being interviewed.

"What do you think of *The Challenges?*" a reporter asked.

"Brilliant!" I said.

"How was it to work with three directors?" another asked.

"Were there three of 'em?"

"You don't know how many directors worked on your picture?"

"I was kidding," I said. "They were great."

"There is death in all three episodes," someone else said. "And you are the one who dies violently. Is it true you made these suggestions, the violent deaths?"

"What do you expect in Spain?"

"What's that?"

"I mean, well . . ." I said, seeing the lack of humor, "I mean, people do get killed in Spain. Like anywhere else. I had nothing to say about what went into the movie."

"You are a draft dodger in one episode. How come you are not in the service?"

"I did my time," I said.

"Should people back in your country dodge the draft?"

"If they got someplace to dodge to. Dodgin' is what it's all about. In the army or out of it."

"Do you think the Vietnam war is just?"

"Yes and no. It's just if I'm not there. It's also just if I'm a general. It's not just if I'm twenty, poor, and dumb."

"Would you please explain?"

"I don't know anything about any war."

"What do you think of your new president, Mr. Nixon?"

"He's a president. And he shits once a day if he's lucky." That made the aggressive blonde next to me pull prissily down on her skirt.

"What's that?" the translator piped up.

"Forget it. I try not to think of governments."

"Are you married?"

"No."

"Why is that?" In Spain, they think everybody should be married.

"Are you married?" I asked.

"Yes," the reporter said.

"Then you know why I'm not married. It's confinin'. Besides, I like men."

They all laughed. I knew I could get them to smile somehow. How could you take any of these interviews seriously? But many did; not only the reporters. The actors, the actresses, would do anything to get a wire-service story.

"Would you like to go to the moon for your country?"

"I got all the excitement I want down here."

"What is your next movie?"

"You'll have to go to the moon to find that out."

They laughed again. We were making progress. But the interview was over. And I stepped down, making way for a seedy Frenchman who, after years of study, looked like he might have found new secrets to the slow dissolve.

In the end, though, underneath the glamour and art, there was the belly of the fish: business. The actor was in the business of himself, the next part. The faded director, the expatriate, the kid director on the make, looked for money for his next picture. The independent producers hunted for American distribution. Deals and more deals, rattling the walls of hotel rooms, some of them luxurious, others drab and littered with half-eaten sandwiches and empty whiskey bottles. They moved decimal points around like chess pieces, constructed deals as if they came out of an Erector set, and now and then they would break for a film or a stray blow job.

But sex, if not quite absent, was mainly illusion. There was the presence of sex, the suggestion of it, but all energy and cunning was spent on the chase for attention, and the chase became orgiastic in itself. The parties boomed long into the night, devoid of sin, notable only for the craning necks, the whispered envy and careful self-promotion. After one party, I awoke on the lawn of a mansion, badly hung over, and squinted up at the bright sky to see the zigzagging trail of a plane writing the name of a movie. You couldn't escape business here.

I was still shaky when I went to something they called a "sidebar event." These were panel discussions in front of an audience of aficionados. Usually there is a main topic—say, violence in film—but it soon races in and out of the corners of many subjects. The auditorium was filled. I was on the panel. I wasn't sure why. I could barely keep my eyes open. It had been going on for a couple of hours when the talk was turned over to the audience for questions. This was what all the aficionados had been waiting for: the stage. There were two types of questioners: the pontificating idiot and the wild-eyed screamer who believed in film as a political weapon. The first framed his questions as if he were building a pyramid. This type wanted to impress someone on the panel, usually a director. When the question finally ended, the director would say one of two things: "What was the question?" or "I never noticed that in my work." Questioners of the second variety were far less refined. One of them had to be carried out of the place.

"Why do you praise capitalism in your films?" he had asked a French director.

"I think you may be mistaken," the director said. "If anything, it may be the other way. But I try not to be political."

"You are a liar!" the questioner said. The director smiled. "You have betrayed your art and your brothers!" continued the screamer. The director smiled again. "You are worthless."

He stammered for more words, and, too angry to find them, pulled something out of a paper bag and heaved it at the director. It was a dead, smelly fish.

The sidebar was over.

Days stumbled into days, and now *The Challenges* was finally to be shown in the Main Hall. There I was up in the box, with Francisco Rabal and his wife, the three directors and their wives. I wanted some company, too. Where was Puffy? I had wired him. He wouldn't miss something like this. Our box was off to the left of the screen. We were the official entry that night, so the box was draped with the flag of Spain. There was an empty box next to us, reserved for General Franco in case he showed up. Before the lights slowly dimmed, total fear had wrapped its fingers around me. The audience was looking up at us. I had been the observer; now I was the observed. The horrible focus was on me. I wanted to yawn. I wanted to piss. I held back the nervous reaction as if I had a team of horses in my hand. The lights dimmed. The film was beginning.

I began to feel better, and now I was watching the audience watch me on the screen. What were they thinking, down there in the dark? The film nut isn't like other fans. He sits alone, even if he is with someone else. He never shares opinions, like fans at a ballpark or a fight. He watches films like he watches his dreams. It is a private act.

How to gauge their reaction? Count the number of bathroom trips, I thought. Listen for someone talking back at the screen; festival fans can be rowdy. What was on their minds? Did they think the photography was nice? If so, it was as Puffy always said: the film and you were a flop because their minds had strayed; the story, the characters, had not held them; the best photography should only be an afterthought.

The first episode was shot at the house of bullfighter Luis Miguel Dominguín. In the end I, an Air Force major, get hit on the head with a baseball bat. Four bathroom visits. It was the weakest episode. Not bad, four visits. The action picked up in the second episode. More hint of sex, more slow-burning evil, on a pampa where fighting bulls are raised. The knives of emotion twist into each character, until I am lying on the hot pampa with a lance in my back, a draft dodger killed by a breeder of bulls. I looked at the blood, at my face, at my chest. It shook me up. Does life imitate art? I wondered. I studied my chest to see if I was holding my breath. Good! I really looked dead. No visits to the bathroom. The audience was quiet.

The third part of the movie came up. I am wearing a mustache. The war has left me in pieces. I am impotent. I believe I am being made a fool of by the women in the house, with whom I have shared sex. Why have they had me smoking so much in these episodes? Puffy liked to say that if a director has an actor smoking, and not doing anything else, it means he doesn't know what to do with an empty character. I attach dynamite to a fuse leading into the house. I walk into the house of women alongside the burning fuse. I come down a long hall and go into the room of women who are laughing at me. I wink at them, and the dynamite goes off, blowing us all to hell. One bathroom visit.

And now I began to feel the fright again, the focus coming back to our box. I didn't want the picture to end. The lights came up fast, and the spotlight fell on our box as the last credit crawled off the screen.

Fear! I looked around hesitantly. Were they flying out of the auditorium? Had they stayed for the credits? "The sure sign of a good film," Puffy once argued, "is if the audience stays for the credits, whether they are standing and looking at them in the aisles or still sitting in their seats."

Where were they? Half the huge crowd were still seated. I had never been so scared in my life. I could feel a drop of water press out between my legs. Then the crowd got to its feet and began to applaud. It was like a magnet to me. Somebody in the box pushed me to my feet. A chill snaked up my back. The applause continued.

I never wanted it to end. I had finally hit the right place at the right time. I could never reach out and touch success in movies. Here it was. Here was where I wanted to be forever.

After the movie, a party for *The Challenges* was held in a decaying castle on a hill outside town. The night was clear and warm, and the wind from the ocean swept gently through the ruins. Festival parties are known for having strange backdrops, but this looked like it had been built by an art director for a movie; seen from a distance, the castle looked like studio scenery. Up close, it was more real, with crumbling stone, gaping holes in walls, and topless rooms. Rolls-Royces and Mercedes-Benzes, begged or borrowed or legitimately owned, Porsches and Citroëns, stopped in front of the castle, spilling out their almost-bare-chested escorts.

Lighted by a hundred Chinese lanterns, the castle vibrated with racing flamenco music, then was soothed by a mourning guitar. It was a scene of faces, heavily mascaraed, of weird shapes, of dress that became even more bizarre as the evening wore on. And always the talk:

"The color surfaces were magnificent, and I—"

"Look at that bitch. She wore the same thing the other night. We all *know* she has tits."

"Movies are the only thing bearable left in the world."

"The cinema should never turn back. Today. Now! Reflect the world."

"My theory is—"

"Yes, wasn't she divine, and—"

"*Maricón*—that's what he is."

"He just picked up and left, and after all I've done for him."

"What did you do for him?"

"I loved him. I don't know what I'll do now."

"*The Rain People* will win; you shall see."

I downed a pair of quick vodkas, and let my eyes scan the party. I was looking for a "live one," a body that didn't talk too much, someone I could share the night with. She didn't have to be pretty. All she had to do was understand, and let me spill all the frustrated years into her, let me become drained of doubt about myself. I wished that Sandra were here; she would understand. Damn, how I missed her!

My eyes didn't get far. They stopped at a man who was slipping carefully through a hole in the wall. There was a sudden pumping of my heart as I walked toward him. We embraced each other. He had lost weight. He looked tired. And he had a patch over his eye.

"You should have told me you were coming," I said.

"I wanted to surprise you, Dean," Garrotte said. He had never called me Dean before.

"Did you see the movie?" I asked.

"Yes. I am glad for you," he said.

"What did you think?"

248

"I know nothing of movies. Music, literature—yes. But movies . . . what can I say? It had—"

"—its moments, right? Not many, but a couple."

"Yes," he said. "But you got killed too much. That, my friend, is a bad habit." He winked with his good eye.

"How's the eye?" I asked. I looked at the patch, saw the scar from the cut taken that night in Africa. The gash climbed up over the patch.

"I had two operations in Locarno. I thought the Swiss doctors might save it. Alas, they are much better with money. The eye is impossible. It is gone."

"I didn't think you'd lose it. It looked bad, but not that bad."

"It was worth it," he said. "For Sandra, anything was."

"Was? You two still together, aren't you?"

He hesitated. "Oh, yes. Nothing will ever change that."

"Where's Puffy?"

"He wanted to come. Something came up."

"I have a lot to talk to you about," I said.

"And I with you," he said, fingering his patch. "There is much to talk about."

"So let's get a drink and start talking."

"No, no, Dean," he said. "It can wait. Wait until tomorrow night, when the festival is over and the awards are made."

"I'm glad you're here. You know how I feel tonight? Sky-high. I'm on my way now."

"Without question, Dean," he said.

That was the third time he had called me Dean.

Coppola's *Rain People* won first prize. I wasn't surprised. It was a fine piece of work, with good performances by Duvall and Caan. Caan was sitting in the audience and accepted the award, the Gold Shell.

I was about to leave when they announced that *The Challenges* was the runner-up. This was the damnedest picture, I thought. It wouldn't go away. I went up to the stage and accepted the Silver Shell, and as the flashbulbs popped, I could only think of the night before. I tried to reach back for the feeling, the big rush, the chill of the highest moment in my life—but there was nothing.

Garrotte was behind the wheel as we headed for the beach at La Concha the next morning. He still looked tired. Looking at his hands on the wheel, I noticed for the first time the age there, the rising ribbons of vein. His hair, that light shock of wheat, had thinned quickly, lifting his forehead and adding years to his face. He seemed preoccupied, as if he were trying to corner a thought. He had something on his mind; he seemed in a vacuum. It was new to me. He had always been quick, sure, precise. He never had any moods. He seemed far away, as he had been the evening after the awards, when I had left him, at two A.M., sitting in the lobby of his hotel, staring at an untouched glass of champagne.

We parked the car and walked over toward the beach, which was shaped like a shell. We sat down on a bench facing the ocean. It was early morning. The streets, clean and bright, were empty. A thin haze began to fade out over the ocean, and the rich green of Santa Clara Isle became sharp and clear. On the beach there were only the squawking birds and the vacant cabañas. The warm wind rustled the plane trees, and Garrotte rubbed his hands as if he had caught a chill.

"It's bad," I said. "Whatever it is, it's bad, isn't it?"

"As bad as it can be," he said, fingering his patch. "But I must know what happened."

"Yeah, but I got to know who," I said. "Have you found who it was . . . who wanted to kill me?"

"We do not know yet. But we are getting close. Puffy and others are getting close."

"That's why Puffy didn't come here?"

"Yes."

"It was all so quick," I said. "I was waiting for the guy in the mountains. I'd sent Sandra away, like you wanted me to. And I waited. Then I decided to make a move. I went down to the village, and there he was, propped up by a tree with his head off. She did it, didn't she?"

"Such a reckless, gentle creature. I should have been tougher. I should have imposed my will on her."

"You know better. She wins any battle of wills."

"Still . . ."

"I told her to keep her goddamned nose out of it. How she did it, I'll never know."

"It was simple. She knew she had to get close. Very close. How could a woman get so close?" He paused. "It's their equalizer. History is full of it."

"Did she tell you?"

"Yes. I dragged it out of her. When she told me, I slapped her. I never hit a woman before."

"Why? Why did she have to—"

"She loved you, Dean."

"But she's going to marry you."

"She thought you didn't need her. She knew I did. That is most important to some women. It's worth more than love to them." He kept his eyes on the ocean. There was a couple walking on the beach. "I needed her badly. Who knows why, when you think about it. I've looked for her all my life. Yes, there have been other women, frivolous women who laugh too much and do not feel too much. But Sandra . . . Once, long ago, I wanted to get married. I had met this young woman in Istanbul. I felt alive. I was tired of scanning the maps for wars, this waving of swords. I wanted to rest now behind the smile, the love on a woman's face. So we left Istanbul, and stood on the deck of the ship, watching the sun catch the white and slender minarets. I thought about the futility of my life, and I suddenly turned to this woman and said, 'Marry me.' She turned to me and laughed. 'Don't be silly,' she said. 'I could never marry you. But I will spend two weeks in Paris with you.' Always there has been a week

251

here, a week there. The changing faces. Until Sandra came along."

"Well, that's all over now," I said. "You can retire. Like me."

"There will be no wedding," he said, once more fingering the patch.

"You can't—"

"She is dead, Dean. . . ."

"What? What the hell are—"

"Sandra is dead. She has been murdered."

His words stuck into my body like tiny pins. The blood rushed to my head. My hands began to tremble. I could feel my face going white. And for a few seconds I was lost in blackness, as if I were underwater and fighting for the surface. I tried to pull together what I had left. I came to the surface, breathing hard and looking out at the wavering horizon. I couldn't speak. There was only rage now.

"A week ago," Garrotte said. "They found her body in the Seine. I would have told you sooner. But I didn't want to destroy whatever success you might have."

"How?" The horizon was a clean, straight line now. My hands were steady. I had loved her deeply. I knew that now.

"It serves no purpose," he said.

"What the hell you talking—"

"I can't talk about it."

"You'd better fuckin' well talk about it," I said, grabbing him by his shirt. He just stared at me. And then I pulled my hand away.

"It was horrible. It was not a killing. The autopsy showed that she had been tortured beyond—"

"In what way?"

"That is all that I will say. I will live with the picture of it in my mind the rest of my life. Why should you?"

"It was because of me and what happened up there in the mountains?"

"Most likely. It was, however, my fault. I should not have allowed her to go to you."

"What's going to be done about it?"

252

"It will be handled. In due time. Without emotion. There is no room for emotion with us."

"In due time? Bullshit! Now!"

"You can't—"

"Don't tell me what I can't do. Tell me what I can do."

"This is an organizational problem. It must be settled wisely and quietly."

"It's my problem now. Don't you people care about anything? Don't *you* care?"

"I loved her," he said.

"Yeah, I know that," I said, sorry that I had hurt him.

"I understand death," he said. "So did she. She had a fine mind. I read to her once from Epicurus:

" 'Become accustomed to the belief that death is nothing to us. For all good and evil consists in sensation, but death is deprivation of sensation. And therefore a right understanding that death is nothing to us makes mortality of life enjoyable, not because it adds to it an infinite span of time, but because it takes away the craving for immortality. For there is nothing terrible in life for the man who has truly comprehended that there is nothing terrible in not living.' "

He paused, and put his hand on my shoulder. "Do you understand?" he asked.

"No," I said.

"She did. Sandra did. She turned to me and said, 'Epicurus is right.' "

I got up from the bench.

"Where are you going?"

"Back to Paris," I said.

PARIS

It's crazy about a town, I thought, the way a pile of bricks, a street or two, with their own sounds and light, will always intrude upon and then remain stuck in your mind whenever you think of what happened there; the luck, good or bad, the face, the moment, becomes the town. It's crazy, too, how when you feel good in a certain place, it will suddenly turn on you and you can never feel the same way about it again. Driving through San Sebastián that morning with Garrotte, I knew I would never want to go back there again. The little town by the sea had been a high for me, but now the low was reflected in every detail: the white emptiness of the streets, the chairs stacked up in front of the cafés, the void left behind by the end of the festival.

Watching the door swing open to Sandra's apartment, I was a stranger in Paris, too. I didn't move from the doorway. I let my eyes wander over the living room: the work of the unknown artists on the wall; the dusty webbing beginning to form on the frames; the big pillows near the bookcase, on which we used to play and rest and love and argue. I could see the Israeli agent sitting on one of the pillows, with a piece of shrimp on his beard. I could see Sandra's bright, angry eyes, the second thoughts going across her face, and then hear the agent's squeaky shoes, outside the door, fading down the hall; out of our lives, I had hoped. Had it all started going bad with the arrival of the agent? It seemed so. Or had it begun long ago, perhaps before she was born, with a set of conditions and emotions that would weigh on her, grow into more conditions and emotions until she would be bent into the wind and headed for a certain place, a certain time, a certain death? Can you ever change course? I wondered. I stayed awhile in the bedroom, listening, thinking, looking at a framed, browned childhood picture of Sandra and her Anna on a hill in Israel. I guessed that after Africa she had finally become comfortable with that picture, so she had put the past up on her bureau. She could look

254

at it and think of Anna again without feeling a sense of shame for herself and hate for Israel; she had settled up with the past. I took the picture and put it in my pocket. I had to leave.

Puffy was waiting for me by the Seine. He had a pocketful of bread sticks, and was throwing pieces of them into the river. The river smelled bad and looked like dirty dishwater.

"What's in there that's still alive and can eat?" I asked.

"I gotta clean out my pockets sometimes," he said. "How you been? Or should it be that Cagney line: 'Whaddaya hear, whaddaya say?'"

"Whatever you hear, whatever you know."

"I didn't think I'd see you again for a long time," he said. "But then again, after it happened, I figured . . ."

"Right again," I said.

"You come to the wrong man. I don't know anything."

"I know you've been on it. Garrotte says he's had you working on it."

"I don't know anything until the old man says I know something."

"Hey, Puffy . . . it's me you're talking to, remember?"

"I don't know your name."

"You breathless prick," I said, without emotion.

"That's not nice," he said flatly.

"It wasn't meant to be," I said.

We stood there, looking into the Seine, not saying anything. He kept popping the chunks of bread sticks into the river. He was throwing harder now.

"Did you see her?" I asked.

"Yeah," he said. "I went to the morgue with the old man. She had been missing for days. It wasn't like her to go off and not tell the old man. He got worried. He had one of his cop friends look into it quietly. Then he got the call. The body was fished out of the Seine. Garrotte was sure it wasn't her. He was still sure she was off somewhere, gatherin' her thoughts. Something like that. You know, maybe she was having some jitters before the marriage. But he went down anyway. On the way, he tried to joke about the foolishness of the trip. Yet you could see he wanted to relieve his mind. They lifted up the sheet; then he sort of had a body spasm that sent him bumping into me slightly. He started to reach out to touch her, and then pulled his hand away. All he said was 'My fault.' "

"What did she look like?" I asked.

"Awww, come on, Dean. I don't want to think about it."

"You act like you've never seen anybody killed before."

"They never killed any of 'em like that."

"What did she look like?"

"Not like Sandra. Not like anything I've ever seen."

"Whaddaya mean?"

"There's a hundred ways of killin' somebody, and just as many to be killed. The worst is when you know you're gonna get it, and that there's not a scrap of hope. Maybe like in the old days, on a pirate's gangplank. You walk out there. You see the water below. You feel the wind. It's not short and sweet. The knowledge, the fact that you know what's comin', makes it last forever."

"Was that—?"

"Worse. She didn't have seconds. She had days."

"The pain, it must've been . . ."

"For one thing, she had every tooth in her mouth pulled out."

"What!"

"There was more. But you're not going to hear it. I've told you enough. I oughta have my ass kicked. A friend's not supposed to tell another friend things like that."

"If you're a friend, help me."

"Come on, Dean," he said, his eyes pained. "I can't tell you a thing. The old man's got his own ideas. He has to be careful. I don't break any rules."

"How close are you?"

"Very close. We got a name. We know where he is. He had help. He had orders. We don't want the help. We don't want the name. We want the root of the thing."

"I want the name."

"Forget it."

He started to walk away. I grabbed his bulky arm. "The name, Puffy."

"What the hell's wrong with you, boy! Whaddaya think you're playin' with. Your guilt don't count."

"Look, Puffy. It's one thing killin' somebody; it's another the way she went out. You don't let that happen to people you care about."

"Lemme put it this way," he said. "Everything is over now. You're off the hook. They don't want you anymore. You're not in danger anymore. It's a trade-off."

"It's a bad fuckin' trade," I said.

"Y'all were crazy. That African thing. I don't know what got into Garrotte. His organization ever got a handle on that African thing, and his ass would be in more trouble than a bull's ass in fly time. He can't be stirrin' things up. Business is business. Y'all played a game. Y'all had your own reasons. Okay. But now it's over. They say it's over. Garrotte says it's over."

"Where's she buried?"

"Père-Lachaise." He pulled out some tierce cards, and began to work numbers onto them. "Should I play a three-number combination, or five?"

"You're not going to tell me any more?"

"Not on your life," he said. "And I—"

"Go on, get outta here," I said, looking away.

"See ya around," he said.

I stayed there awhile, looking at the ugly river and thinking of what I would do next. Without a name, there wasn't much I could do. I was starting to leave when I noticed a piece of yellow at my feet. It was one of Puffy's tierce cards. There were three numbers on it. I was going to leave it there, but the scribbling on it made me curious:

ROOM 215 HOTEL DES INVALIDES.

Puffy had broken the rules.

I went out to David's clinic. I wanted to talk to him about her. There was that strain between us, I knew, but maybe now we could be at ease with each other. He had been fond of Sandra, had even seemed to depend on her at times for her help, for her sensitivity to his work, for her caring about him. I got out of the taxi and looked toward the lawn: the swing, the same lost kids, the new girl who was playing with them now.

I walked into David's office. He had his nose in a book, and when he looked up, he seemed startled to see me.

"What's wrong?" I asked.

"Nothing. It's just that . . . I haven't seen you in so long."

"I should have called," I said.

"No, no, that's all right," he said. "You're welcome here; you know that."

"Well, I just stopped by to see how you were. Mainly, I wanted to tell you that I want you to have her things."

"Certainly," he said.

"She didn't have anybody, you know. Just us."

"I'll miss her," he said.

"You know—paintings, some furniture. Things you can use. If not here, maybe back at your apartment."

"She had no training," he said. "No real knowledge of the work. But she had a way with these children. Invaluable."

"When was the last time you saw her?"

"Oh, not in quite a spell. I began to resent her absence."

"You know she was going to get married."

"Yes. I thought Garrotte would finally bring some sense of permanence to her life."

"What d'you mean?"

"I don't know, exactly. You never did with Sandra. There was this odd duality about her. Sometimes I'd have this feeling that she was as bewildered and in need of as much guidance and patience as our children here. And then, at other times, there was this presence of hers, that rigid independence and control that overwhelmed you. I don't know. I can't explain it. How do you like that?"

"Doctors aren't perfect."

"She never seemed to be troubled. But, then again, maybe I didn't pay enough attention."

"Did she talk to you much? I mean about herself?"

"No. She talked about the kids, about me and my work. I could never pin her down. She resented the questions. I asked her once what she wanted to do with her life, and she said, 'Nothing.' She said it in such a way that you knew she meant it.

"I felt afraid for her sometimes, as if she were on the edge of some calamity. I felt much of the same thing in medical school. Guys pushing themselves to an exploding point. In over their heads. Unable to brake their lives. They didn't belong. Yet they pushed and pushed their limits, until they cracked. And they never knew why or for whom. It wasn't devotion to medicine. Sandra seemed to be pushing limits, invisible limits. We'll never know, will we?"

"She ever do anything that made you feel this way?"

"No. It was only a feeling."

"Yeah, that's all it was."

"Why? Why suicide, then?"

"I . . . I don't know," I said, coming up short at the word "suicide." I wanted to change the subject.

"So, how's it going out here?" I asked. "No more high-priced specialists? No more visiting firemen fuckin' up the colors?"

"Oh, you mean that black-and-brown incident. No, no more of that. I've become more aggressive. I think I'm doing pretty well. And besides, the money has been coming in nicely."

I was going to ask him about the monthly twenty-five hundred I had noticed in the bank statements, but thought better of it; that was none of my business.

"I've done a lot with your help," he said. "The results are slow in child psychology. But I'm on top of a couple of breakthroughs. I'm working on one of the papers now. It will produce surprise in the field, to put it mildly. The progress I am making with some of the worst cases has been unheard of."

He was becoming excited. I envied him. I envied him because of the definition he was able to have of his life. I seemed to be without definition. I let my mind wander over the years. Here, at least, David's work, his progress, was something that could be counted. I had helped him. It was the only flower still alive among all the wreckage.

"I'll see ya," I said. "It was good seeing you again. I'll keep in touch."

"Yes," he said. "Let's go out and have a long talk one night."

"We'll do that," I said, leaving.

I never wanted to see him or the clinic again. It was enough to know that the flower was there.

Puffy's help was all that I had needed. But I still had to match a face with the room number. Whoever belonged to the room was my man; Puffy's information was probably only an hour old. How to make his face, without exposing my own? I just couldn't walk up to his room, or hang around in the halls. Besides, I didn't want to risk any work in the hotel. I needed some time with him, some conversation in a quiet place.

I studied the hotel for a moment, but nothing clicked in my mind, until I noticed a pay phone. I called the operator for information, using rough French.

She gave me the number, and I dialed the hotel.

"Room Two-fifteen," I said. I let it ring once, and hung up. I dialed the hotel again.

"Say," I said to the room operator. "I wanted room Two-fifteen. Mr. Johnson. An American. He said this was his room number. You must have given me the wrong number."

"Room Two-fifteen," she said. "That room is Monsieur Mikalokov."

"Oh, I'm sorry," I said. "He must be staying somewhere

else." I thought a moment. How do I get him out of his room, down to the lobby? I tapped the phone with my index finger, and finally it came to me. I dialed the American Express office. Did they have the number of a limousine service? I got it, and dialed the service.

"This is Monsieur Mi-kalo-kov," I said. "Room Two-fifteen, Hôtel des Invalides. I need a car and driver to go to Orly Airport. One hour. I will be at the desk."

The man was writing on the other end. "Yes. Orly."

I took a seat in the lobby, and waited for the show. The driver arrived, and walked up to the desk. I could see the clerk call up to Two-fifteen. He put down the phone and said something to the driver. The driver became annoyed, and the two argued for a couple of minutes. He had made a trip for nothing. Monsieur Mikalokov, room Two-fifteen, did not want service to the airport. What kind of trick was this? The clerk picked up the phone again, no doubt explaining the problem to Two-fifteen. The driver paced in front of the desk. Soon, Mikalokov was down at the desk, looking like he had just been awakened. It was nine A.M. He was waving his arms. I got up and left, not waiting for the outcome of the dispute. I had my face.

After that, it was only a matter of time, the way it always was: watching, waiting to move into an easy, catlike lope; no sweat, no backfire, just nice and easy like. He came along without any trouble. They always do, the good ones. They never waste motion. They pick their spot. He'd play it out.

Besides, he never had much of a choice, seeing the black hole of the gun peeping out from the newspaper wrapped around my hand and stuck up under his chin. He was sensible; I would have been, too. Just go along, see how he plays it, his eyes kept saying. What was I up to? After all, I could have done him right there, on the dark and empty street down from his hotel. Maybe he thought I didn't want to kill him. It was midnight. He had made a habit of going for a coffee at midnight, at a *tabac* a couple of blocks away. Any kind of habit is a bad habit.

I moved him behind the wheel of my rented car. It was a Mercedes; I wanted lots of room. I let the rolled paper fall off the gun, and pressed the black hole under his eye, and carefully slid around into the backseat. I had two heavy pieces of rope back there, one short piece already worked into a loop. I dropped the loop over his head, and tightened it with my other hand. Then I climbed over to the front seat. I threw the keys into his lap.

"Start it up," I said, looking into his big craggy face, sharply boned, perfect for the movies. His hands were working at the rope around his neck.

"Too tight?" I said.

"Yeah," he said. "It's scraping my neck."

"Here, let me loosen it some. You gotta be comfortable behind a wheel. Just reach in back of your neck and loosen it. Slowly. I wouldn't want to yank on this end of the rope." He moved his hands to the back of his neck.

"That better?"

"Yeah," he said.

"Now, let's go," I said. "Not fast. Not slow. Easy does it. We got a lot of time."

"Where are we going?"

"Oh, we're going for a drive into the country, and then we're going to take a walk. Night air will pick you right up. You don't need coffee. Makes you nervous. I never touch it at night."

He eased the Mercedes away from the curb. His hands were big on the wheel. Were they the ones? Had they done the job on Sandra's mouth?

I told him to make a right, then some more turns before we were on the road out of Paris.

"You got a good face," I said. "You ever been in movies?"

"No," he said.

"You missed your calling. What's the name? Monsieur . . . Wait a minute; lemme see now. Monsieur . . . Oh, hell, I can't pronounce it. I'll just call you Monsieur Jones."

"What's your problem?" he asked.

"Monsieur Jones. Whadda you, a Russian? Hungarian? I don't know. Corsican? Naaah."

"Czech," he said.

"That's too bad. I kind of liked the Czechs. Fought like hell in the Second War. Out of Paris, are ya?"

"Maybe."

"Yeah, it's Paris, all right. Between you and the Corsicans, there aren't enough pies for your hands." I could see his hands relax on the wheel.

"Feelin' better, huh?" I said. "Yeah, there's nothin' to be excited about. We're just gonna have a little talk. I got nothin' against you."

"I never saw you before," he said.

"Of course not. You're a pro, aren't you, Monsieur Jones?"

"What's a pro?"

"You know what a pro is, Jonesy. Somebody calls, gives you a name. Bang! Bang!"

"I don't know what you're talking about."

"Movin' too fast now." He had the speedometer up to 110 kilometers per hour. "Can't have that, can we? We get a ticket. And then Jonesy has me on the spot. Bring it down to eighty. We don't have far to go."

"What do we have to do with each other?" he said.

I gave the loop around his neck a tug. "Down to eighty," I said. The car slowed. "You'd better take care of those ears. Awful thing, not bein' able to hear."

"I hear ... I hear," he said. "Look!" He held his neck, and then pointed to the speedometer.

"Oh, I'm sorry," I said.

He got his breath back. "You do not have to play. Get to the point."

"I don't like to play, Jonesy," I said. "But you like to play, don'tcha? You a dentist, Jonesy?"

"Are you crazy?" he said. I could see his mind tracking something. "A . . . a dentist. That's a laugh."

"Yeah, it sure was. Wanna tell me about it?"

"What? Tell you about what?"

"The girl."

"What girl?" he said. I saw some big trees to the right. They were a couple hundred yards off the road.

"Stop, and back it up. Then turn into the field when I tell you to."

He did as he was told. I led him out of the car by the rope, with the noose tight around his neck. "Just walk over there by the big tree and we're going to sit down and have a quiet talk."

The moon was bright. You could see a single light in a farmhouse maybe a quarter mile away, flanked by more big trees. And, faintly, you could hear a cow mooing at the moon. I propped him up against the tree, but first I tied his hands with my end of the rope, so that his head was pulled forward. I squatted next to him.

"You know, it's a pleasure to work with a real pro, Jonesy," I said. "No panic. There you are . . . cool, *sooo coool.* It's a pleasure, I'll tell ya."

"You are wrong," he said, his head bent down by the rope, his words coming hard.

"Naah, I'm not wrong," I said. "You've been wrong. But I'll tell ya . . . there's a way out for you. Just a few answers, and all you have to put up with is a long walk back to town. Hell, you'll probably be able to get a lift back anyway."

"I have no answers."

"How ya know until I ask?"

"Go ahead . . . and . . . ask."

"The girl."

"I don't know about any girl."

"You see . . . here we are, back where we started, Jonesy. We'll be here all night at this rate. I'm afraid I'll have to be a little tougher with you."

I went to the backseat of the car for the big, heavy rope. I came back, stood him up, and wrapped him tight, body and feet. I put him back down on the ground, and then threw the other end of the long rope over the thickest branch.

"You're a fool, Jonesy," I said, pulling slowly, with all the strength I had, until he was up in the air, head down. I raised him some. He was face to face with me now. I held on to the rope with both hands, and leaned into it with my shoulder.

"Great exercise," I said. "Rejuvenates the whole body. I hear it's the big thing now. People all over standin' on their heads. You can feel the blood, can't you? You'll be a new man."

"I can't—"

"Do you know me, Jonesy? My name is Dean Selmier."

"Never . . . heard of . . . you."

"Let's say we're in the same line of work. But I'm not all that crazy about it. You like it, don'tcha?"

"Let me . . . down, please. My head . . ."

"The girl, Jonesy. How long did she live?"

"Six . . . six days."

"Did you kill her?"

"No . . . why me? There were . . . three others."

"How was she killed?"

"She . . . died . . . on . . . us."

"Were you the dentist?"

"No . . . I didn't have anything to . . . do with it. It was . . . one of the others."

"What else you do to her?"

"I can't tell you . . . any more."

He was grappling for a last ounce of control. He wasn't going to admit to having tortured her. That would cost him his last chance to live, and he knew it.

"Why . . . why the girl?" I asked.

"Why? You ought to know. I don't know. They . . . don't tell you . . . why. We waited for her in . . . town. She'd been . . . away. Up on a . . . mountain in Spain."

"How did you know about a mountain?"

"I . . . don't know."

"Sure you do. Your head can't take much more of this. I wanna let you down in a minute."

"They just . . . said . . . some doctor in town. Call him."

"Who?"

"I . . . don't know. I never saw . . . him."

"Who told you? Who told you to kill her?"

"I . . . never met him either. I just go . . . to Copenhagen."

"Where?"

"Tivoli . . . I worked for him twice before. Get instructions in Tivoli."

"How?"

"At the band shell. The music . . . is over. The players leave . . . I look for . . . the sheet music left . . . behind . . . on one stand. It has . . . instructions."

"Why didn't you just kill her? What were you after?"

"Nothing. That is . . . way . . . they work. The others. They were in charge. They were . . . wild."

"Were they Czechs, too?"

"No . . ." He began to pass out. I let the rope go, and he fell to the ground. I sat him up, so the blood would flow back from his brain. He came around, and I let him rest there.

"I . . . didn't think you would kill me," he said, smiling thinly. "You know how it is. We just . . . do a job."

"Naah, you got it all wrong, Jonesy. That wasn't a job. If you'd put a bullet in her, I could live with that." Quickly, I strung him back up again. I looked into his face. "I could live with that. Maybe she had it coming. It comes with the work. Sooner or later. But you were a pack of animals. It wasn't clean, Jonesy."

"I swear . . ."

"You get off on that stuff, don'tcha? The screams. The new ways to get the screams."

"I . . . only pulled one tooth. That's the truth. I . . . wanted . . . told them to get rid of her. They . . . wouldn't listen."

"Wanted to see how it felt, eh, Jonesy? One tooth. One too many. What else you do?"

"We stripped—"

"I don't want to know, goddamn you!"

I pulled a penknife out of my pocket, holding on to the rope with one arm. He had slipped down from face level. I opened the knife, and pulled him back up to my eyes again.

"You . . . you going to cut me down? Please cut me down," he pleaded.

"Yeah, I'm gonna cut you down, Jonesy," I said, the flash of a picture going through my mind.

Dimly at first, and then as clear as anything that I can ever recall in my life. Mr. Frank, the fourth-grade teacher, has taken us to Kingen's Meat Packaging Company. I am eleven years old. It seems like I have walked into another world. There are big men all around, wearing white smocks. A conveyor, with dozens of pink pigs hung upside down, trussed up and squealing, moves past. Now the pigs are in front of the men. One big man flicks a long blade twice at each pig. There are two spurts of blood with each flick, and one spurt splashes onto a man's face. He wipes his face quickly, and goes back to the next pig floating by.

I turn away. I am sick.

"What's the matter?" asks Mr. Frank.

"They can't do that! Don't let them do that!"

"Sure they can," he says, rubbing my head.

I ran the knife into and across his jugular. The blood gushed out, and I jumped back. I tied my end of the rope tightly around the foot of the tree. And I walked away, leaving Monsieur Jones to bleed his miserable life away.

PÈRE-LACHAISE, FEBRUARY 1970

We were in the backseat of his chauffeured Rolls, heading for the cemetery, Père-Lachaise, where Sandra was buried.

Garrotte had put her there; the place had served his idea of an Old World send-off. The prince and the beggar, I thought, looking at Garrotte. He had a light-gray topcoat on, with a black velvet collar and expensive black gloves. I had my collar up around a heavy sheep coat, and my boots, I could see, would never see spring; I find it hard to part with old boots. It was a cold, bright morning, and I didn't much like the trip. I don't like cemeteries. They are pointless, because when you're dead, you're dead, and rare marble and flowers don't make you less dead. But I had to go to Père-Lachaise. Once.

"You're looking better," I said. "If it wasn't for all that serious stuff you got on."

"I suppose it's required," Garrotte said, his head turned away, his good eye staring at the passing flow of Paris. "As you will see, the French take the grave seriously. It is part of the idolatry of the past, my dear Selmier." I wasn't Dean to him anymore. That was good. He was moving back to his old self.

"If you ask me, I think the whole town is a cemetery. I never used to think that."

"Ha! What a curious fellow. A creature of pure emotion, both touching and terrible. I have never met anyone who proclaims such outward disinterest. And feels so much. And doesn't even know it. You know nothing of architecture, history, not much of the world you live in. A man who flies only by his senses. Yet, with all critical certainty, Paris is now a cemetery to you. The truth is that you may be right."

"I only know what I feel," I said.

"It is ugly; that is certain," he said. "And what is left can barely be seen through the gas fumes."

"That's everywhere. Not only Paris."

"True, but here it is more noticeable. The promise of beauty is being drowned by Coca-Cola and Cinzano. The marketplace . . . it has the slovenly taste of a bad dinner guest with a shovel in his hand."

"I'm glad to see you're sharp again," I said. He turned his head from the window.

"Yes," he said, looking at me, "I feel better. And you? You appear to be at one with yourself. Serene. That might be the word."

268

"Almost," I said. "Not quite. I'll be better after I take a trip."

"Good. Revenge is a foolish motive. Where are you going?"

"Up north. Scandinavia, most likely. I'd like to look around up there."

"And your film work?"

"I'll keep at it. I have to."

"And me?"

"I'll stay in touch. I'm not fond of it, you know. But then again . . . I am suddenly drawn into it. I remember a line from a play I was in. 'Somebody's trampling on my shadow.' It always seems to be that way with me." The car moved past Les Invalides, the site of Napoleon's tomb. He looked at it as if he had never seen it before.

"France is a hothouse of monuments," he said. "Five hundred, I think the latest count was." He came back to me. "You are a valued friend. Always remember."

"Why don't you quit?" I said. "You have it all."

"I would have," he said, "with her."

"Well, if you don't get out, get this car bulletproofed. I don't have to know much to see that this business is going to become nastier. If that's possible."

"What does it matter?" he said. "The majority of men die like dogs. Very unheroically. We are not an heroic species. So what is the difference? A bullet? Or starvation? Or persecution? All ways are bad. And there are many. To kill the spirit, that is the most popular. There are those who are dead and do not even know it."

"I guess so," I said.

"Back there—Napoleon. He would have much preferred a bullet or a lance through the heart. But he died slowly, before he was dead. You know, his uniform was always dark green. On Saint Helena, it became so worn and bleached by the sun that it lost its color. He wanted another uniform. But the green cloth they gave him was not pure. It ran into a yellow, like the rind of a melon. He could not stand for this, so he took his old uniform and turned it inside out. How pathetic for a master of kings. Sitting on a lonely island with a turned uniform. For him, that was the cruelest death."

Finally, we drew up in front of the cemetery. He told his driver to wait, and we started through the gate. An old woman stood there selling shoestrings and cheap statuettes. We walked along the cobblestone paths, winding up and down hills; the breath came out of our mouths in little streams. Squirrels ran up trees, and there were the squawks of birds. And cats. Hundreds of them.

"They are all here," Garrotte said. "The pride of France. Victor Hugo. Balzac. Edith Piaf. Molière. This is the most glorious earth in the world."

Maybe, I thought. But it wasn't like any cemetery I had ever seen. The ones in America were modest in comparison. This place was like an old walled city. I watched the old women playing with children along the narrow lanes. There was no death here. Statues stood starkly against the hard cold sky. Gesturing men in homburgs. Mothers with children in their laps. Women in ballroom gowns. Angels of all shapes and sizes, blowing trumpets or playing harps. Every re-creation of life and beyond that could be made out of marble or stone was here. We walked among the strange forms and shapes, in and out of the stitching of tombstones, with their small hanging lamps that would be lit on All Souls' Day. We saw the pictures: brown photographs of whole families, or of a husband, or a wife, the figures smiling or waving, moments gone but not released by someone who could not let go—like myself.

"Here she is," Garrotte said.

There were still dozens of baskets of flowers around the tomb. He had bought them all, I was sure. Who else would have sent them? She had nobody. He stooped down, and began to pick at the loose petals on the marble. Then he pulled out his handkerchief and began rubbing at what he thought was a spot on the surface. There wasn't any spot. He needed to do something with his hands. The tomb was strong and had clean lines. He had done well by her. There was no celebration of life here. That would have been out of character for him. And for her.

"Who was here for the burial?" I asked.

"Just Puffy and I," he said, still stooping. "We got a rabbi to say a few words." He rooted about for a while, pulling a weed here and there.

"By God!" he said. "I still can't believe it. Sandra . . . dead."

"Neither can I," I said.

"She seemed so indestructible."

"I know."

"But I knew better. She looked that way only if you were not looking closely. Up close, there were moments. I could always see. She reminded me of a big bird. A raven. Dark and drifting. With a broken wing. That is one reason why I wanted to marry her. I wanted to protect her wing." He stood up. "I must leave. I've been here too much of late. It seems that my bones have become powdered, too."

"Do you mind?" I said. "I want to stay a moment. I'll take a taxi back to town."

"Of course," he said. He walked over, and took my hand. "Take care of yourself, my friend," he said.

I watched him go down the hill and fade into the tangle of statuary. I pulled out the picture I had taken from her apartment, the little girl and her Anna. I placed it on the tomb, and then sat down on the marble surface. I sat there for a long time, drifting. My thoughts were but fragments, but I could see well. I could see the funny hats. I could see her face. And that was all I would ever need. I wouldn't come back, I told myself. Never again.

Winter shadows ribboned the cobblestone walks as I neared the gate. What was up ahead for me? An appointment in Tivoli. Maybe. Soon. I didn't know. Perhaps Madrid. Let the past rest. Madrid: where I could get lost among the whores and the vodka, among all the penny-arcade refugees exiled by that Universal Bitch called Movies; the Bitch who only yawned and picked lint out of her belly button when we tipped our caps for love; all those actors and directors, good and bad, beaten and half whipped, sentenced forever to low budgets and parts that were spit out of a cheap grinder like horse meat. Life was not San Sebastián, with a spotlight on your box, with the blood racing through you like a cataract. Life was an evacuated town on a silent street.

I nodded to the decaying witch at the cemetery gate. She tried to push a statue in my hand. I hadn't looked at her closely before, but now she looked like one of those strange forms pulled down from above a tomb and placed here in front of me. I gently moved her bony hand away, but she held on, cackling, exposing her bloodless gums and looking straight into my eyes. Her face was rotting timber. She had a dry sore under her eye.

"I'm sorry," I said, pulling away.

She cackled after me as I made my way to the cab, screeching something in French and pointing her finger at me.

"Go to hell, you old bat!" I yelled out the taxi window, for no reason except that I had to. "I'm a finisher! I know how to finish! You hear me? I'll finish!"

Chronology of Films
in Which Dean Selmier Has Appeared

1966	Maybe You Don't Like It
1968	The Challenges (with Francisco Rabal)
1969	The Ring (with Maria Luisa San José)
1969	Gallos de Pelea
1969	Patton (with George C. Scott)
1970	The Glass Ceiling (with Carmen Sevilla)
1970	The Hunting Party (with Oliver Reed and Candice Bergen)
1970	Murders in the Rue Morgue (with Jason Robards, Michael Dunn, and Lilli Palmer)
1971	Mecanismo Interior (with Maria Mahor)
1971	Capitán Apacha (with Lee Van Cleef)
1971	Man in the Wilderness (with Richard Harris)
1972	The Blood-Spattered Bride (with Alexandra Bastedo)
1973	The Name Is Rupert (with Michael Dunn) (never shot)
1974	School of Death
1974	Take a Hard Ride (with Fred Williamson, Jim Brown, and Catherine Spaak)
1975	El Paranoico